What's Science all about?

written by Alex Frith, Hazel Maskell,
Dr. Lisa Jane Gillespie & Kate Davies

Illustrated by Adam Larkum

Designed by Stephen Moncrieff, Tom Lalonde,
Samantha Barrett, Anna Gould,
Steve Wood & Brenda Cole

Science consultants: James Williams,
Dr. John Rostron, Dr. Margaret Rostron,
Dr. John Spokes, Laura Parker,
Toby Swan & Dr. Lisa Jane Gillespie

Edited by Rosie Dickins & Jane Chisholm
Series advisor: Tony Payton

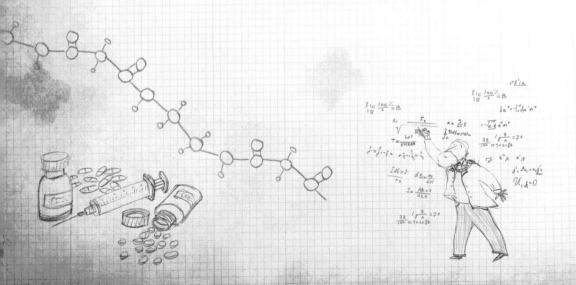

What's Science all about?

All about science

Have you ever wondered what fire is?
Or why things fall to the ground?
Or what's alive and what's not?

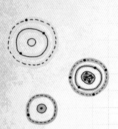

Scientists have asked all these questions,
and many, many others too. They've
found the answers using science — a way
of learning about the world by watching,
coming up with ideas and testing them.
And there's still lots left to learn.

Science is also the name for all the
knowledge that scientists have gathered
so far. This is usually divided up into
three main branches, each dealing with
a different kind of knowledge: biology,
chemistry and physics.

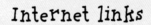

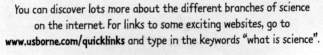

Internet links

You can discover lots more about the different branches of science
on the internet. For links to some exciting websites, go to
www.usborne.com/quicklinks and type in the keywords "what is science".

Contents

What's Biology all about?

Contents

Part 4: Where did life come from?

Part 5: Life on Earth

Internet links

You can find out lots more about biology on the internet. You can use a virtual microscope to look at cells, watch baby chicks hatch and flowers bloom, zoom into the DNA of a human hand and ask a biologist a question. For links to these websites, and many more, go to **www.usborne.com/quicklinks** and type in the keywords "what is biology".

When using the internet, please follow the internet safety guidelines shown on the Usborne Quicklinks website. The recommended websites in Usborne Quicklinks are regularly reviewed and updated, but Usborne Publishing Ltd is not responsible and does not accept liability for the content or availability of any website other than its own.

what's biology all about?

Biology is all about life – what it is, how it works and why it is the way it is. It covers all forms of life, from the largest living plants and animals to tiny life forms that are much too small to see; and it's also about where these life forms came from, how they've changed over time, and how they exist side-by-side all over the Earth today.

Here are some of the big questions that keep biologists busy...

what is life?

It's normally pretty easy to tell if something is alive, especially if you can see it without a microscope. But biologists study far weirder, tinier things, which may act as if they're alive in some ways but not in others. Even experts often disagree over whether these things are alive or not.

From big to small

Living things come in all sizes. The smallest are so tiny that you can't see them without a microscope, but the biggest are gigantic – such as blue whales, which can be as long as 16 men lying head to toe.

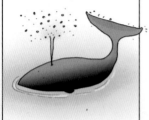

Of all living things, one of the very biggest is a huge fungus in North America. All you can see of it is scattered patches of mushrooms, but below the ground it stretches for miles.

A jug of sea water can contain tens of thousands of different kinds of life.

This creature, called *Paramecium bursaria*, is shown about a thousand times larger than real life. Without a microscope, you wouldn't be able to see it at all. It usually lives in stagnant ponds.

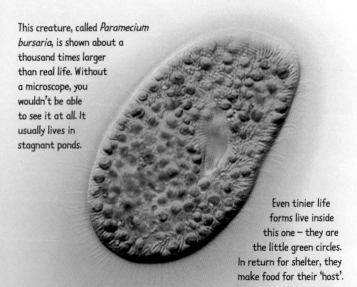

Even tinier life forms live inside this one – they are the little green circles. In return for shelter, they make food for their 'host'.

How does it work?

There are some processes that all living things do – although they don't all do them in the same ways. Biologists look deep inside living things to learn how they work – right down to the tiny strands of chemicals that make them what they are.

This is a strand of a chemical called DNA (deoxyribonucleic acid). It contains the instructions that make living things what they are.

Where did it come from?

Some biologists study the remains of ancient living things – some over 3,500 million years old – to piece together a history of life. No one knows how the very first living things formed, but biologists are trying to find out.

What are people?
We might like to think we're special, but to a biologist we're just another kind of animal. Specifically, we're a type of ape.

Where can you find it?

Living things are found in most places on Earth. Hot, wet places are packed with millions of life forms, and even the coldest or driest areas are almost always home to some. But if life exists on any other planets, we don't know about it.

Antarctica is one of the coldest places on Earth, but Emperor penguins can survive and raise their chicks there.

what do biologists do?

Biology is such a huge subject that most biologists specialize in just one area. Here are some of the different kinds of biologists...

Botanists study how plants grow and live.

Microbiologists study living things that are too tiny to see without a microsope.

Zoologists study all kinds of animals.

Geneticists study the chemical codes that define and shape all living things.

Palaeontologists study records of living things that were around long before us.

Ecologists study how living things exist together.

Marine biologists study life in seas and oceans.

What's biology ever done for us?

People have been studying living things for centuries – even if they haven't always called it 'biology'. Their discoveries have made our lives safer, longer and healthier. Here are a few examples...

Hospitals are much safer since experiments showed that keeping things clean prevents germs from causing infections.

Biologists have developed medicines and vaccinations which help to beat diseases. Their studies of the human body have made complex operations possible too.

Food can be stored safely for longer because scientists discovered germs, and came up with ways to keep food germ-free.

Drinking water became much safer once scientists understood how to rid it of harmful germs.

Louis Pasteur (1822–1895) was a great French scientist who developed the first vaccinations for anthrax and rabies. He also found a way of heating food and drink to kill the germs in them – called 'pasteurization' after him.

Joseph Lister (1827–1912) was a Scottish doctor who realized that wound infections were caused by germs. He made hospitals much safer by developing germ-killing antiseptics.

Discoveries of codes, or 'genes', that make us what we are may pave the way for medical breakthroughs in the future.

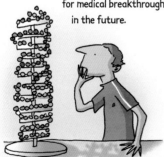

Today, biologists are helping to save animals and plants by studying how they live and what threatens them.

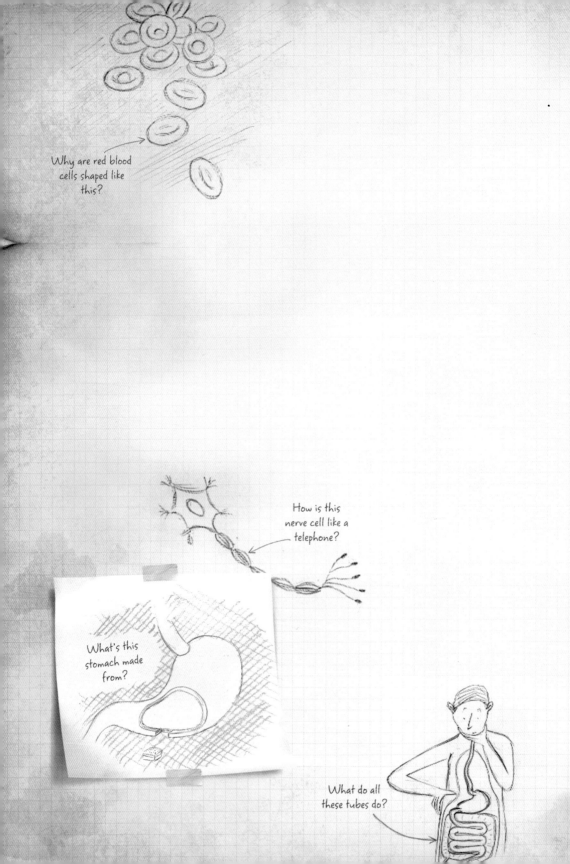

Part 1
What's life?

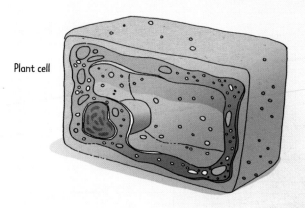

Plant cell

Our planet is teeming with billions of
different life forms – from gigantic whales to
minuscule microbes. To make sense of it all,
the first thing biologists do is define what is
and isn't alive. Then they sort living things
into categories, to understand the similarities
and differences between them. And to see
how life works, they look at cells – the basic
units that make up nearly all living things.

How can we tell what's alive and what's not?

What links a monkey, a mite and a mushroom? On the surface you wouldn't spot many similarities, if you could even see a mite at all. But they actually have seven things in common with each other, and with every other living thing.

Biologists call these the seven **life processes**...

Moving plants

Put a pot plant on a sunny window sill. After a few days, look at the direction in which its leaves are facing.

WHAT'S CHANGED?
You should find that the plant's leaves have moved to face the light.

WHY?
Plants need sunlight to make food.

Movement

All living things can move by themselves, even plants – they just move very slowly.

I'm winning!

Nutrition

All living things need food. Animals eat plants or other animals, and plants make their own food using sunlight.

Respiration

All living things release energy from food, in a process called respiration. Most need oxygen to do this.

Waste not...

The most obvious form of excretion might seem to be poo – but actually, poo doesn't count. It's mainly made up of leftover food that the body can't use, rather than waste chemicals that have been made inside the body.

Excretion

All living things need to get rid of waste chemicals that they have made. They excrete them in sweat or urine, or by breathing out.

Reproduction

All living things make new versions of themselves. If they didn't, they would soon die out.

A few plants have very quick reactions. This Venus Flytrap can snap its leaves shut in one tenth of a second.

Sensitivity

All living things can sense what's going on around them. Even though plants don't have eyes or ears, they still react to things such as sunlight.

Artificial life?

Humans have created very lifelike robots. Some can do several, or even most, of the seven life processes. But no one has ever created a robot that can grow or reproduce.

One day you'll be as big as me.

Growth

All living things grow. Some grow to a certain size, then stop. Others carry on growing throughout their lives.

So to count something as alive, you must be able to answer 'yes' to all seven categories on this checklist...

Plant

Movement	Yes – slowly
Nutrition	Yes – makes food using sunlight
Respiration	Yes – releases energy in cells
Excretion	Yes – gases and water
Reproduction	Yes
Sensitivity	Yes – to light
Growth	Yes

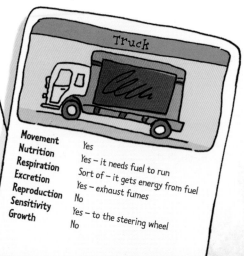

Truck

Movement	Yes
Nutrition	Yes – it needs fuel to run
Respiration	Sort of – it gets energy from fuel
Excretion	Yes – exhaust fumes
Reproduction	No
Sensitivity	Yes – to the steering wheel
Growth	No

How do biologists divide up living things?

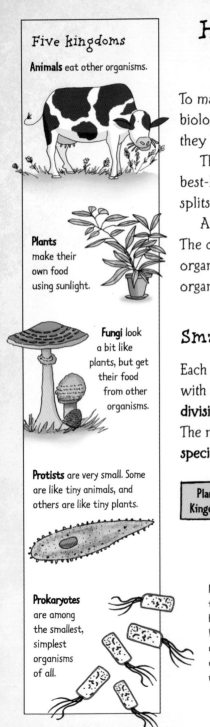
To make living things, or **organisms**, easier to study, biologists separate them into groups, according to what they have in common. This is called **classification**.

There are different systems of classification, but the best-known is called the five-kingdom system, which splits living things into five huge groups, or **kingdoms**.

Animals make up one kingdom, and plants another. The other three kingdoms are fungi, simple tiny organisms called prokaryotes, and more complex tiny organisms called protists.

Smaller sub-groups

Each kingdom is split up into smaller and smaller groups, with more and more in common. The first group is a **division** (for plants) or a **phylum** (for everything else). The next groups are **class**, **order**, **family**, **genus**, and finally **species**. Every kind of living thing has its own species.

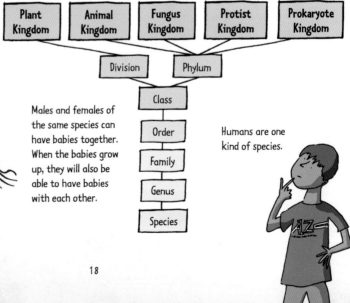

Plant Kingdom · Animal Kingdom · Fungus Kingdom · Protist Kingdom · Prokaryote Kingdom

Division — Phylum

Class

Order

Family

Genus

Species

Males and females of the same species can have babies together. When the babies grow up, they will also be able to have babies with each other.

Humans are one kind of species.

18

What's in a name?

Species have different names in different countries. So to avoid confusion, biologists have one scientific name for each species.

Here is an example of how a single species can be separated out from the whole Animal Kingdom...

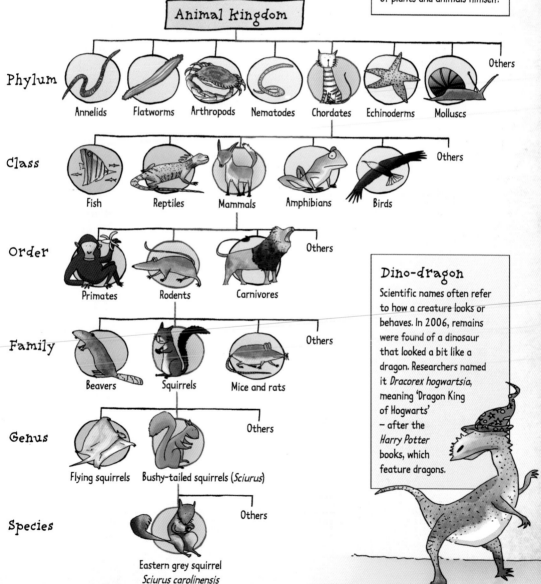

Animal kingdom

Phylum
Annelids · Flatworms · Arthropods · Nematodes · Chordates · Echinoderms · Molluscs · Others

Class
Fish · Reptiles · Mammals · Amphibians · Birds · Others

Order
Primates · Rodents · Carnivores · Others

Family
Beavers · Squirrels · Mice and rats · Others

Genus
Flying squirrels · Bushy-tailed squirrels (*Sciurus*) · Others

Species
Eastern grey squirrel *Sciurus carolinensis* · Others

Dino-dragon

Scientific names often refer to how a creature looks or behaves. In 2006, remains were found of a dinosaur that looked a bit like a dragon. Researchers named it *Dracorex hogwartsia*, meaning 'Dragon King of Hogwarts' – after the *Harry Potter* books, which feature dragons.

The Animal Kingdom

The Animal Kingdom isn't just made up of animals like dogs and dolphins that are easy to recognize. It also includes some you might not think of as animals at all, such as corals and sponges.

What they all have in common is that they get their food from eating other organisms, rather than making their own food, like plants. Animals are also made up of lots of cells, instead of just one.

Animals with backbones

Most of the biggest, heaviest animals are **vertebrates**. This means they have a backbone (made up of bones called vertebrae) to support their bodies. But, although they're the easiest animals to spot, they only make up 3% of the Animal Kingdom.

There are eight classes of vertebrates (of which four are kinds of fish), and they are all grouped into one phylum, called **chordates**. Some are warm-blooded, which means they can control their body temperature. Others are cold-blooded, meaning they can't control their body temperature, and get warmth from the Sun.

New discoveries
Around 15,000 new species of animals are discovered and named every year.

What's this?
Splitting organisms into groups may seem easy, but it's nearly impossible to get a group with no exceptions!

One animal that doesn't quite fit is the platypus. It's a mammal, but it also has a duck-like bill and lays eggs.

Birds are vertebrates with wings and feathers. They lay eggs with hard shells, and are warm-blooded.

Mammals are warm-blooded, hairy vertebrates that give birth to babies rather than laying eggs. Mothers produce milk for their babies to drink.

Reptiles are cold-blooded vertebrates with scales. They live on land and usually lay leathery eggs.

Fish are water-dwelling vertebrates, with scaly skin and gills for breathing. They lay small eggs, and are cold-blooded.

Amphibians are vertebrates that can live on land, but lay their eggs in water. They are cold-blooded.

20

Spineless creatures

The other 97% of animal species are cold-blooded creatures without backbones, called **invertebrates**. Many have soft, squishy bodies, often surrounded by hard shells. Invertebrates are usually much smaller than vertebrates, although there are some very big invertebrates in the sea, such as squids with tentacles much longer than the tallest person.

Each group of invertebrates has its own phylum. Here are just a few...

Nematodes are worm-like creatures with no body segments.

Annelids are worm-like and have body segments.

Arthropods have segmented bodies, jointed legs and hard shells. They make up 80% of all animal species, including insects, centipedes, millipedes, spiders, scorpions and crabs.

Molluscs have soft bodies and include snails, octopuses and squid.

Flatworms have flat bodies with no segments.

Echinoderms live in seas, and have tough bodies. They include starfish.

Water-dwelling **cnidarians** have sack-like bodies. They include jellyfish and corals.

Sponges have very simple bodies, which don't even have brains or muscles. They live on the sea floor and hardly move at all.

Rotifers are among the tiniest animals in the world. Most can only be seen with a microscope.

Are spiders insects?

You might think that spiders are insects, but they aren't! Insects and spiders are both arthropods, but they are in different classes.

Insects all have six legs and make up their own class. Spiders belong to a class with eight legs, called **arachnids**, along with ticks, mites and scorpions.

The Plant Kingdom

Life on Earth relies on plants, because they make their own food – which can then be eaten by other living things. They make sugars using sunlight, water and a gas in the air called carbon dioxide. To make food, they also need a substance inside them called **chlorophyll**, which is what gives them their green colour.

Almost all plants contain tubes for moving food and water around. Most also reproduce by making seeds, which usually contain a tiny baby plant and some food for it, surrounded by a protective case.

Red Giant

The tallest living thing is a redwood tree in California that's more than 115m (379ft) high – over 63 times higher than a man. This tree is named 'Hyperion', after a giant from Greek mythology.

Seedy plants

Seed-bearing plants can be divided into two groups: **angiosperms** and **gymnosperms**.

Most plants are **angiosperms** – which means they grow flowers, and their seeds develop in fruits. All angiosperms are in the same plant division.

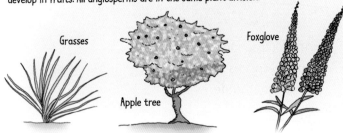

Grasses

Apple tree

Foxglove

Thieves

Plants can break the rules too. Dodder is a brownish plant that has hardly any chlorophyll. Instead of making its own food, it winds itself around other plants and steals theirs.

Dodder

Gymnosperms don't grow flowers, and their seeds often form in cones. Here are the four gymnosperm divisions...

Conifers (including pine and fir trees)

Ginkgoes (of which only one species is found today)

Cycads (including palm trees)

Gnetophytes (certain woody plants)

which plants don't make seeds?

Some plants reproduce using **spores**, which are simpler than seeds. Here are some examples of spore-bearing plants.

Bryophytes are very simple plants that mostly live in damp, shady areas. They are split into three divisions – liverworts, mosses and hornworts.

Ferns and horsetails are the most complex plants that reproduce using spores. They are all in the same division, called *Pteridophyta*.

Liverwort

Bracken
(a fern)

Horsetail

Hart's-tongue fern

Moss

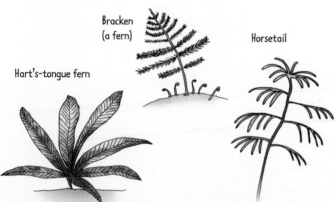

what about the other kingdoms?

The other three kingdoms in the five-kingdom system contain organisms that can be much harder to spot.

Fungi grow underground or in damp, dark places. Most are made up of masses of tiny threads which feed on dead matter or living organisms. Fungi include mushrooms, moulds and single-celled yeasts.

Protists and prokaryotes are so tiny that you can't see them. They are all around, on your skin, in water and the air, and on everything you touch. Prokaryotes are very small, simple organisms. Protists are larger and more complex, and act a bit like tiny animals or plants. Some even join together to form colonies, such as seaweeds.

Just the tip

Toadstools are just a small part of a kind of large underground fungus. The fungus sends up toadstools to release spores above the ground, where they are scattered by the wind.

What are living things made from?

Life comes in an astounding range of shapes and sizes, but nearly all living things are made up of tiny living units called **cells**. Some organisms are only made up of one cell, and others are made of millions upon millions of them.

In organisms with many cells, different cells do different things – from carrying food to creating seeds or babies. Each cell has a particular shape to help it do its job as well as possible. But, although cells can look very different, most contain the same basic structures.

What's in an animal cell?

Here you can see the structures that are found in most animal cells.

The cell in this picture has been enlarged several hundred times. Cells are usually so small that you can't see them at all.

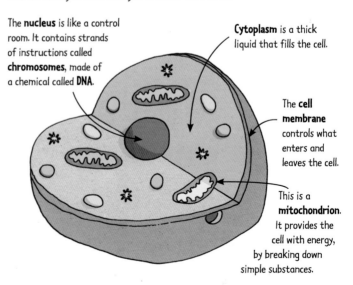

The **nucleus** is like a control room. It contains strands of instructions called **chromosomes**, made of a chemical called **DNA**.

Cytoplasm is a thick liquid that fills the cell.

The **cell membrane** controls what enters and leaves the cell.

This is a **mitochondrion**. It provides the cell with energy, by breaking down simple substances.

How many cells?

You have between 50 and 100 million million cells in your body.

Just one drop of blood contains over 250 million cells.

How many types of cell are there?

There are over 200 kinds of cells in the human body alone, including these...

Red blood cells carry oxygen. Their flat, curved shape allows them to hold lots of it.

White blood cells fight germs.

Long nerve cells carry messages around the body.

What about a plant cell?

Plant cells usually have all the structures found in an animal cell, and a few extra ones too.

This diagram shows a cell that comes from the top of a leaf.

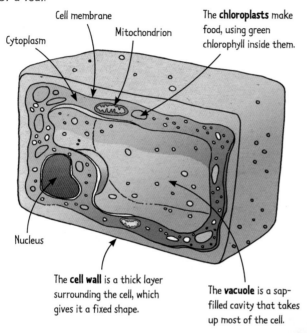

Cell membrane

Cytoplasm

Mitochondrion

The **chloroplasts** make food, using green chlorophyll inside them.

Nucleus

The **cell wall** is a thick layer surrounding the cell, which gives it a fixed shape.

The **vacuole** is a sap-filled cavity that takes up most of the cell.

This photograph shows magnified plant cells, taken from a leaf. The green dots inside the cells are chloroplasts.

Can I see cells?

You can look at some bigger cells using a home microscope. This experiment shows how to look at onion cells.

1. Cut an onion in half, then in half again. Separate the layers.

2. Snap one layer in half.

3. Peel off a thin sheet of onion 'skin'.

4. Put it on a slide, add a drop of water and cover it.

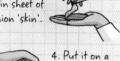

5. Fasten the slide under the clips. Turn the lenses so the smallest one is in position.

6. Use the knobs to lower the lens, then look through the eyepiece to focus the image. You should see rows of cells.

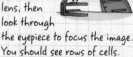

If you can't see the cells, try a longer lens – but take care not to knock the slide!

How do your cells stick together?

How do these...

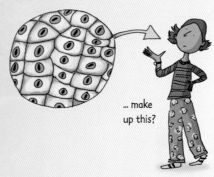

... make up this?

Cells are really small, but they band together to make big, complex organisms, such as humans. And, even though they have different jobs and shapes, joining up is the same step-by-step process for them all.

Cells

This photograph was taken with a powerful microscope, and has been artificially coloured. It shows fat cells joined together to make a tissue that stores energy and keeps the body warm.

Cells group together with other cells of the same type.

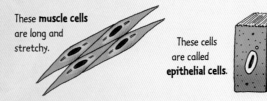

These **muscle cells** are long and stretchy.

These cells are called **epithelial cells**.

Tissues

Together the cells make something called a tissue. There are many different tissues, including **muscle tissue**, and **epithelial tissue** which lines much of the body's insides.

Most epithelial tissue is thin and delicate.

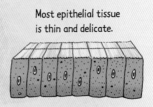

Muscle tissue can contract (bunch up), creating movement.

Organs

Different tissues group together to make **organs**. An organ is a structure – such as the **stomach**, **heart** or **intestine** – which does a particular job in the body.

This is a picture of a stomach. Part of it has been cut away, to show the layers of tissue inside.

This is a cutaway of a tube called the intestine, which transports food and water through the body. It too is made of layers of tissues.

Plant organs

Some common plant organs have been labelled on this photograph of a tulip.

Flower

Leaf

Stem

Roots

Systems

Organs group together to make **systems**. Humans have 10 systems, including the **digestive system**.

Oesophagus

Small intestine

Stomach

Large intestine

The digestive system deals with breaking down food and getting rid of the leftovers.

Organisms

Different systems combine to make an **organism**, which can carry out all seven life processes. (See pages 16-17 for a reminder of what these are.)

A human is one kind of organism.

Where do cells come from?

New cells are made when an existing cell splits into two. One cell can divide many times, to make thousands of 'daughter' cells. Plants and animals need all these new cells either to grow bigger, or to replace old or damaged cells.

How do they divide?

Animal cells mostly divide through a process called **mitosis**, in which a series of splits ends with two cells. Each has a full set of instructions inside its nucleus.

First, the information in the cell copies itself, and coils up into X-shapes.

This picture only shows two **chromosomes** (sets of instructions in the nucleus). Human cells really have 46.

The membrane around the nucleus vanishes. The information splits into two, and moves to either end of the cell.

New membranes form around each set of information.

The cell begins to split into two, each with its own nucleus.

The two halves end up as two completely separate cells.

Plant cells divide in a very similar way.

Flaking skin

The top layer of your skin is made of old, dead cells. Try sticking a piece of sticky tape to the back of your hand. Then peel it off, and you'll see bits of dead skin stuck to it.

Splitting cells

If a single cell divides into two, and each divides again, then there'll be four cells. Then if these four divide, there'll be eight. How many divisions would it take to reach 1,024 cells?

The answer is at the bottom of the page.

Why are they called cells?

Cells were discovered in the 17th century, by a scientist called Robert Hooke. Hooke used early microscopes to see that cork was made of tiny chambers. He called them 'cells', after the small, bare rooms where monks lived.

Answer: from the first division, it'll take 10 sets of division to reach 1,024 cells.

What about the very first cell?

Every plant and animal starts off life as just one single cell, which contains the instructions for everything the organism will ever be. This cell divides again and again, starting a chain of cell divisions that can create something millions and millions of times its size.

Most new animals and plants are formed from two special 'half-cells' called **gametes** – one from the mother, and one from the father. Gametes form through a special process of cell division called **meiosis**, which produces cells with only half the usual information.

When gametes come together, the two halves fuse to make a new, complete cell, called a **zygote**. This starter cell contains the instructions to build a brand new organism which will combine features from both its parents.

STEM CELL SCIENCE

Most adult cells can only make copies of themselves – they can't change what *kind* of cell they make. But some cells are different...

Special 'stem' cells can turn into many other kinds of cell. Scientists think stem cells could be used to treat some illnesses and to grow replacements for damaged organs. In 2007, scientists found a way to turn normal adult cells into stem cells. This was a giant break-through, which could lead to many medical advances.

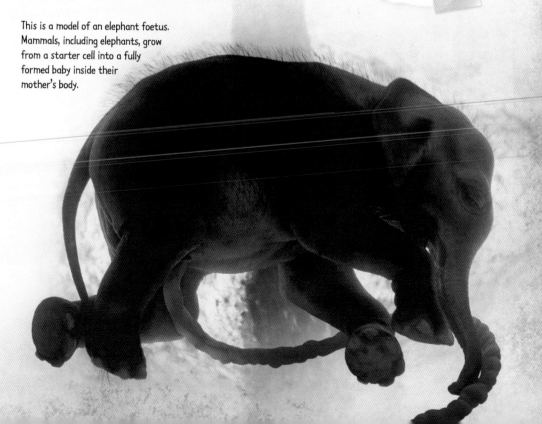

This is a model of an elephant foetus. Mammals, including elephants, grow from a starter cell into a fully formed baby inside their mother's body.

The smallest living things

Plants and animals contain many different cells that work together. But some of the smallest living things are made up of just one cell, and others are so simple that they don't even count as a cell. **Viruses**, the very smallest organisms, are so basic that scientists are still arguing over whether they're really alive at all.

Most single-celled organisms and all viruses are so tiny that they can only be seen with a microscope. They are called 'micro-organisms' or **microbes**. Some microbes cause diseases, and are often called germs.

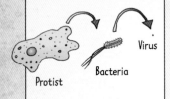
Viruses

Of all the organisms in the world, viruses are the simplest and strangest. They can't carry out the seven life processes alone. Instead, they get into the cells of another organism, or **host**, and use the systems there. So viruses are only alive when they're inside a host. When they are by themselves, scientists say they aren't really alive at all, but 'dormant' (or 'sleeping'). A virus is nothing more than a strand of DNA, or a similar chemical called RNA, surrounded by a protective coat. When it invades a host cell, the DNA or RNA hijacks the cell and forces it to make copies of the virus. When the host cell is full of copies, it bursts. The new viruses are released, and will infect the next cells they come into contact with.

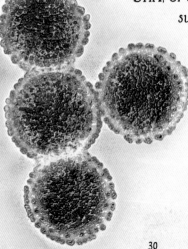

This is a photograph of highly magnified influenza viruses. The viruses have been coloured artificially.

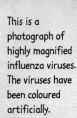

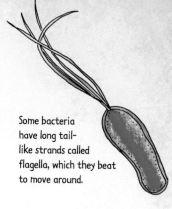

Bacteria

Bacteria are prokaryotes – very basic cells which lack many of the usual cell structures. They don't even have a nucleus. Instead, their DNA (which is tightly coiled up) floats freely in their cytoplasm. But they are much more complex than viruses, and are definitely alive.

Bacteria are vital for our survival, as they break down dead organisms so chemicals in them can be reused by other living things. Bacteria are useful in other ways, too – for example, some bacteria live inside our bodies and help us to digest food.

Some bacteria have long tail-like strands called flagella, which they beat to move around.

Protists

Protists have complex cells, rather like plant or animal cells. Most are made of just one cell, but others join together to form colonies. There are several different kinds of protists...

Protozoa are single cells similar to animal cells. They eat by engulfing smaller organisms, such as bacteria.

Algae are mostly single plant-like cells. Most have chloroplasts, so they can make food from sunlight.

Some algae join into big groups to form seaweeds. These look like plants, but the cells are all similar and don't have specialised jobs.

Hungry protozoa

Protozoa eat bacteria and other protists. To reach its prey, this protozoan pushes part of itself forward and pulls the rest after.

It surrounds the prey with part of its body.

The prey is swallowed up, broken down and absorbed.

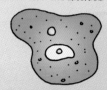

Dangerous microbes...

Most microbes are harmless, but some cause diseases. The most deadly, such as the virus which causes HIV, can kill tens of millions of people. Here are some more examples...

Some **bacteria** attack individual cells inside the body, or produce harmful waste products called toxins. They can cause sore throats, food poisoning,

meningitis, pneumonia and a deadly disease called cholera which spreads through food and water.

Protists can cause diseases such as amoebic dysentery, caused by protozoa attacking the intestine's lining, and malaria, in which protozoa injected through mosquito bites invade the liver and red blood cells.

This photograph, taken with a very powerful microscope, shows viruses attacking a bacterium called *Escherichia coli* (or *E. coli*). Some viruses are attached to the cell's surface. Others have already injected themselves into the cell.

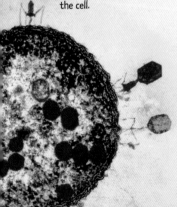

Overall, however, most bacteria and protists are harmless or even helpful. But **viruses** are only ever destructive, causing illnesses from colds to rabies. The worst kinds can kill millions – the Spanish flu of 1918-19 caused more deaths than the First World War. There are so many strains of each virus that it's impossible to become resistant to them all.

...and how we beat them

Humans have been fighting off dangerous microbes for as long as we've been around, and we're very good at it. Our defences include nose hairs and tough skins to block germs, stomach acid to kill them in food, and tears to wash them from our eyes.

If these defences fail, then germ-busting **white blood cells** swing into action. There are two main kinds of white blood cells: **phagocytes** (which engulf germs), and **lymphocytes** (which make structures called **antibodies** that disable germs).

Phagocytes break down germs, and also sweep up any poisonous waste that they make.

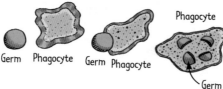

Germ Phagocyte Germ Phagocyte Phagocyte

Germ

The antibodies made by lymphocytes latch onto microbes. Each kind of antibody fights a particular germ.

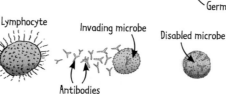

Lymphocyte Invading microbe Disabled microbe

Antibodies

Once your body learns to make an antibody, it remembers how to make it, so if the same kind of microbe attacks again, your body quickly produces the antibodies to fight it off. This means you won't catch the same disease again; you'll have become **immune** to it.

Heat can help to slow down invading germs too, and also helps some white blood cells to do their job. That's why your body temperature often rises when you're fighting off an illness.

But even though our bodies are pros at fighting disease, sometimes they need outside help. That's where medicine comes in...

Avoiding germs

Here are some ways you can avoid picking up or passing on germs...

Many germs travel in droplets in your breath, so cover your nose and mouth when you sneeze or cough.

Germs also cling to your skin, so washing your hands helps to avoid spreading them.

Germs can lurk in raw food. You can kill them by cooking food properly.

New germs can grow on cooked food, but low temperatures slow them down. So it's safest to keep food in the fridge.

Marvellous medicines

Here are some of the scientists whose brilliant breakthroughs saved millions of lives...

EDWARD JENNER AND VACCINATION

DEADLY SMALLPOX USED TO BE ONE OF THE MOST FEARED OF ALL DISEASES.

PEOPLE KNEW THAT IF THEY SURVIVED SMALLPOX, THEY WOULDN'T CATCH IT AGAIN. IN ANCIENT CHINA, PEOPLE INHALED OLD SMALLPOX SCABS, TO TRY TO CATCH A MILD VERSION. BUT THIS WAS VERY RISKY.

BUT MILKMAIDS HARDLY EVER CAUGHT IT.

AN 18TH CENTURY DOCTOR, EDWARD JENNER, NOTICED THEY OFTEN CAUGHT MILDER COWPOX INSTEAD.

Does cowpox make them immune to smallpox?

JENNER DECIDED TO TEST THIS THEORY WITH A RISKY EXPERIMENT.

FIRST HE INJECTED A BOY WITH COWPOX...

...WHICH DIDN'T MAKE HIM TOO SICK.

THEN HE INJECTED THE BOY WITH SMALLPOX.

If he dies, I'll be tried for murder.

LUCKILY, THE BOY DIDN'T GET ILL.

It works!

NEWS OF THE DISCOVERY SPREAD, AND HUGE NUMBERS OF LIVES WERE SAVED.

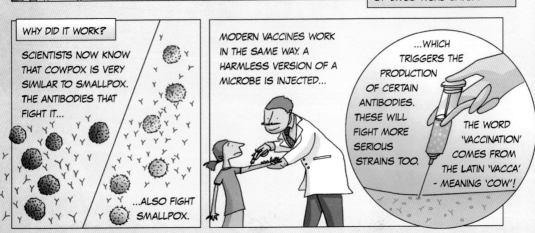

WHY DID IT WORK?

SCIENTISTS NOW KNOW THAT COWPOX IS VERY SIMILAR TO SMALLPOX. THE ANTIBODIES THAT FIGHT IT...

...ALSO FIGHT SMALLPOX.

MODERN VACCINES WORK IN THE SAME WAY. A HARMLESS VERSION OF A MICROBE IS INJECTED...

...WHICH TRIGGERS THE PRODUCTION OF CERTAIN ANTIBODIES. THESE WILL FIGHT MORE SERIOUS STRAINS TOO.

THE WORD 'VACCINATION' COMES FROM THE LATIN 'VACCA' - MEANING 'COW'!

ALEXANDER FLEMING AND ANTIBIOTICS

ALEXANDER FLEMING WAS A BRILLIANT BIOLOGIST...

...BUT HE COULD BE RATHER MESSY!

ONE DAY HE WAS LOOKING AT SOME OLD EXPERIMENTS WITH BACTERIA, WHEN HE MADE AN ASTOUNDING DISCOVERY.

The mould growing on this dish has killed all the bacteria around it!

HE RESEARCHED THE BACTERIA-KILLING CHEMICAL THAT THE MOULD HAD MADE, AND NAMED IT PENICILLIN.

THEN HE LOOKED FOR A CHEMIST TO TURN IT INTO A MEDICINE.

BUT HE DIDN'T HAVE MUCH LUCK.

A DECADE LATER, TWO SCIENTISTS CALLED HOWARD FLOREY AND BORIS CHAIN USED HIS RESEARCH...

FLOREY

CHAIN

...TO MAKE A VERSION OF PENICILLIN THAT COULD KILL BACTERIA INSIDE HUMAN BODIES.

THEY HAD CREATED THE FIRST ANTIBIOTIC.

PENICILLIN STOPPED COUNTLESS SOLDIERS FROM DYING OF INFECTED WOUNDS IN THE SECOND WORLD WAR.

AT THE END OF THE WAR, FLEMING, FLOREY AND CHAIN WERE JOINTLY AWARDED THE NOBEL PRIZE FOR THEIR WORK...

...AND ANTIBIOTICS HAVE BEEN SAVING LIVES EVER SINCE.

Part 2
How do human bodies work?

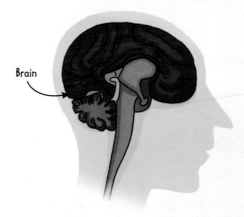

Brain

The human body is so complicated that it's taken biologists centuries to unlock its mysteries, and they're still making new discoveries. Like all animals, human bodies are made up of systems that control everything from breathing and moving to making babies. Fortunately, these systems are so good at their jobs that most of the time we don't even notice they're there. But one thing makes humans very different from other animals — our tremendously powerful brains. They make us the most intelligent species on Earth.

Shape and movement

The human body gets its shape from its **skeletal system**, or skeleton. Without this bony framework, you would collapse into a heap.

Your skeleton also protects your organs from damage, and helps you to move around.

Bony bodies

Most adult humans have 206 bones in their body – over half in just their hands, wrists and feet. Each hand and wrist has 27 bones, and each foot has 26.

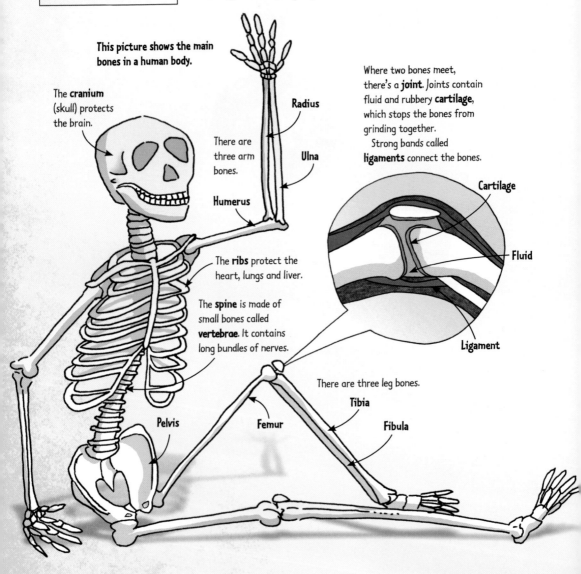

This picture shows the main bones in a human body.

The **cranium** (skull) protects the brain.

Radius

There are three arm bones.

Ulna

Humerus

The **ribs** protect the heart, lungs and liver.

The **spine** is made of small bones called **vertebrae**. It contains long bundles of nerves.

Where two bones meet, there's a **joint**. Joints contain fluid and rubbery **cartilage**, which stops the bones from grinding together.

Strong bands called **ligaments** connect the bones.

Cartilage

Fluid

Ligament

Pelvis

Femur

There are three leg bones.

Tibia

Fibula

How do you move?

Moving seems so simple that it's easy to take for granted. But behind every movement is a complex series of actions, which rely on muscles in your body.

The muscles you use to move around are made up of long, thin cells. Tough cords called **tendons** connect the muscles to the bones on either side of a joint. When you move, the muscle cells get shorter, or **contract**, bunching together to make the whole muscle shorter and fatter. This pulls the bones together.

Muscle cells can only contract – they can't make themselves stretch out to be long and thin again. So muscles usually work in pairs, where only one contracts at a time. As one muscle in the pair contracts, it makes the other stretch. These are called **antagonistic pairs**.

Mighty muscles

Some of our muscles only move when we want them to. Others are out of our control, but these aren't usually attached to bones. Some keep working all the time, such as the heart muscle which pumps dozens of times every minute.

Up, down and all around

The joints in your elbow and knee are different from your shoulder and hip joints. Move your body to see if you can work out how.

You should find that your shoulder and hip joints let you circle your arm and leg, while your elbow and knee only allow your forearm and calf to swing back and forth.

Here's the reason...

Shoulders and hips have **ball and socket joints**. These allow movement up, down and sideways.

Elbows and knees have **hinge joints**. These only let the bone move up or down, not sideways.

Biceps

Triceps

The **biceps** and **triceps** are an antagonistic pair.

Biceps

Triceps

When the **biceps** contracts, it pulls the forearm up, and the triceps gets long and thin.

When the **triceps** contracts, it pulls the forearm down and straightens out the biceps.

But how does the decision to move get made and communicated to the muscles? It's all down to our brilliant brain and hard-working nerves...

Inside the brain

Your **brain** issues commands for all the actions you choose to take, and for many you don't think about, such as controlling your body temperature. A brain is really a gigantic network of thousands of millions of nerve cells, or **neurons**. Each neuron is joined to many others, and new connections are always being made. These connections store your memories, and enable you to think. But it's all so complex that scientists are still finding out how it works.

The **cerebrum** is used for thinking.

The **cerebellum** controls balance and movement.

The **thalamus** receives signals from the body.

The **hypothalamus** keeps the body running smoothly.

The **brain stem** connects to the rest of the body.

From the brain to the body

Nerves also stretch down your spine and around your body, and whizz electrical signals to and from your brain. When a signal reaches the end of one neuron, a tiny amount of a chemical passes the signal to the next one, until the message reaches its target. Along with your brain, these nerves make up the **nervous system**.

All in your head

Sensations such as touch or pain feel as if they're in your body, but really they're all in your head. Nerves in your body send signals to your brain that it interprets as sensations.

Sometimes, a person who has an amputated limb still feels sensations from it. These are made by the brain, which makes them feel as if they come from the missing limb. This is called Phantom Limb Syndrome.

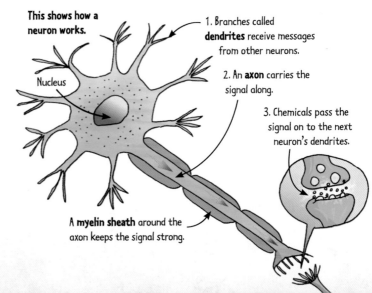

This shows how a neuron works.

Nucleus

1. Branches called **dendrites** receive messages from other neurons.

2. An **axon** carries the signal along.

3. Chemicals pass the signal on to the next neuron's dendrites.

A **myelin sheath** around the axon keeps the signal strong.

Are all neurons the same?

No. There are three main kinds of neurons in your body – all with different jobs.

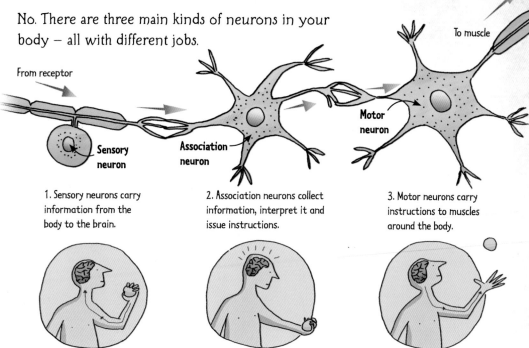

From receptor

To muscle

Motor neuron

Sensory neuron

Association neuron

1. Sensory neurons carry information from the body to the brain.

2. Association neurons collect information, interpret it and issue instructions.

3. Motor neurons carry instructions to muscles around the body.

How quickly does it happen?

Messages flash along your nervous system at very high speeds. It only takes a fraction of a second for a signal to travel to your brain and be interpreted, and for an instruction to be issued. There's such a tiny time lag that we don't even notice it.

But in an emergency, even this split second could be crucial. So, to speed things up even more, neurons running down the spine can issue a command for instant action, called a **reflex**.

This is why you react to some things before you've even realized they're happening. Examples include dropping hot objects, or blinking if something gets in your eye.

Mysterious brain

One of the biggest mysteries about the human brain is how it's aware of what it's thinking. This is called **consciousness**. It's what lets us be aware of ourselves, and our actions and decisions. We don't know if any other animals have this ability.

I wonder what she's thinking?

Sensing the world

People have five main ways of sensing what's going on in the world around them...

Sight

Light sources send out rays of light. When these rays hit an object, they are altered by it. If they then bounce into your eye, structures called **receptors** send the details recorded in the rays to the brain to interpret.

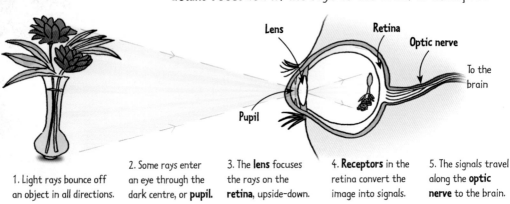

Lens

Retina

Optic nerve

To the brain

Pupil

1. Light rays bounce off an object in all directions.

2. Some rays enter an eye through the dark centre, or **pupil.**

3. The **lens** focuses the rays on the **retina**, upside-down.

4. **Receptors** in the retina convert the image into signals.

5. The signals travel along the **optic nerve** to the brain.

Hearing

Hearing relies on vibrations, called sound waves, that travel through the air. When these enter the ear, they are processed and sent to the brain.

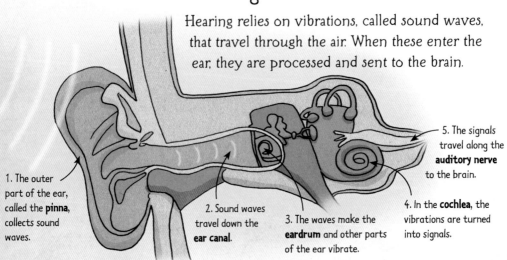

1. The outer part of the ear, called the **pinna**, collects sound waves.

2. Sound waves travel down the **ear canal.**

3. The waves make the **eardrum** and other parts of the ear vibrate.

4. In the **cochlea**, the vibrations are turned into signals.

5. The signals travel along the **auditory nerve** to the brain.

Touch

Your skin contains millions of receptors which respond to sensations such as heat, pressure and pain. The signals they pass to your brain are what creates the sense of touch. Sometimes, the signals make you feel pain, for example if you burn yourself.

Although pain is unpleasant, it's a useful warning that something's wrong. It helps you to react quickly to avoid what's hurting you, and reminds you to protect the damaged part of your body.

Smell and taste

A smell is made up of tiny particles floating in the air. When you breathe in, they touch millions of thread-like receptors deep inside your nose. Different receptors react to different particles, turning the information into signals which whizz off to the brain.

Taste comes from particles in food. The tongue recognizes tastes, although it can only detect five kinds – sweet, salt, sour, bitter and savoury.

But, as you eat, particles from the food drift up your nose, adding to the sensation. So the receptors on your tongue and in your nose work together to create taste.

Busy brain

Your brain receives so many different signals that it has to use shortcuts to interpret them. This means it sometimes makes mistakes. For example...

... these gorillas look different sizes, but in fact they're identical. Your brain thinks the top gorilla is further away – and as things in the distance look smaller, it thinks the top gorilla must be enormous.

Taste test

Try this experiment to see how smell affects your sense of taste.

1. Grate some fruit and vegetables, such as apples and carrots, into separate bowls.

2. Close your eyes, hold your nose and ask a friend to feed you some from each bowl.

3. Can you tell which is which? What about if you do it without holding your nose?

Body fuel

Your body is an incredibly complex machine and, like any machine, it needs fuel to power it. This fuel comes from the food you eat, which gives your body the energy it uses to keep running, as well as chemicals it needs for growth and repair.

The process of breaking down and absorbing food is called **digestion**. The system that deals with it is called the **digestive system**.

What happens when you eat?

Your teeth grind up the food in your mouth, and mix it with chemicals in your spit called **enzymes**. These start to break down the food.

After swallowing, the chunks pass quickly down the **oesophagus** into the stomach.

The **stomach** releases enzymes, and acidic juices to kill any germs. Soon the food is churned into a liquid.

The food passes, a bit at a time, into the **small intestine**. There, enzymes break it down even further, until the tiny particles can pass through the intestine's lining into the bloodstream.

Leftovers, such as tough parts of fruits and vegetables, pass into the **large intestine** – along with water, dead cells from the intestine, and mucus that has helped move food along. Water is reabsorbed here. Solid waste moves to the **rectum** and passes out of your body as **faeces** (or poo).

This diagram shows a human digestive system.

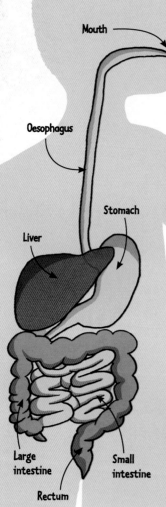

Mouth

Oesophagus

Stomach

Liver

Large intestine

Small intestine

Rectum

How does your body use food?

Once food particles pass into the bloodstream, they are carried to cells all around the body. Some particles are used to build new cell parts, and others – made of a special sugar called **glucose** – are used for energy.

Some particles are stored in the **liver** for later use, or converted into other useful substances there.

What kinds of foods are there?

Foods are made of combinations of different types of substances. Here are some of the main groups...

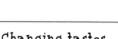

Long tube
The small intestine is small and narrow, but it's really, really long – about four times the length of your whole body.

Proteins are chemicals that the body needs for growth, repair and making new cells.

Carbohydrates contain sugars, which provide energy.

People can't digest **fibre**, but its bulk keeps food and water flowing through the intestines.

Minerals and vitamins are chemicals that the body needs. There are many different kinds.

Fats provide energy, keep you warm and are used in building new cells.

Changing tastes
Take a big bite of white bread, and chew it for several minutes. Don't swallow it! Does the taste change?

What happens?
If you keep chewing the bread for long enough, you should find it slowly starts to taste sweeter. That's because it's been broken down into sugars by an enzyme in your spit.

45

Lungs and smoking

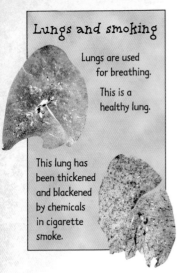

Lungs are used for breathing.

This is a healthy lung.

This lung has been thickened and blackened by chemicals in cigarette smoke.

How do you turn food into energy?

To release energy from food, cells need a gas from the air, called **oxygen**. This is so vital that we take over 20,000 breaths of it every day.

How do you get oxygen from air?

Air is only about one fifth oxygen; the rest is made up of other gases, such as nitrogen. But your **respiratory system** can deal with taking in oxygen and getting rid of other gases (especially **carbon dioxide** – see opposite).

When you breathe in, air travels down a pipe at the back of your throat, called the **trachea**. (This is separate from the oesophagus, and a flap at the top called the **epiglottis** stops food from entering it.)

Then the air passes along tubes called **bronchi** into big, spongy organs called the **lungs**.

Inside the lungs, the bronchi split into smaller and smaller tubes, which finally end in millions of tiny, moist sacs called **alveoli**.

Oxygen passes through the alveoli's thin walls into the bloodstream. Only about a quarter of the oxygen in each breath is absorbed.

This shows the human respiratory system.

Epiglottis

Trachea

Bronchi

Lung

Lung

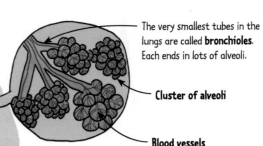

The very smallest tubes in the lungs are called **bronchioles**. Each ends in lots of alveoli.

Cluster of alveoli

Blood vessels

Respiration at work

Respiration – or releasing energy from food – is one of the seven life processes. In humans, this happens when glucose from food reacts with oxygen. As energy is released, the glucose and oxygen are turned into water and carbon dioxide (a gas). This can be written as a word equation, like this:

glucose + oxygen → water + carbon dioxide + energy

This reaction takes place in every living cell in your body, as each cell releases its own energy.

Feeling the burn

When you exercise, you need more oxygen than normal for respiration. If you don't get enough oxygen, an acid builds up, which causes a burning sensation in your muscles.

See the difference between the air you breathe in and the air you breathe out.

BREATHING IN:
21% oxygen
78.96% nitrogen and other gases
0.04% carbon dioxide

BREATHING OUT:
16% oxygen
78.96% nitrogen and other gases
5.04% carbon dioxide

Making a noise

Breathing out isn't just useful for getting rid of waste gas. It's also how you talk, sing and shout.

La la laaaaa

Clearing the waste

Cells need the energy from respiration, but they don't need the carbon dioxide or most of the water. These unwanted leftovers, or **waste products**, are taken away in the blood and used elsewhere or got rid of.

Your body uses water as sweat to keep you cool, or as tears in your eyes. It gets rid of extra water as urine when you go to the toilet. Meanwhile, all the carbon dioxide is carried to your lungs and breathed out.

Air flowing up your trachea passes folds called vocal cords, making them vibrate. This makes a noise, which you control by relaxing or tightening the cords, and moving your mouth and tongue.

Vocal cords (as seen from above)

Open (low pitch)   Closed (high)

The blood highway

From the top of your head to the tips of your toes, every cell in your body is connected to your **circulatory system**, which is made up of blood, the tubes which carry it, and your heart. This system acts as a conveyor belt, carrying oxygen, waste and chemicals from food all around your body. It also helps protect you from injury and disease.

This photograph shows a human heart. The white lines are blood vessels carrying the heart's own supply of oxygen-packed blood.

Changing blood

Blood vessels in your limbs may look bluish green, but it's just an illusion caused by the skin layers. Blood is always red. But blood carrying lots of oxygen is bright red, while blood that's not carrying oxygen is darker.

How does blood get around?

'Circulate' means 'to go around', and that's what blood does in your body. It travels in tubes called **blood vessels**. Some are as wide as your thumb, and others are thinner than a sheet of paper. It takes lots of blood vessels to reach each cell in your body. Laid out end to end, they would stretch several times around the Earth.

This picture shows the contents of a blood vessel, roughly 3,000 times bigger than in real life.

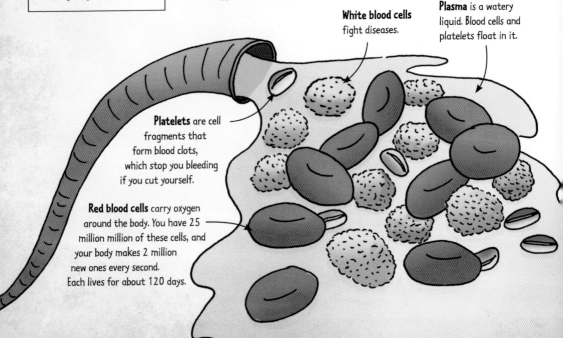

White blood cells fight diseases.

Plasma is a watery liquid. Blood cells and platelets float in it.

Platelets are cell fragments that form blood clots, which stop you bleeding if you cut yourself.

Red blood cells carry oxygen around the body. You have 25 million million of these cells, and your body makes 2 million new ones every second. Each lives for about 120 days.

What makes your blood move?

Your blood's journey around your body is controlled by your **heart** – the circulatory system's hard-working pump. The heart is only the size of a fist, but it beats around 100,000 times a day. Each beat squeezes blood-filled chambers inside the heart shut, forcing the blood to race from the heart to the lungs or rest of the body.

Counting beats

You can measure the rate at which your heart beats by resting two fingers on the inside of your wrist. Count how many beats you feel in a minute while sitting. Then try counting while doing different things, such as walking or lying down, or after running.

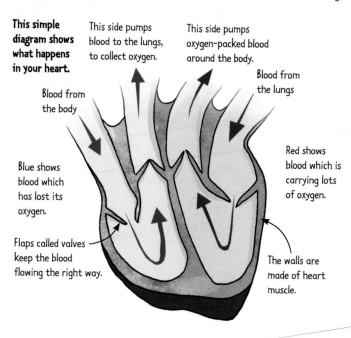

This simple diagram shows what happens in your heart.

This side pumps blood to the lungs, to collect oxygen.

This side pumps oxygen-packed blood around the body.

Blood from the body

Blood from the lungs

Blue shows blood which has lost its oxygen.

Red shows blood which is carrying lots of oxygen.

Flaps called valves keep the blood flowing the right way.

The walls are made of heart muscle.

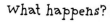

What happens?

You should find your heart rate speeds up when you're more active. This is because your body needs more oxygen, and makes more carbon dioxide to be breathed out.

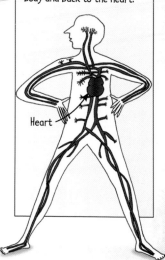

Your circulation

Arteries (shown in red) and veins (shown in blue) stretch out to all parts of the body. It takes just 45 seconds for blood to travel all around the body and back to the heart.

Heart

Vanishing vessels

The vessels leading away from the heart are called **arteries**. They are quite thick, but they split gradually into thinner and thinner tubes. The smallest of these, called **capillaries**, have very thin walls. Food and oxygen pass through these walls into your body's cells.

Cell waste passes through the walls in the other direction. As capillaries fill up with this waste, they form larger tubes called **veins**. These lead back to the heart.

Reproduction

A baby begins when two special cells called **gametes** fuse. This is called **sexual reproduction**. One gamete, called a **sperm**, comes from a man. The other, an **egg**, comes from a woman. Human reproductive systems make gametes and bring them together. A woman's reproductive system also carries the developing baby.

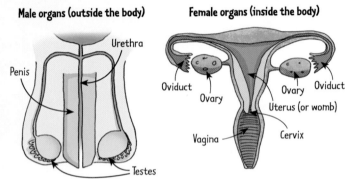

Male organs (outside the body)

Female organs (inside the body)

Male and female

A male gamete (or sperm) is long and thin. It has a nucleus at the front, and a long tail.

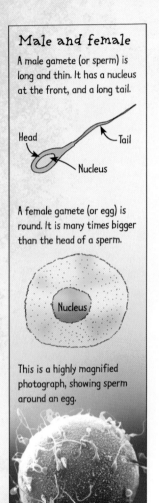

A female gamete (or egg) is round. It is many times bigger than the head of a sperm.

This is a highly magnified photograph, showing sperm around an egg.

Time of the month

If the egg doesn't fuse with a sperm within a few days, then the extra lining of the uterus breaks down. Blood from it leaks out through the woman's vagina for several days. This is called having a period, or **menstruation.**

Basic baby ingredients

Sperm are made in a man's testes, which hang in a sac outside his body. The slightly cooler temperature there is ideal for sperm production.

A woman is born with lots of eggs already in her ovaries. When she grows up, an egg leaves one of her ovaries about every 28 days, and moves along the oviduct. Meanwhile, her uterus' lining gets extra thick, so it's ready if the egg is **fertilized** (joins with a sperm).

The gametes join through sex. When a man and a woman have sex, the man pushes his penis into the woman's vagina. Muscle movements force millions of sperm out through his urethra into the woman's body. The sperm then swim up to the oviduct. If an egg is there, just one sperm will fuse with it.

Pregnancy and birth

1. The egg and sperm fuse into a single cell, called a **zygote**.

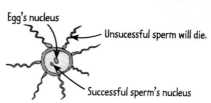

Egg's nucleus

Unsucessful sperm will die.

Successful sperm's nucleus

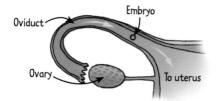

Oviduct

Embryo

Ovary

To uterus

2. The **zygote** splits again and again to form a ball of cells. Now called an **embryo**, it travels to the uterus.

3. The embryo attaches itself to the lining of the uterus, which provides it with food and oxygen. The cells continue to divide rapidly.

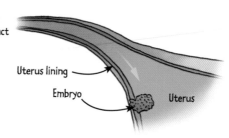

From oviduct

Uterus lining

Embryo

Uterus

Food and oxygen passes from the mother to the baby through a disc-like **placenta**.

The **umbilical cord** joins the embryo and placenta.

Embryo

Uterus

Protective sac

4. After about 2 months, the embryo has a head, arms and legs, and a protective watery sac has formed around it. It is now called a **foetus**.

5. After about 9 months, the baby is ready to be born. The protective sac breaks, and muscle spasms, or contractions, start. These push the baby out of the mother's body, through the cervix and vagina.

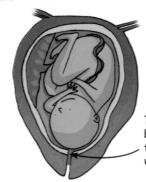

The baby will be pushed out through the cervix, which is here.

How do cells know what to do?

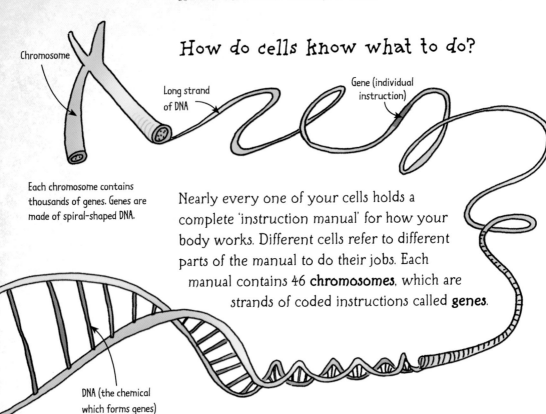

Chromosome

Long strand of DNA

Gene (individual instruction)

Each chromosome contains thousands of genes. Genes are made of spiral-shaped DNA.

DNA (the chemical which forms genes)

Nearly every one of your cells holds a complete 'instruction manual' for how your body works. Different cells refer to different parts of the manual to do their jobs. Each manual contains 46 **chromosomes**, which are strands of coded instructions called **genes**.

Each manual of 46 chromosomes holds over 200,000 genes, which control how you look, how your body works, and even how you act. All humans share similar genes – they're what make us human – but slight differences mean we're not all the same.

DNA dilemmas

Scientists have just started to unravel the mysteries of genes and DNA, and their work has helped to treat many terrible illnesses.

But some people worry about where their research may lead. For example, should parents be allowed to choose their children's genes to prevent them from inheriting diseases? How about making their child cleverer or better looking? And who would be able to choose – all parents, or just the richest ones?

Where did your genes come from?

Children get their genes from their parents. Each sperm and egg holds a unique set of 23 chromosomes, created by rearranging a parent's genes, then halving them. If gametes fuse, these sets join to form a full 'manual'.

As children get their genes from their parents, they usually look like them. Children also tend to look like their brothers and sisters, who share very similar genes.

Pushy genes

Each of the 23 chromosomes that a child gets from one parent is matched by one inherited from the other, to give 23 pairs of mirrored genes. If the genes in a pair contradict each other, only one – called the **dominant** gene – may be used. The other is said to be **recessive**.

For example, the gene for a cleft (or dimpled) chin is dominant over a gene for a smooth chin.

This diagram shows how different genes for cleft or smooth chins can combine.

I have two 'cleft chin' genes.

I have one 'cleft chin' gene and one 'smooth chin' gene.

I have two 'smooth chin' genes.

Here, only the person with two recessive 'smooth chin' genes will have a smooth chin.

But don't write off recessive genes. They may not be used, but they can still be passed on. So two parents with cleft chins can have a child with a smooth chin if they both carry a recessive gene for smooth chins.

Genetic genius

The first scientist to make a close study of how characteristics are passed on was an Austrian monk called Gregor Mendel, who lived in the 19th century.

He experimented with breeding pea plants, and noticed patterns in the results. He came up with the idea of dominant and recessive characteristics.

Boy or girl?

Your genes determine whether you're male or female. Women have two 'X' chromosomes, and men have one 'X' and one 'Y' chromosome. The egg always has an X chromosome, and the sperm can have either an X or a Y.

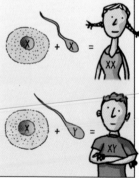

This diagram shows how dominant and recessive genes can be passed on in different combinations.

Parents

I have one 'cleft chin' gene and one 'smooth chin' gene.

I have one 'cleft chin' gene and one 'smooth chin' gene.

Children

I have inherited two 'cleft chin' genes.

I have inherited one 'cleft chin' gene and one 'smooth chin' gene.

I have inherited two 'smooth chin' genes.

What about other animals?

Other animal species must do the same things that humans do to survive, from eating and breathing to having babies. But they have developed a huge range of strange and startling ways of doing these – as you can see from the examples below.

All animals

For a reminder of the seven life processes common to all living things, turn to page 16. In addition, all animals need to eat to survive.

Skeletons and movement

Animals need to move and support their bodies. Vertebrates have skeletons, but invertebrates (who don't have backbones) keep their shape in other ways.

Fluid fillings

Some invertebrates, such as worms, are packed with fluid. This keeps their bodies firm, and gives the muscles something to push against.

Fluid

Muscle

Hard homes

Many soft-bodied molluscs, such as snails, live inside hard shells. The shell gets bigger as the animal grows.

Shark skeletons

Most vertebrates have bones. But sharks, rays and skates have skeletons made of a tough, lighter material called cartilage – from their spines to their fins.

Outer cases

Arthropods have protective cases, called 'exoskeletons' – 'exo' means 'outside'. Exoskeletons don't stretch, so growing arthropods cast them off to make new, bigger ones.

Boneless bodies

Octopuses don't have skeletons or shells, just very strong, muscular arms and a hard beak for eating. Their lack of bones makes them extra-flexible.

Coral reefs

Coral is made up of tiny animals called polyps. Each has its own miniature exoskeleton, and new polyps build up over the remains of older, dead ones.

Nerves and brains

Almost all animals have nerves which let them move and react to things around them. But some of the simplest animals don't have brains.

Simple jellyfish

Jellyfish have no brains and very simple nerves, which react automatically to what's around them.

Nervy insects

Insects have 'command centres' of large nerve clusters throughout their bodies. Some don't die for a long time even if their heads are cut off.

Clever molluscs

Octopuses, squid and cuttlefish (above) are very smart – they have the most complex brains of any invertebrates.

Loose cells

Sponges are the simplest animals. They don't have a brain or nerves, so their cells act separately from each other.

Senses

Humans mostly use sight to get around. But other creatures rely on different senses – including some senses that we don't have at all.

Glowing eyes

Many night animals have a reflective layer at the back of their eyes. As light reflects back out, receptors in the eye have a second chance to pick it up.

Super scents

Wolves and dogs have a super-sensitive sense of smell. For every smell receptor that a human has, they have over twenty.

Echolocation

Bats make high clicks, and listen for the echoes* to bounce back. From these, they can work out what's around them.

Ear

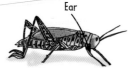

Feeling the way

Many night mammals have touch-sensitive hairs called whiskers. Some can even sense air currents moving around things.

Scattered senses

Many insects have senses in strange places. Crickets hear through their knees, and flies have taste sensors on the ends of their feet.

Electricity

Sharks, such as this hammerhead shark, use nerve cells in their skin to sense tiny electric pulses made by other animals.

Compound eyes

Most insect eyes are made of lots of lenses. These eyes can't see as clearly as ours, but can see over a wider area and detect movements more quickly.

Eating and digesting

All animals need to eat and digest food. But they have different ways of eating it and breaking it down.

Spit soup

Flies cover food with their spit, which breaks it down into a soupy liquid. Then they slurp it up.

Gobblers

Birds gobble food whole and store it in their crop. Then it moves to their stomach and gizzard to be digested.

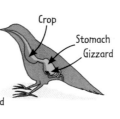

Crop

Stomach

Gizzard

Grazing

Grass is hard to digest, so grazers such as cows and sheep have four sections in their stomachs. Their food is broken down a little more as it passes through each section.

Filter feeders

The biggest whales and sharks only eat tiny organisms. They take huge mouthfuls of seawater, then squeeze out the liquid and swallow what's left.

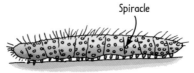

Breathing

All animals, no matter where they live, need oxygen for respiration.

Spiracle

Skin and mouths

Most full-grown frogs and toads can breathe through their skin and the lining of their mouths.

Breathing holes

Insects don't have lungs. Instead, they have holes called spiracles in their exoskeletons, which let in oxygen and release carbon dioxide.

Super lungs

Birds have extra-efficient lungs, which keep fresh and used air separate. This helps the lungs to absorb more oxygen from the fresh air.

Fishy breathing

Oxygen dissolves in water. The water enters fishes' mouths and passes over the gills, which absorb oxygen, a bit like underwater lungs.

Hole in the head

Whales and dolphins breathe in and out through holes on their heads. Some whales can hold their breath for up to 90 minutes when they dive.

The gills are under this flap.

Blood and circulation

Animals must move substances such as oxygen, food and waste around their bodies. Many vertebrates transport these in red blood, but other creatures have different kinds of blood, or even none at all.

Bloodless animals

Some animals, such as flatworms, have such simple bodies that they don't need blood. Instead, nutrients and oxygen pass directly from cell to cell.

Hollow cavity

Arthropods, such as beetles and spiders, have a wide hollow in their bodies. Blood flows through it, carrying food and oxygen to the organs.

The hollow surrounds the organs.

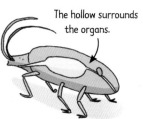

Hearty beasts

Octopuses have three hearts. Two pump blood to the gills, and the third sends it around their bodies.

The hearts are at the back of the head.

Reproduction

Animal reproduction almost always needs a male and female gamete to fuse. But the ways in which it happens varies hugely – as do the ways in which different animal species treat their children.

Fatherless sons

Female Komodo dragons (a kind of lizard) can have male babies without mating, by making gametes that fuse with each other. But they have to mate with a male to have female babies.

Water babies

Most fish release their eggs and sperm into the water, and the gametes join there.

Queen of the hive

Many insects, such as ants, live in huge groups. Just one female, called the queen, lays all the eggs.

Stage-by-stage

Frogs, toads and many insects go through three stages as they grow – egg, larva and adult. The larva often looks completely different from the adult.

Eggs

Adult

Larva

Beating the odds

Sea turtles lay lots of eggs, then abandon them. Most of the unprotected babies will die, but there are so many that some usually survive.

Eggs

Baby mammals develop inside their mothers' bodies. But in most other animals, mothers lay eggs and their babies develop inside those.

Eggs laid on land have shells, so the insides stay moist.

Eggs laid in water, such as frogspawn, are usually much smaller and softer.

Part 3
How do plants work?

How a seed grows

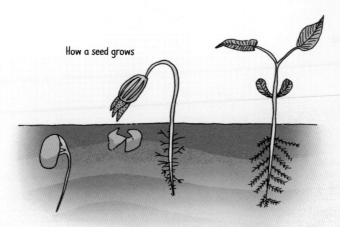

Plants carpet the Earth, from mosses in
the freezing Antarctic wastes to grasses and
shrubs in the hottest deserts. In fact, there
are so many plants on our planet that from
space, much of the land looks green. These
plants are vital to our survival, making
both the oxygen that we need to breathe
and the food we need to eat.

where do plants live?

Warm, damp places such as rainforests are home to over half of all known plant species. There are far fewer kinds of plants around the icy poles, but forests grow even around the Arctic circle, and there are mosses in Antartica. Some tough plants survive high up on mountains, where the air is cold and the soil is thin, or in hot places where it hardly ever rains.

But there are a few plantless places – dark caves, where there is no light to make food, or deep, dark seas and oceans.

Counting plants

Scientists have discovered over a quarter of a million plant species so far – and they are still finding new ones all the time.

Another one!

Ocean 'plants'

Seaweeds look like plants, but really they're much simpler organisms without roots or veins. Instead, each cell takes what it needs straight from the water.

How do plants grow?

Plants grow from sections called **meristems**, where specially adaptable cells divide to make all the different kinds of cells the plant needs. Each plant has lots of meristems, found just behind their root tips and in their stems, especially in their buds.

Many plants grow upwards from a meristem at the tip of their stem. But tips may be eaten or damaged, so other plants, including grasses, grow from meristems that lie close to the ground. These plants can grow back quickly after being grazed or mown.

The bud at the stem's tip is called the **terminal bud.** It contains a meristem.

This plant is called St John's Wort. It grows in all kinds of places, especially grasslands.

60

Plant parts

This chrysanthemum has a typical plant structure – but not all plants have all of these parts.

Flowers are where gametes are made. These flowers are colourful and scented to help attract insects, which spread gametes between plants.

Leaves collect carbon dioxide and sunlight, which they use to make food.

The **stem** is stiff, and holds the plant upright.

Below ground, the **roots** collect water and nutrients, and anchor the plant firmly in the soil.

what do leaves do?

Plants make food in their leaves. The process is fuelled by energy from sunlight, and it's called **photosynthesis** – 'photo' means 'light' and 'synthesis' means 'putting together'.

During photosynthesis, water and carbon dioxide react together to make a sugar called glucose (the food) and oxygen (a waste product). Biologists write this as a word equation, like this:

Plants from dry places, such as this one from an African desert, often store water in their leaves.

carbon dioxide + water (+ light energy) → glucose + oxygen

This happens in parts of plant cells called **chloroplasts**.

Falling leaves

Deciduous trees lose their leaves before winter. This prevents water loss at a time when ground water may have frozen into ice, which trees can't use.

Evergreen trees don't shed their leaves over winter, as their small, waxy leaves hardly lose any water over the cold months.

what's in a leaf?

Leaves are mostly made up of long **palisade cells** along the top, and round **spongy cells** in the centre. Both have chloroplasts, but palisade cells have more. The surfaces of leaves are covered by thin epithelial cells.

Water flows from the roots up the stem and into the leaves. If it's not used in photosynthesis, it escapes as water vapour. This is called **transpiration**.

This picture shows the structure of a leaf.

The blue holes are **stomata** – pores in a leaf's surface which allow gases and water vapour to flow in and out.

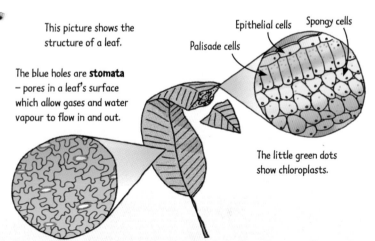

Epithelial cells   Spongy cells

Palisade cells

The little green dots show chloroplasts.

Why do leaves change colour?

Leaves are usually green because of **chlorophyll** – a green substance inside the chloroplasts which transfers energy from light into a form the plant can use.

Leaves also contain other substances, which can be red, yellow or orange. Usually the green chlorophyll masks the other colours, but in autumn, the chlorophyll in many trees' leaves breaks down, revealing all the other colours.

Do plants need oxygen?

Just like animals, plants need oxygen to **respire** (release energy from food) and they make carbon dioxide as a waste product. But overall, plants make much more oxygen through photosynthesis than they use up respiring – so there's lots left over for us.

Plants keep respiring all the time, but most only photosynthesize during daylight hours. So at night they only release carbon dioxide, rather than using it up.

Amazing algae

Algae in rivers, lakes, seas and oceans also release oxygen through photosynthesis – though they are protists, not plants. Together, they produce even more oxygen than all of the land plants.

Slow build-up

The amount of oxygen created each year is only small compared to the total amount in the air – but it has been building up over a long time. So the oxygen you breathe today may have been made thousands of years ago.

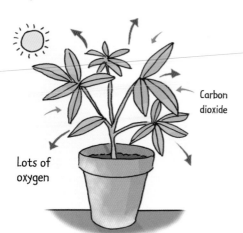

This plant is respiring and photosynthesizing. Overall, it is using up carbon dioxide and producing oxygen.

Carbon dioxide

Lots of oxygen

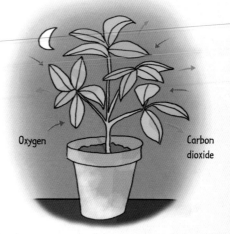

This plant is just respiring. It is using a small amount of oxygen, and releasing a small amount of carbon dioxide.

Oxygen

Carbon dioxide

Rootless plants

Mosses, hornworts and liverworts don't have real roots, or tubes to transport water and food. Instead they absorb water through their surface, so live in damp places.

water guzzlers

Some trees absorb more than enough water to fill a bath tub every day.

Meat munchers

Some plants get extra nutrients from animals. For example, insects often fall down the slippery sides of this pitcher plant, and down into a pool of liquid. Then their bodies break down into nutrients that the plant absorbs.

Collecting ingredients

Plants usually absorb water and nutrients through tiny hairs on their roots. These **root hairs** are so small, they slip between tiny particles of soil.

Most root hairs grow near the end of the root. As the root grows longer, old hairs wither and new ones grow further along. At the tip of the root there's a hard cap, which protects the root as it pushes through the soil.

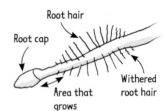

Root hair

Root cap

Area that grows

Withered root hair

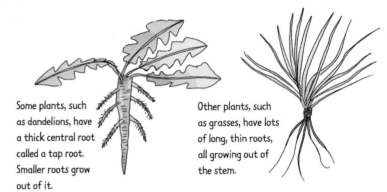

Some plants, such as dandelions, have a thick central root called a tap root. Smaller roots grow out of it.

Other plants, such as grasses, have lots of long, thin roots, all growing out of the stem.

Rooting out a meal

Some plants store food in underground roots, leaves or shoots. Many use it to shoot up quickly in spring. The stores can also provide a tasty meal for animals.

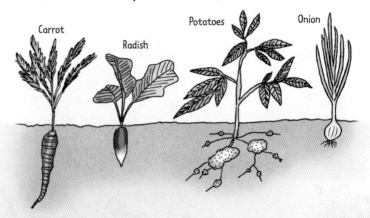

Carrot

Radish

Potatoes

Onion

Transport tubes

Most plants have tissues called the **xylem** and **phloem**, for transporting water and food. Xylem tissue is made of tubes which carry water up from the roots. Phloem tissue is made of tubes which carry food all around the plant.

Xylem and phloem tissues run through plants in clusters called **vascular bundles**. These support the plant – especially the woody walls of the xylem tubes.

This is a close-up across the middle of a typical plant stem. The colours have been added to show the different parts.

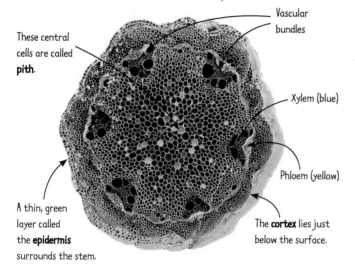

These central cells are called **pith**.

Vascular bundles

Xylem (blue)

Phloem (yellow)

A thin, green layer called the **epidermis** surrounds the stem.

The **cortex** lies just below the surface.

Why do plants droop?

A healthy plant's cells are packed with watery liquids, making them expand right up to their cell walls and push against each other. This force keeps the plant firm.

But if a plant loses too much water, the cells shrink and stop pushing against each other. So the plant goes limp and wilts. This often happens in summer, when heat dries out the soil.

Dying xylem

To see xylem tubes for yourself, try this...

1. Put some water in a container. Add enough food dye to colour it.

2. Snap the bottom end off a stick of celery.

3. Put the celery in the water. Leave it for at least an hour.

Look at the end of the celery that's been in the water. You should be able to see where the xylem has taken up the coloured water.

Xylem tubes

Tree rings

In trees, xylem and phloem tissue grows in rings. Xylem rings are easy to see, and a new one grows each year.

Phloem rings cluster beneath the bark.

Xylem rings (one per year)

How do plants reproduce?

Most plants use flowers to reproduce. Flowers contain the female gametes, or **ovules**, and the male gametes, or **pollen**. When an ovule and a grain of pollen (often from another flower) join, they form a seed which can grow into a new plant.

What's in a flower?

This picture shows a typical flower structure...

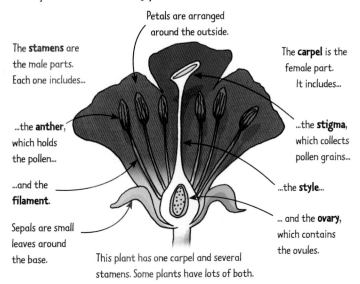

Petals are arranged around the outside.

The **stamens** are the male parts. Each one includes...

The **carpel** is the female part. It includes...

...the **anther**, which holds the pollen...

...the **stigma**, which collects pollen grains...

...and the **filament**.

...the **style**...

Sepals are small leaves around the base.

... and the **ovary**, which contains the ovules.

This plant has one carpel and several stamens. Some plants have lots of both.

How are seeds made?

A seed begins when a pollen grain lands on a stigma. The grain grows a tiny tube through the style to the ovary. Then the grain's nucleus travels down the tube, and merges with the nucleus of an ovule, fertilizing it.

The fertilized ovule divides many times to make a tiny plant embryo. A protective coating surrounds it, forming a seed. Many seeds may form inside an ovary.

Pollen power

When plants spread their pollen to other flowers, it's called pollination. It can happen in different ways:

Insect pollination

Many flowers make a juice called nectar to attract insects. Pollen clings to the insects, and they carry it to new flowers.

Water pollination

Water plants may use water currents to spread their pollen.

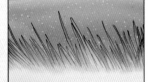

Wind pollination

Some plants have long anthers which scatter pollen as they sway in the wind.

From flower to fruit

As seeds develop in the ovary, the petals around the flower wither. The ovary swells and becomes a fruit.

Sowing the seeds

A plant must spread its seeds far and wide, so its own patch of soil isn't overrun. Some plants make fruits that are fluffy or have 'wings' to catch the wind. Others have pods which explode open to scatter their fruits.

Plants also use animals to spread their seeds. Sticky fruits, or fruits with hooks, can catch a ride on passing creatures. Other fruits are eaten by animals, who spit out the seeds or spread them somewhere else in their poo.

How do seeds grow?

If a seed lands in the right spot, with enough light, soil and water, then it **germinates**, or starts to grow.

Far and wide

Pea pods dry up, then suddenly split open. The seeds burst out.

Fruits such as this are ideal for hooking onto fur or hairs.

The wind carries these light seeds far away from their parent plant.

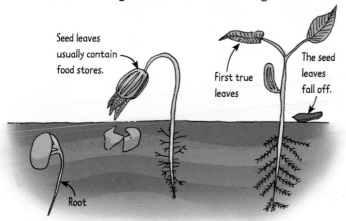

Seed leaves usually contain food stores.

First true leaves

The seed leaves fall off.

Root

When plants first start to grow, they have simple 'seed' leaves. Plants with two seed leaves are called **dicotyledons**, and those with one are **monocotyledons**.

Ancient seeds

Some seeds can wait for years to grow into a plant.

In 2005, scientists managed to grow a date palm from a 2,000-year-old seed.

They've named it 'Methuselah' after the oldest person in the Bible.

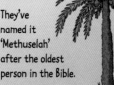

Simple spores

Liverworts, mosses and ferns don't make seeds. Instead, they reproduce using gametes and **spores** (which are much simpler than seeds). It's a two-part cycle. First, the gametes fuse and grow into structures that make spores; then the spores grow into structures that make gametes. Biologists call this **alternation of generations**.

The brown dots on the underside of these fern leaves are full of spores.

Here you can see how moss plants reproduce...

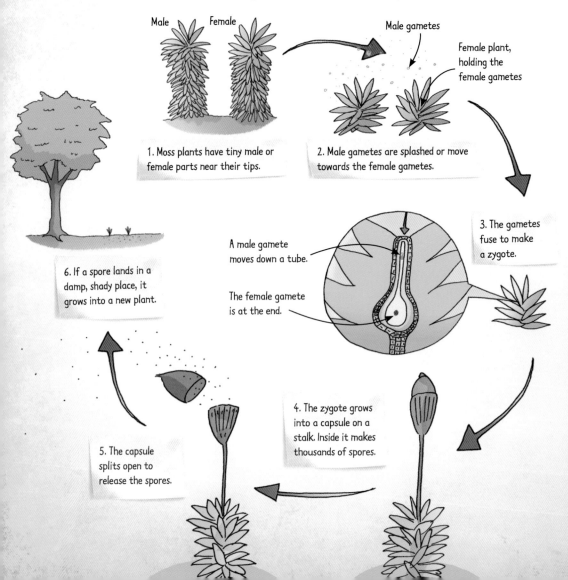

Male   Female

Male gametes

Female plant, holding the female gametes

1. Moss plants have tiny male or female parts near their tips.

2. Male gametes are splashed or move towards the female gametes.

A male gamete moves down a tube.

3. The gametes fuse to make a zygote.

The female gamete is at the end.

6. If a spore lands in a damp, shady place, it grows into a new plant.

5. The capsule splits open to release the spores.

4. The zygote grows into a capsule on a stalk. Inside it makes thousands of spores.

Cloned copies

Many plants can also reproduce by making exact copies of themselves, called **clones**.

Some plants send out long shoots, or **runners**, which put out stems and roots to make new plants. When the new plant is established, the runner withers away.

This strawberry plant has copied itself by sending out runners to either side.

Other plants use underground food stores to make copies of themselves. These stores may sprout into new plants, or split to produce two plants rather than one.

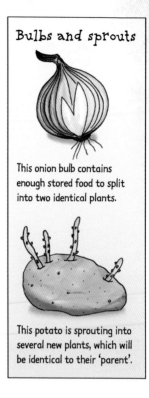

Bulbs and sprouts

This onion bulb contains enough stored food to split into two identical plants.

This potato is sprouting into several new plants, which will be identical to their 'parent'.

From bulbs to shoots

Garlic bulbs are food stores that grow into copies of their parent. See how the cloves shoot up into plants...

1. Separate out two cloves from a bulb of garlic.

2. Plant the cloves in a pot full of soil, so that the rounded end is pointing downwards.

3. Put the pot somewhere sunny, and water it every day.

4. After about two weeks, you should see new shoots starting to grow from the cloves.

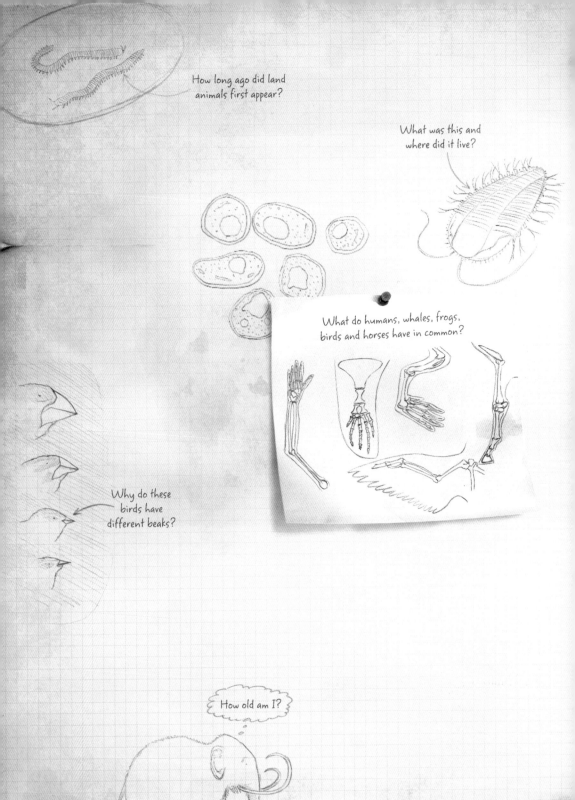

Part 4
Where did life come from?

Early amphibian

Over the past few centuries, biologists have
discovered a huge amount about early life,
and how it developed into the organisms we
know today. Their discoveries have challenged
previous ideas of humans' place in the world,
and even today much of their work still
sparks arguments and debates.

How did life begin?

Life in a lab

In 1953, scientists Harold Clayton Urey and Stanley Lloyd Miller set up an experiment to recreate the conditions and chemicals on early Earth. Within just a week, some of the most basic building blocks of life, called amino acids, had formed.

Since then, other experiments have produced more complex building blocks – but never a living organism.

Are we aliens?

Some scientists think the chemicals needed for life were carried to Earth on an asteroid. A few even think that the first living cells arrived like this, after forming elsewhere.

Experts aren't sure exactly how and when life first began. But they have lots of ideas...

Most biologists think the first living things formed in early oceans, which were steaming hot and toxic. They think that chemicals in these oceans reacted together again and again – fuelled by sunlight, lightning bursts, volcanic eruptions or hot underwater vents – until they formed molecules which could copy themselves.

Scientists have found traces of living things dating back over 3,500 million years. These ancient organisms were simple water-dwelling bacteria, which trapped particles of mud or sand to form long-lasting stone structures known as **stromatolites**.

Although early microbes such as these were pioneers on a hostile Earth, they had all they needed to thrive – including, eventually, the ability to make their own food by photosynthesis. This produced oxygen, which slowly began to build up in the atmosphere.

What happened next?

Gradually, early microbes developed into more complex life forms. After hundreds of millions of years, some had banded together to make 'multicellular' organisms, in which different cells did specialized jobs. This began a long process of change, which is still going on today.

These stone clumps are made by bacteria. Long ago, structures like these may have been the only signs of life on Earth.

Reading the records

Very few ancient organisms left any record of their existence. But some fragments have survived, and they provide enough evidence for experts to piece together a history of life. The oldest records are stony remains called **fossils**, which can last for many millions of years.

How do fossils form?

1. An organism dies. Its body may decay, but the hard parts remain.

2. The remains are covered by mud, which gets thicker and thicker.

3. The mud hardens into rock. Water and dissolved minerals drip through.

4. Minerals slowly soak into the remains, turning them to stone.

5. The remains are now a fossil. Above, the land slowly changes.

6. Sometimes, the rock wears away or shifts, exposing the fossil.

Sadly, most remains are eaten or rot away before they turn to stone. In particular, those with soft bodies hardly ever become fossils; and remains on land are rarely covered by mud quickly enough. Even when fossils do form, many stay buried deep underground.

Trapped alive

Sometimes animals get caught in sticky situations, such as tar pits or plant sap. As their gooey prison hardens, they are preserved inside.

This termite was trapped in sap 35 million years ago. The sap has hardened into amber.

Trace fossils

Long-dead animals may leave behind other traces, such as tracks, burrows, nests or droppings. These records are called 'trace fossils'.

A large 'sail-backed' reptile left these footprints over 250 million years ago.

From then to now — life's history

This timeline shows how life on Earth developed. Most early creatures were very different from those that are around today.

What happened on land...

Meteorites smash into the Earth.

Vapour from volcanoes falls as rain.

The surface of the Earth gets very cold... then thaws.

The seas freeze.

The Earth forms.

Oxygen slowly builds up.

About 4,600 mya

600 mya

Single-celled organisms live in the oceans.

Some cells start to photosynthesize.

Some cells group together into simple organisms.

...and under the sea.

A long, long day

Picture the Earth's lifetime as a single day. These are, roughly, the times of events throughout the day.

- At midnight, the Earth forms.

- At about 04:10, the first living microbes appear.

- Animals develop hard parts just after 21:00.

- Dinosaurs first roam the Earth at about 22:45.

- Modern humans appear at around 4 seconds to midnight.

A normal human life span would be over in a thousandth of a second.

The first cells with a nucleus appear.

Early organisms are soft and don't leave much of a trace.

Jellyfish-like animals scrape food from the ocean floor.

74

Timeline guide

MASS EXTINCTION
These boxes show the dates of mass extinctions — when many species died out at once.

This timeline stretches back to thousands of **millions of years ago** — shortened to **mya**.

Land-dwellers are shown above the timeline. Sea- and ocean-dwellers are shown below it.

Plants quickly become taller and taller.

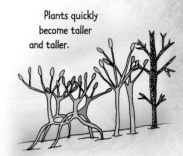

The land gets warmer again. Nothing lives there.

Early land plants

Millipedes

Algae creep onto land.

The first plants develop...

MASS EXTINCTION

...and the first land animals follow.

550 mya   500 mya   450 mya   400 mya

The first fish form.

Many species start to form hard body parts.

Seas and oceans are packed with life.

Early fish don't have jaws.

This animal has a simple support down its back.

Fish with jaws

These chalky tubes are made by animals called cloudinids.

Hard-shelled trilobites scuttle through the seas.

The remains of this species and many others are preserved in a mudslide, now called the 'Burgess Shale'.

Sea floors are home to many kinds of animals, including corals and molluscs.

Worm-like animal

WHERE DID LIFE COME FROM?

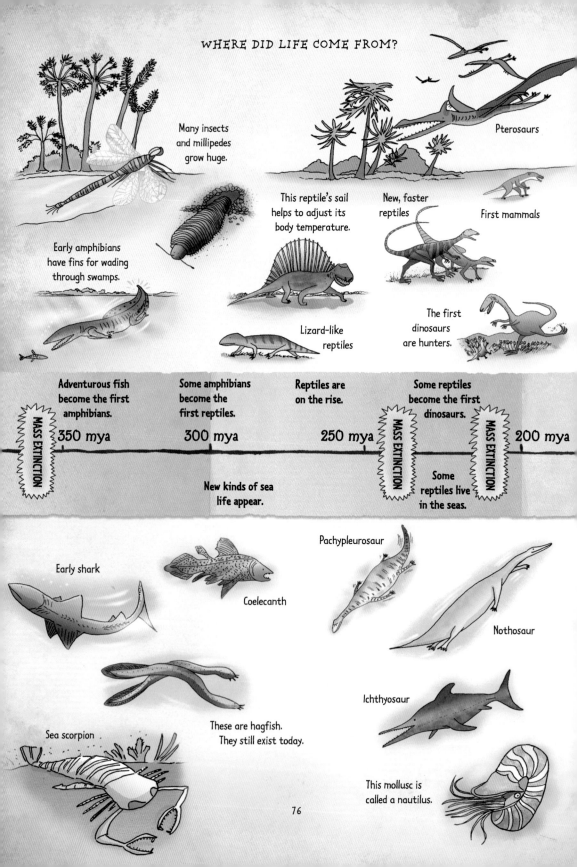

Many insects and millipedes grow huge.

Pterosaurs

This reptile's sail helps to adjust its body temperature.

New, faster reptiles

First mammals

Early amphibians have fins for wading through swamps.

Lizard-like reptiles

The first dinosaurs are hunters.

Adventurous fish become the first amphibians.

Some amphibians become the first reptiles.

Reptiles are on the rise.

Some reptiles become the first dinosaurs.

MASS EXTINCTION

350 mya

300 mya

250 mya

MASS EXTINCTION

200 mya

MASS EXTINCTION

New kinds of sea life appear.

Some reptiles live in the seas.

Early shark

Coelecanth

Pachypleurosaur

Nothosaur

Ichthyosaur

These are hagfish. They still exist today.

Sea scorpion

This mollusc is called a nautilus.

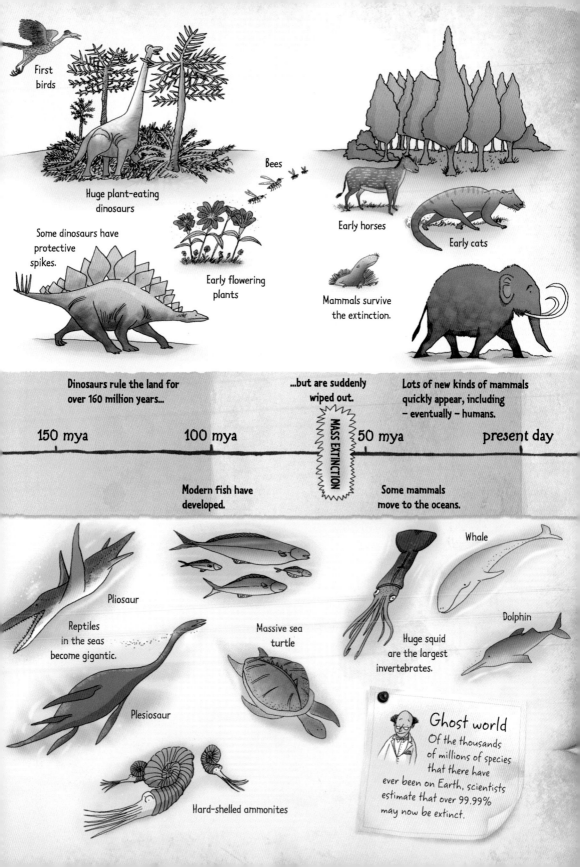

First birds

Huge plant-eating dinosaurs

Bees

Some dinosaurs have protective spikes.

Early flowering plants

Early horses

Early cats

Mammals survive the extinction.

Dinosaurs rule the land for over 160 million years...

...but are suddenly wiped out.

Lots of new kinds of mammals quickly appear, including – eventually – humans.

150 mya   100 mya   MASS EXTINCTION   50 mya   present day

Modern fish have developed.

Some mammals move to the oceans.

Pliosaur

Reptiles in the seas become gigantic.

Massive sea turtle

Whale

Huge squid are the largest invertebrates.

Dolphin

Plesiosaur

Hard-shelled ammonites

Ghost world
Of the thousands of millions of species that there have ever been on Earth, scientists estimate that over 99.99% may now be extinct.

How do new species form?

New species keep appearing – and they don't come out of nowhere. Instead, existing species gradually change and develop into new ones. This is known as **evolution** and it links all living things in a long chain that stretches back to the very first microbes.

Where's the evidence?

A new species will share many features with its ancestors, even if it looks very different. To tell how a species evolved, experts trace these features back through the history recorded by fossils. It's a patchy record, but it shows strands of similarities running through huge numbers of organisms.

More evidence can be found inside organisms alive today. Very different species may have hidden similarities, inherited from a common ancestor. For example, many vertebrates have similar skeletons, suggesting they all evolved from a single species.

Hairy reflex

Goosebumps, the tiny bumps we get on our skin when we're cold or scared, are a reflex inherited from our ancestors.

These bumps appear when muscles raise hairs on our skin. In furry animals, this traps warm air, or makes the animal look bigger. But it's useless in us humans.

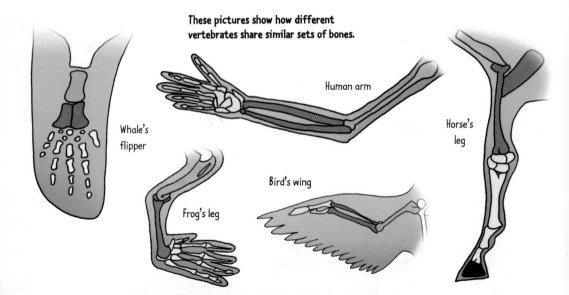

These pictures show how different vertebrates share similar sets of bones.

Whale's flipper

Human arm

Horse's leg

Frog's leg

Bird's wing

How does evolution happen?

When a male and female gamete fuse, it almost always produces an individual with a unique set of genes. For example, some gene combinations may result in longer legs or bigger flowers.

Natural resources such as food, water and shelter are always limited, with lots of organisms trying to use them. Species compete with other species to get what they need, and members of the same species compete with each other. Some have genes that make them better suited to where they live. They usually live longer, while others go hungry, get eaten or die out.

The organisms that live longest tend to have the most children. Some inherit their parent's helpful genes, and so have more children of their own. Slowly the helpful genes spread and, after many generations of the best genes being passed along, a new species evolves. This is known as **natural selection.**

Who discovered it?

Charles Darwin (1809-82) and Alfred Russel Wallace (1823-1913) were the first scientists to come up with the theory of evolution by natural selection. In 1859, Darwin published his ideas in a ground-breaking book, called *On the Origin of Species.*

At the time, most people believed all living things had been designed by a creator. They were shocked by Darwin's idea that life's 'design' was really down to competition, inheritance and time.

People are still arguing over evolution today, but it has been consistently supported and built upon by new discoveries, including how genes work.

Growing up tall

Some early grazing mammals ate leaves. Longer-necked ones could eat leaves that others couldn't reach.

The grazers with longer necks had more children, so the gene for long necks spread.

After millions of years, the grazers could reach the tree-tops. They had become giraffes.

Drifting genes

As well as natural selection, evolution can happen by chance. A gene may change in a way that doesn't give any benefits, but may spread anyway. Or if a disaster wipes out most of a species, the survivors may be lucky rather than well-adapted. This kind of random evolution is known as 'genetic drift'.

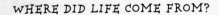

How fast does evolution happen?

Evolution is happening all the time, but it's usually very slow. Sometimes species don't change for hundreds of millions of years. But sometimes, evolution suddenly speeds up...

The Earth's landscape is always changing, as immense underground forces push up new islands and mountain ranges. When this happens, species may be split up into separate groups. Each group evolves to suit its new home and, within just a few thousand years, may be on its way to becoming a separate species.

How can extinctions speed it up?

Every so often, huge numbers of species die out at once, in **mass extinctions**. Scientists think there have been at least five of these.

Mass extinctions may happen if the climate changes, if sea levels rise or fall, or if dust from an asteroid collision or volcano blocks out heat and light from the Sun. Species unable to adapt to the new conditions die out, and a wave of new species evolves to fill the gaps.

For example, scientists think the earliest mammals were small mouse-like creatures, and remained so for over 150 million years while dinosaurs ruled the Earth. But the dinosaurs died out in a mass extinction about 65 million years ago, probably when debris from an asteroid collision blocked light and heat from the Sun.

Just a few million years after this, mammals had started to evolve into many new forms, such as cats, horses and monkey-like primates.

Specialized beaks

The Galapagos Islands, west of South America, are home to over a dozen species of finches. They all evolved from the same ancestor, but each has developed a different shaped beak, suitable for getting food on its island.

Ground finches have big, blunt beaks for crushing seeds and nuts.

Tree finches have sharp, thin beaks, for snatching insects up from crevices.

Vegetarian finches have large, strong beaks for nipping fruits, leaves and buds.

Record extinction

The worst mass extinction took place about 250 million years ago. About three quarters of all living species died out, including about 96% of sea-dwellers. Scientists call it the 'Great Dying'. They aren't sure why it happened.

mya stands for 'millions of years ago'. ya stands for 'years ago'.

what about humans?

This timeline shows how scientists think humans evolved.

270 mya

Some reptiles develop a sail on their back, which lets them control their body temperature.

200 mya

They evolve into the first, small mammals.

125 mya

Some mammals begin to give birth to their babies.

65 mya

An asteroid hits the Earth, causing mass extinction.

58 mya

The mammals quickly evolve into lots of different species, including tree-dwelling primates.

Mammals survive, probably because they can control their body temperature and don't need much food.

35-25 mya

The first monkeys evolve, followed by the first apes.

7-5 mya

In Africa, some apes begin to walk upright.

2.5 mya

Some develop larger brains, and learn to make tools.

1.5 mya

A species evolves called *Homo erectus*. They learn to hunt and make fires.

200,000 ya

The very first modern humans, *Homo sapiens*, evolve.

Present day

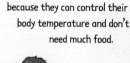

10,000 ya

Humans spread around the world. Eventually they start to make towns, farms...

... cities...

... and books!

Part 5
Life on Earth

The Earth is home to tens of millions of species, living everywhere from rainforests to mountains, cities and the deep blue sea. The study of where they live, how they've adapted to fit there and their reliance on their neighbours is called **ecology**.

Adapting to home

The area where an organism lives is called its **habitat**. Habitats can be any place, from mountaintops to ocean floors, and any size, from a rotting log to a forest. The conditions in a habitat, including temperature, rainfall and soil quality, are described as the **environment**.

Organisms evolve to become well-suited, or **adapted**, to the environment where they live. In fact, many are so well-suited to their environment that they couldn't survive being moved anywhere else.

This habitat has a light, airy, salty and sandy environment.

Awful Arctic?

Temperatures below -30°C (-22°F) and thick snow would finish off most living things. Yet to Arctic organisms, these conditions are perfectly normal...

Polar bears have thick fur and layers of fat to keep out the cold. They're so good at staying warm that they hardly lose any heat at all.

It's hard to walk on the soft snow. Ptarmigans have feathered feet, to spread out their weight and stop them sinking into snowdrifts.

Some Arctic plants look like cushions – the outer layers protect the insides from winds and cold.

Desperate desert?

Most deserts are bone-dry and blistering hot during the day. But some organisms thrive in this unforgiving habitat...

Camels only need to drink about once a week. Their noses reabsorb most of the vapour in their breath, and they hardly ever sweat.

Many desert animals come out at night, when it's cooler. Jerboas leave their burrows at dusk and may bound over long stretches of sand to find food.

Lots of desert plants spring up during the short rainy seasons. They grow, flower and make seeds in just a few weeks, before the water dries up.

Who does what for whom?

A habitat is usually shared by many species, from
microbes and plants to powerful hunters such as lions.
All the organisms of a single species in a habitat are
called a **population**, and all the populations together
are a **community**. An entire community, along with its
habitat, is known as an **ecosystem**.

Planet-wide

Ecosystems don't have fixed
boundaries – they may be as small
as a blade of grass, or as big as
an entire country. The biggest
ecosystem of all is the planet
– where the community is every
single animal, plant and microbe.

The relationships between different populations
are very complex, as each plays a part in keeping the
ecosystem running smoothly. Even the biggest, fiercest
hunters rely on the plants and microbes around them.
So if just one species is removed, the knock-on effects
on all the others can be devastating.

Here you can see an ecosystem in the African grasslands.
Note how each kind of organism relies on all the others.

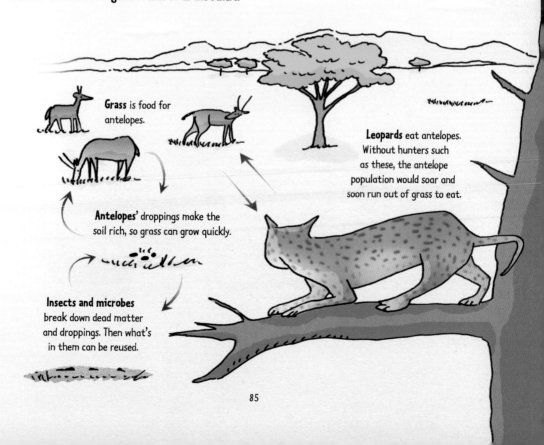

Grass is food for
antelopes.

Leopards eat antelopes.
Without hunters such
as these, the antelope
population would soar and
soon run out of grass to eat.

Antelopes' droppings make the
soil rich, so grass can grow quickly.

Insects and microbes
break down dead matter
and droppings. Then what's
in them can be reused.

Safe as houses

Sea anemones have stingers on their tentacles, to keep predators away and catch prey. Some small fish have become immune to the stings, and use anemones as safe havens.

Deadly weapons

Although species may depend on each other, the day-to-day lives of individuals tell a very different story. For most, life is a constant battle to avoid being eaten while finding enough to eat. As a result, many species have developed an amazing array of weapons and defences – from lethal poisons and razor-sharp claws, to hard shells and protective prickles.

Claiming a slot

Each habitat has a limited set of **resources**, such as food, water, space and shelter. The way a species uses these is called its **niche** (a 'niche' means a space or crevice). A species' niche includes where it lives, what it eats and what time of day it comes out.

No two species can share the same niche. If they tried, one would be more successful and drive the other out. The losing species would have to carve out a new niche for itself, or else it would die out.

But species can share the same resources – as long as they don't use them in exactly the same way. For example, giraffes and rhinoceroses spend their days grazing on leaves, but giraffes eat from treetops while rhinoceroses browse on low bushes. And owls and kestrels both hunt for small rodents, but owls do it at night and kestrels do it during the day.

In fact, there are so many ways of using resources that huge numbers of species can live side-by-side – as long as each has its own separate niche.

Different slots

Lions and leopards are very similar animals, and they eat the same food. But they use what's around them in different ways...

Leopards are smaller than lions, and live alone. They climb trees, and hide food up there from lions and other groups of hunters.

Lions live on the ground, in groups. Their large build and teamwork make them the dominant hunters.

Ecosystem meltdown

Species are usually so well-established in their niches that ecosystems are very stable – as long as the conditions remain the same. But any changes – such as disease, climate change or the arrival of a foreign species – can be disastrous. Even if just one species is affected to begin with, the results can soon spread across the whole ecosystem.

Are all species equally important?

Not always, no. Although all species in a community have important roles, a single species may hold the key to it all. This species may do something that affects the habitat, keeps a balance between other species, or provides shelter or food.

For example, elephants are vital to African grasslands, as they clear away trees and stop forests from growing. And in flat North American prairies, ground squirrels build huge burrows that provide shelter for other species.

These species are called **keystone species**, after the top 'keystone' in an archway, which holds the other stones in place. But ecosystems are so complex that it can be hard for biologists to work out which, if any, is a keystone species.

Australian species

Australia is an isolated country with very unusual native animals.

For example, almost all Australian mammals, such as kangaroos and koalas, give birth very early and carry their tiny babies in pouches.

But through the centuries, humans have brought over foreign species such as dingoes (wild dogs) and rabbits. These have taken over most niches, and many native species have now become extinct.

Thylacines like this one were wolf-like hunters that became extinct after dingoes took over their niche.

Sea otters are a keystone species in many coastal areas, where they are the only animals that eat sea urchins.

Without them, sea urchins quickly multiply and destroy the ecosystem.

What's for dinner?

In an ecosystem, energy from food is constantly being passed between organisms. Animals that get their energy from eating other animals are called **carnivores**, and those that get it from plants or algae are called **herbivores**. Humans and all other animals that eat both animals and plants are known as **omnivores**.

Plants and algae are called **producers**, because they produce their own food through photosynthesis. The food they make is vitally important – it's the fuel that powers all the other organisms.

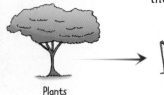

Latin names
Carn- is from the Latin for 'flesh', **herb**- is from the Latin for 'plants', **omni**- is from the Latin for 'all', and **vore** is from the Latin for 'to devour'.

You can show who eats what by making a line of organisms, called a **food chain**. Food chains start with the producer, and lead up to the top carnivore.

This is an example of a food chain. The arrows point from what's being eaten, to who's doing the eating.

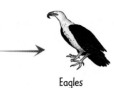

Plants   Insects   Meerkats   Eagles

Each ecosystem contains many different food chains, which can be linked together in a **food web**.

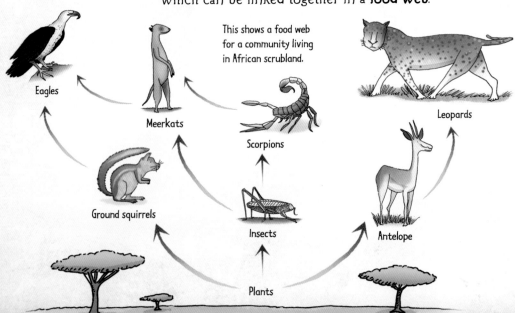

This shows a food web for a community living in African scrubland.

Eagles

Meerkats

Scorpions

Leopards

Ground squirrels

Insects

Antelope

Plants

How many, and how big?

To show the size of the different populations in a food web, biologists sometimes draw a stack of bars called a **pyramid of numbers**. The length of each bar reflects how many of that species there are. Each species eats what's in the bar below it.

Here's an example of a pyramid of numbers:

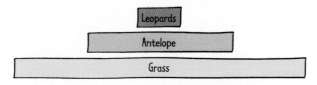

Each species needs lots of what it eats, so each bar is shorter than the one below it. And if the producers are small plants such as grass or algae, their bar will be the longest of all.

But, sometimes, the producer may be a big plant such as a tree, which by itself provides food for many animals. Then, the pyramid of numbers looks like this:

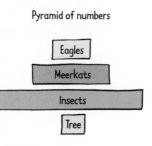

Pyramid of numbers

In this case, a pyramid showing the physical size and weight of each population gives a clearer idea of what's going on. This is called a **pyramid of biomass**.

Pyramids of biomass are always widest at the bottom.

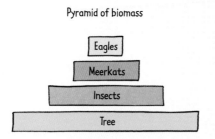

Pyramid of biomass

Poisoned chain

Sometimes man-made poison or waste gets into a food chain, like this...

Small fish eat food tainted with very small amounts of a poison called mercury.

A medium-sized fish eats lots of small fish – and mercury starts to build up in its body.

A top predator eat lots of medium fish. The mercury builds up to dangerous levels.

How do humans fit in?

Like all animals, humans compete with other species; but it's no longer a fair fight. For millenia we've altered our habitats to suit us, often threatening the species that live alongside us. Here are just some of the problems we've caused, and some possible solutions.

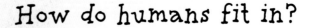

Then and now

For every person who lived a thousand years ago, it's estimated there are more than 22 alive today. The current human population is 6,700 million, and scientists predict it's going to carry on growing and growing...

Habitat destruction

The problem: Habitats such as grasslands and forests are cleared to make space for towns, cities and farms. Some forests are cut down for wood.

The results: Species lose their homes and food sources. With nowhere to live and nothing to eat, many die out.

Plan of action: Huge reserves that no one may build on have been set up, as well as protected 'green belts' around cities. Some farmers leave wild areas free on their land, to give wild animals somewhere to live.

Lifeless lake

Unnaturally high levels of nutrients in this lake have caused huge amounts of algae to grow. When the algae die, bacteria use up oxygen in the water to break them down, suffocating all the fish.

Pollution and waste

The problem: Factories, power plants and cars release harmful chemicals and gases. Farmers and gardeners may also use fertilizers to make plants grow better, and pesticides to kill pests. We throw away lots of waste.

The results: Chemicals may harm ecosystems, especially in rivers and lakes. Some gases combine with water in the air to make acidic rain, which kills plants and animals. Mountains of waste are building up.

Plan of action: Experts are finding ways to reduce the production of harmful gases. Some farmers no longer use harmful chemicals. Many countries have campaigns to cut waste, and lots can be recycled.

Climate change

The problem: We burn fuels such as coal and oil to get energy to run everything from cars to factories.
The results: Burning these fuels releases gases such as carbon dioxide, which traps heat from the Sun. Most experts agree this affects weather, making the Earth warmer. Many species can't adapt to the new climates.
Plan of action: Some countries have agreed to reduce their carbon dioxide production by using less coal and oil. Less harmful energy sources can be used instead, such as wind, moving water and the Sun.

Polar bears hunt seals on sheets of sea ice that form each winter. But recently the ice has melted more and more quickly. This makes it hard for polar bears to hunt, and many may end up starving or drowning.

Why should I bother with biology?

As far as we know, the only life in the entire universe is right here on this planet. Yet because of us, species are disappearing at an alarming rate – making many experts think we're causing the next mass extinction.

The study of biology has helped us to understand life, and now biologists are vital in learning how to protect it. So bothering with biology could, quite literally, mean the Earth to future generations.

Safe havens

This family of cheetahs lives on a big nature reserve in Kenya. There, they are protected from poachers and can live and hunt naturally. Without dedicated workers to set up and manage reserves like this, we'd have lost far more species.

Biology through the ages

People have been studying living things for thousands of years, even though they only began to describe what they were doing as 'biology' about 200 years ago. Here is the story of biology so far, including the most influential biologists and their breakthroughs and achievements.

from 8500 BCE

Early farmers learn how to grow plants and keep animals. They find that by choosing the best plants and animals to breed from, they get more food.

about 590-40 BCE

A Greek thinker called Anaximander writes *On Nature*, explaining his ideas about how the natural world came to be. Sadly, no copies survive today.

about 460-377 BCE

Greek doctor Hippocrates argues for a scientific approach to diagnosing illnesses, which were more often blamed on magic or spirits.

about 384-22 BCE

A Greek thinker named Aristotle develops theories based on his observations of the natural world, including an early system of classification.

about 130-200

Greek doctor Claudius Galen studies the human body. He's not allowed to cut up corpses, so many of his ideas are wrong. But people believe them for over a thousand years.

1025

Persian scholar Ibn Sina (or 'Avicenna') finishes his encylopedia, the *Canon of Medicine*. It is used to teach doctors for many centuries.

1480s-1519

Leonardo da Vinci is allowed to dissect human bodies. He bases hundreds of sketches on his observations.

1610s-20s

William Harvey proves that blood moves around the body in a one-way system. He also guesses that embryos form when a sperm and egg fuse.

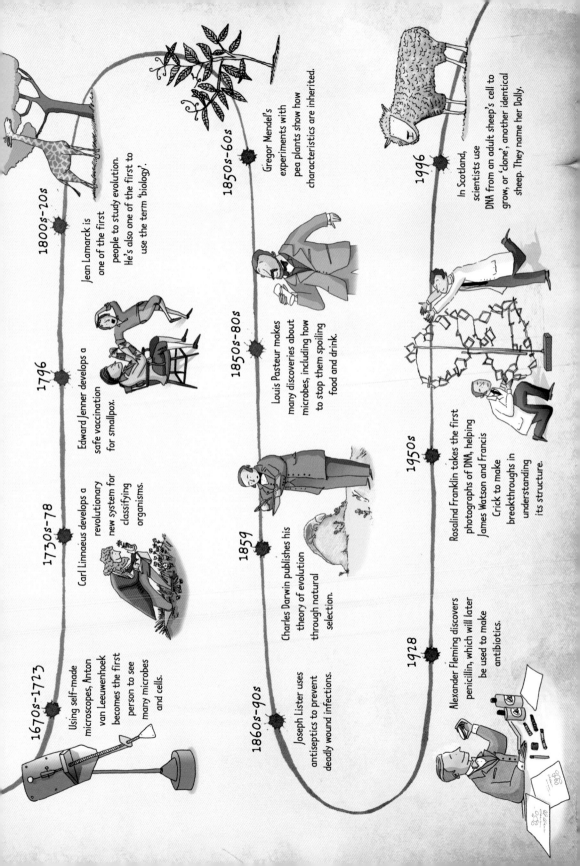

1670s–1723
Using self-made microscopes, Anton van Leeuwenhoek becomes the first person to see many microbes and cells.

1730s–78
Carl Linnaeus develops a revolutionary new system for classifying organisms.

1796
Edward Jenner develops a safe vaccination for smallpox.

1800s–20s
Jean Lamarck is one of the first people to study evolution. He's also one of the first to use the term 'biology'.

1850s–60s
Gregor Mendel's experiments with pea plants show how characteristics are inherited.

1859
Charles Darwin publishes his theory of evolution through natural selection.

1850s–80s
Louis Pasteur makes many discoveries about microbes, including how to stop them spoiling food and drink.

1860s–90s
Joseph Lister uses antiseptics to prevent deadly wound infections.

1928
Alexander Fleming discovers penicillin, which will later be used to make antibiotics.

1950s
Rosalind Franklin takes the first photographs of DNA, helping James Watson and Francis Crick to make breakthroughs in understanding its structure.

1996
In Scotland, scientists use DNA from an adult sheep's cell to grow, or 'clone', another identical sheep. They name her Dolly.

What's Chemistry all about?

Contents

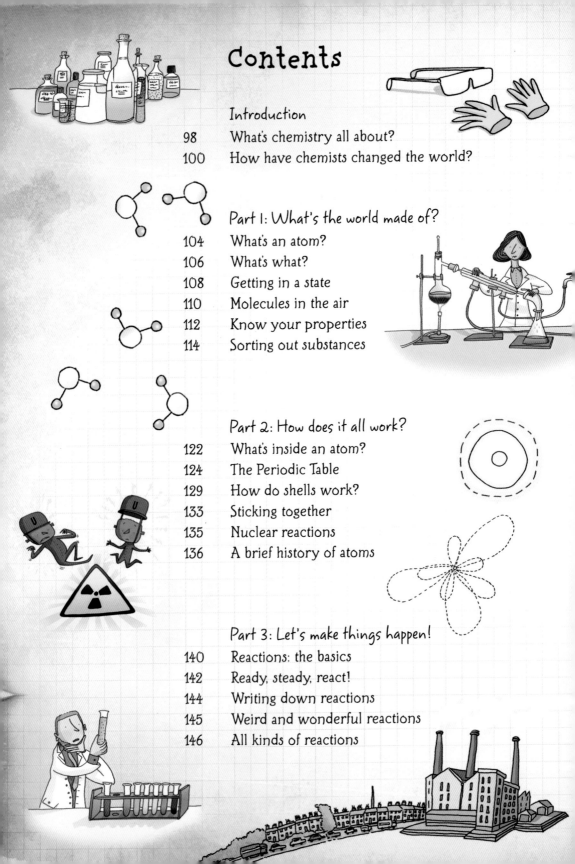

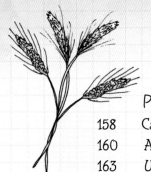

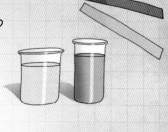

Part 4: How is chemistry useful?

Part 5: Our chemical Universe

Internet links

You can find out lots more about chemistry on the internet. You can find out about every single element, do experiments in an online lab, and build your very own molecules. For links to these websites, and many more, go to **www.usborne.com/quicklinks** and type in the keywords "what is chemistry".

The links are regularly reviewed and updated, but Usborne Publishing cannot be responsible for any website other than its own. Please follow the internet safety guidelines displayed on the Usborne Quicklinks website.

What's chemistry all about?

Chemistry is all about different types of stuff – or **substances**, to use a scientific word. It's about what substances are, what they can do, what's inside them and how they can change. Chemists study all kinds of substances – from everyday things, like mud and smoke, to rare, deadly ones like strong acids and explosive powders.

Chemists are constantly asking questions and doing experiments to find the answers. The answers may reveal what something is made of, or show what it can do. Here are some of the questions chemists ask...

Lab rules

Chemists don't always wear white coats. But if they're working with messy substances, they wear clothes that they don't mind getting dirty. And if they're using dangerous substances, they wear gloves and goggles for protection.

What on earth IS this?

What exactly IS this stuff?

How do you really know what anything is? A bottle of liquid labelled 'water' might not really contain water. To find out what a mystery substance is, a chemist asks more questions.

How heavy is it?

What does it DO?

Different substances do different things. For example, pure water boils at 100°C. Chemists call this one of the **properties** of water. Other properties include toughness, and how easily it mixes with other substances.

Do things dissolve in it?

What happens if you heat it up?

Is it just one thing?

Some substances are made of just one thing, but others are a mixture of various different things. A chemist might need to break something down into its different parts before working out what each part is made of.

What is this gooey stuff?

I think it's a mixture.

Can I change it into something else?

Many substances can be used to create other substances. Sometimes they will change if you heat them up, but mostly they change when they are mixed with other substances. This change is called a **reaction**.

What happens if I mix this with this?

What can I change this into?

What makes it change?

Can I change it back again?

Finding all the answers

Chemists know a lot about substances, but they don't know everything. Ever since people began doing experiments, they've discovered more and more new substances, and more ways to use them.

Turn the page to find some of the interesting and useful inventions that chemists have been responsible for.

Things chemists don't know... yet.

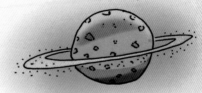

What about all those substances on alien planets? Are they like the ones on Earth, or are they completely different?

How have chemists changed the world?

Chemists are always experimenting with substances, mixing them together, heating them up, and testing them to see what they can do. And sometimes this results in remarkable inventions. Here are just a few of the amazingly useful things that chemists have given to the world.

Batteries

A battery provides electricity. Inside, pieces of two different metals are placed apart in a liquid or paste. The metals react with the liquid, making an electric charge flow.

Some of the earliest experiments with batteries were performed by Italian Alessandro Volta in 1791. Turn to page 250 to find out more about Volta.

Volta's first experiment gave him a shock.

Silver spoon

Tin rod

Salt water

Matches

Matches are tipped with a mixture of substances that will catch fire when struck against a rough surface.

Early matches caught fire too easily. The first 'safety matches' were invented in 1827 by Englishman John Walker.

Petrol engine

Engines are machines that make things move – such as cars. But they need power to operate. In 1870, Austrian scientist Siegfried Marcus hit upon the idea of using petrol as a fuel to make an engine run – an early version of a motor vehicle.

The colourful story of mauve

One day in 1856, chemist William Perkin was cleaning up after a messy experiment, when something strange happened...

Perkin called his new colour 'mauve'. At the time, there was no cheap way to manufacture purple dye.

I'll wash this gunk out with alcohol.

Ooooh! It's gone a lovely purple colour.

I can make some serious money out of this...

Mauve became fashionable after Queen Victoria wore it.

White paint

Paint contains coloured substances called pigments. The pigment titanium dioxide is bright white, and is used in house paints.

Titanium dioxide occurs naturally, and has been used to manufacture paint since the 1920s.

Antifreeze

A chemical called ethylene glycol is the main ingredient in liquid antifreeze. It forms a layer of liquid on a car windscreen and won't freeze even when it's very cold.

Non stick pans

In 1938, American Roy Plunkett was trying to make a refrigerator chemical, but instead his experiments produced a useful new plastic. His team called it Teflon®.

When they get hot, most things become sticky – but Teflon® doesn't. It is used to coat cooking pans.

Inhalers

Since the 1960s, many people with asthma have used inhalers to help them during an attack. Inhalers contain the substance salbutamol, which relaxes the breathing muscles and stops the attack.

Heat packs

A liquid called sodium acetate is very useful to mountain climbers. They carry small packs filled with it on their hikes. When they want to warm up, they press a button on the pack which releases solid sodium acetate into the liquid. This makes the liquid turn into crystals, and gives out heat.

Light-sensitive substance

Digital cameras

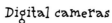

When you take a photo, light entering a digital camera causes a chemical reaction in a light-sensitive substance. This reaction produces an electric charge.

The camera changes this charge into a code and uses a series of codes to store or display the photo.

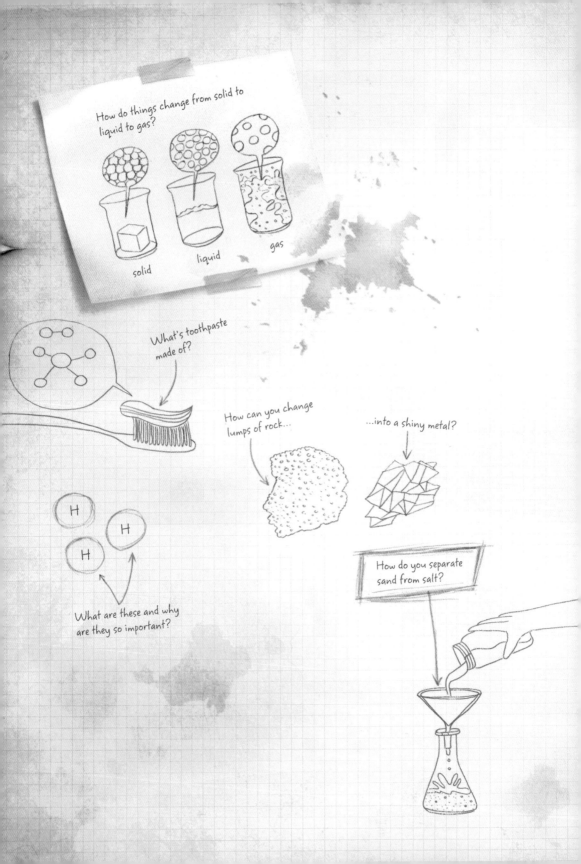

Part 1:
What's the world made of?

The Universe is full of a wide range of different substances – from hard, shiny metals and beautiful, crystal diamonds, to soft, bendy plastics and black, crumbly coal. But, deep, deep down, everything is made of the same thing – mindbogglingly tiny specks called **atoms**. Read on to find out more...

What's an atom?

Meet your first atom...

Chemists often draw atoms as simple circles. This circle with an 'H' in it represents a single atom of an element called hydrogen.

You can think of atoms as incredibly small building blocks. There are 117 kinds of atom. Substances can be very simple or quite complicated, depending on how many kinds of atom they're made of. The simplest substances, called **elements,** are made of only one kind of atom.

Gold is an element. A bit of gold dust scraped from a gold bar is made up of billions of individual gold atoms.

Simple symbols

Chemists use symbols for each different kind of atom so they can write them down quickly. You can see a list of them all on pages 124-125.

Even huge blocks of gold only contain individual gold atoms. But atoms in most other substances stick together in groups of two or more atoms called **molecules**.

What are molecules?

Molecules are made when atoms make links called **bonds** between each other. For example, oxygen atoms bond in pairs to make molecules of oxygen – which is found naturally in the air.

Atoms don't have to bond with the same kind of atom. A molecule of water is made of two atoms of hydrogen bonded with one atom of oxygen. Although water – like every other substance – is made of atoms, there's no such thing as an atom of water. That's because the smallest amount of water you can have, that is still water, is a *molecule*. Because water contains more than one kind of atom, it's not an element – it's something called a **compound**.

Meet your second atom...

An *atom* of oxygen

...and your first molecule.

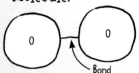

A *molecule* of oxygen

Forming compounds

Compounds can only be created when substances mix together and undergo a **chemical reaction** (you can find out more about this on page 128).

A reaction can make elements bond together and form an entirely new chemical substance, which behaves differently from the elements that made it.

Do reactions always happen when you mix substances?

No. Elements and compounds can also mix without reacting or bonding together. This creates another kind of substance known as a **mixture**. Most things in our world are mixtures. For example, air is a mixture of gases, and mud is a mixture of soil, stones, leaves and all sorts.

Compound sketch

Chemists draw compounds by showing the atoms they are made of. A water molecule can be drawn in two ways:

Like this:

H   O   H

O - Oxygen

H - Hydrogen

Or this: Bond

H   O   H

It can also be written using symbols like this: H_2O.

Elements are made of only one kind of atom. This is a molecule of nitrogen, with two nitrogen atoms in it.

Compounds are made of more than one kind of atom bonded together.

They can be quite complicated, like this molecule of sulphuric acid.

In a mixture, such as mud, different elements and compounds are jumbled up, but they haven't bonded with each other.

Bits of plants and animals

Stones and rocks

Air

Water

Mud is a mixture of many different substances.

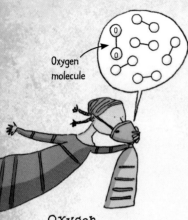

Oxygen molecule

what's what?

All the substances in the Universe are elements, mixtures or compounds. Here are a few examples...

Carbon dioxide

Carbon dioxide is a **compound** of carbon and oxygen. It's a gas in the air which plants use to make food.

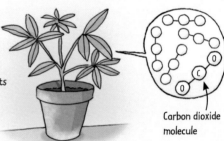

Carbon dioxide molecule

Oxygen

Oxygen is an **element**. It's one of the gases in the air we breathe. It reacts easily with other elements, which means it's also found in many compounds.

Iron oxide molecule

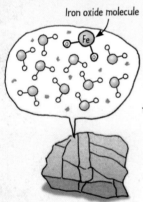

Iron ore

Iron ore is a **mixture**. It's mostly a compound called iron oxide, mixed with some other bits. It can be dug out of the ground, and then processed to extract pure iron.

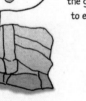

Water molecule

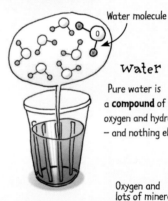

water

Pure water is a **compound** of oxygen and hydrogen – and nothing else.

Oxygen and lots of minerals

Salt

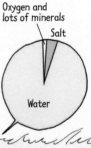

Water

Sea water

Sea water is a **mixture**. It's mainly water, but it also has salt and oxygen and other bits dissolved in it. Fish breathe the dissolved oxygen through their gills.

Milk

Milk is a **mixture** of lots of compounds. It's mainly water, with a mix of fat, sugar and minerals such as calcium, which we need for healthy teeth and bones.

Other minerals
Calcium
Fat
Sugar

Water

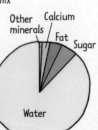

WHAT'S THE WORLD MADE OF?

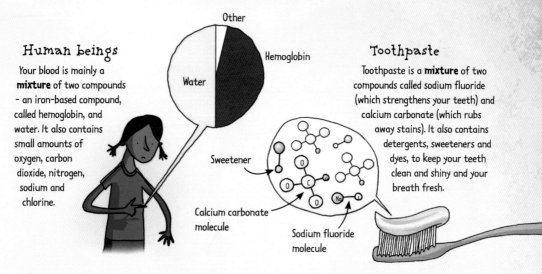

Human beings

Your blood is mainly a **mixture** of two compounds – an iron-based compound, called hemoglobin, and water. It also contains small amounts of oxygen, carbon dioxide, nitrogen, sodium and chlorine.

Other

Hemoglobin

Water

Toothpaste

Toothpaste is a **mixture** of two compounds called sodium fluoride (which strengthens your teeth) and calcium carbonate (which rubs away stains). It also contains detergents, sweeteners and dyes, to keep your teeth clean and shiny and your breath fresh.

Sweetener

Calcium carbonate molecule

Sodium fluoride molecule

Vinegar

Vinegar is often used to flavour food. Its chemical name is ethanoic acid. It's a **compound** of carbon, hydrogen and oxygen.

Ethanoic acid molecule

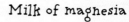

Milk of magnesia

Milk of magnesia is a **mixture** of two compounds: magnesium hydroxide and water. Magnesium hydroxide cancels out stomach acids that can cause indigestion. The water is just to make it drinkable.

Magnesium hydroxide molecule

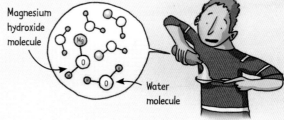

Water molecule

Acetone

Acetone is a **compound** of carbon, hydrogen and oxygen. It's a liquid that can be used to remove nail varnish or to weaken glue.

Acetone molecule

Glues

Most glues are **mixtures** of some sticky, runny compounds (such as cyanoacrylate, which contains carbon, hydrogen, oxygen and nitrogen) and smelly liquids (such as ethyl acetate which contains carbon, hydrogen and oxygen) that slowly dry and harden.

Ethyl acetate molecule

Cyanoacrylate molecule

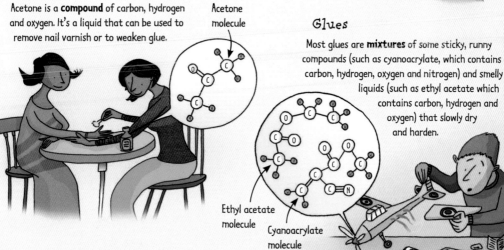

Meet mercury

Mercury is the only metal that is liquid at room temperature. It won't freeze until -39°C, and it doesn't boil until it reaches an incredibly high 357°C.

Mercury is often used to measure temperature. As mercury gets hotter, it expands. When it's inside a thermometer with markings on the side, you can see exactly how much the mercury expands, and that tells you what the temperature is.

Absolute cold

Chemists think that if you could make the temperature really low – as low as -273.15°C – atoms would stop moving completely. They call this absolute zero. They can make things very nearly, but not quite, this cold – so we don't know for sure.

Getting in a state

Substances can exist in one of three different **states**; as a **solid**, **liquid** or **gas**. Most substances can be found in all of these states – but not at the same time. Take water, for example. It's usually a liquid, but it can also be a solid (ice) or a gas (steam) – it all depends on the temperature.

Why does temperature matter?

One of the strangest things that chemists have discovered is that nothing is ever completely still. Take a solid block of wood. You may not be able to see it moving, but in fact the atoms and molecules it's made of are constantly fidgeting and moving around. How much they move depends on how much heat there is.

When molecules are cold, they don't have much energy, so they sit tightly packed and form a solid. But even then they vibrate slightly, in their fixed positions.

Molecules that are a bit warmer have more energy and move away from each other, forming a liquid. They can move enough so the liquid can flow.

Really hot, energetic molecules can fly far apart from each other. This is what's going on in a gas.

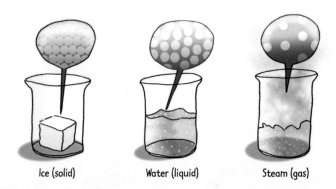

Ice (solid)   Water (liquid)   Steam (gas)

Changing state

Most substances have their own temperature at which they change from one state to another. For example, ice will **melt** (or liquify) from solid ice into liquid water at 0°C. This temperature is water's **melting point**. Water will **boil** (or evaporate) into steam at 100°C. This is water's **boiling point**.

These changes can be reversed by cooling down the substance; a gas that gets cold enough **condenses** into a liquid and a liquid **solidifies** into a solid.

Quick change

Some substances, such as moth balls, go straight from being a solid to a gas, without ever becoming a liquid.

This is called **sublimation** and it's why moth balls disappear into thin air, leaving only a smell behind.

How does ice make drinks cold?

What happens when water boils?

You don't usually notice air molecules knocking into you. But sometimes they move more quickly than normal. That's what wind is.

Molecules in the air

Air is made up of atoms and molecules of different gases. They're constantly rushing about, bashing into things. This creates something called **air pressure**.

You need air pressure to hold yourself together. Inside your body, blood pumps around and pushes outwards, but air pressure pushes back. It's this balance which stops you from bursting out of your skin.

How does pressure affect state?

The amount of pressure on a substance affects how free its molecules are to move around. So changing the pressure can sometimes cause a change of state, even without a change in temperature.

For example, squeezing a gas into a really tight space puts extra pressure on the gas. This can turn some gases into liquids, and make them stay that way.

At very low temperatures nitrogen gas becomes a liquid. This liquid can be stored in a pressurized container to stop its molecules from spreading out and becoming a gas again, even if the container is then kept at room temperature.

When liquid nitrogen is released from the container, at room temperature, it immediately turns back into a gas.

Water pressure

Water is heavier than air, so under water there's more pressure than on land.

The deeper you go, the stronger it gets.

Deep sea submarines need incredibly thick hulls to cope with the pressure of the water pushing all around them.

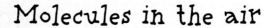

The yellow canister contains liquid nitrogen. As it is poured out, it turns into a gas. To do this, it takes heat from the molecules in the air. In turn, this makes **water vapour** in the air condense into water and this appears as a white mist.

How do we know about this?

Gases always spread out to fill whatever space they're in. This makes them really tricky to catch and study. 17th-century Irish chemist Robert Boyle was one of the first people to manage it.

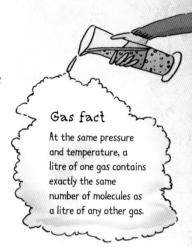

First, he invented a perfectly airtight container he could fill with air (with help from his physicist friend, Robert Hooke). Then, he built a pump that could suck the air back out again. By experimenting with this pump, Boyle discovered he could make a gas take up less space by putting pressure on it – and vice versa.

Gas fact

At the same pressure and temperature, a litre of one gas contains exactly the same number of molecules as a litre of any other gas.

How Boyle made a balloon get bigger – without blowing any extra air into it.

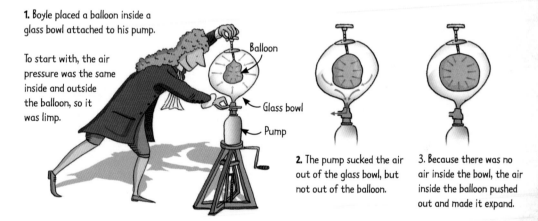

1. Boyle placed a balloon inside a glass bowl attached to his pump.

To start with, the air pressure was the same inside and outside the balloon, so it was limp.

Balloon

Glass bowl

Pump

2. The pump sucked the air out of the glass bowl, but not out of the balloon.

3. Because there was no air inside the bowl, the air inside the balloon pushed out and made it expand.

Boyle used his pump for other experiments, too. He proved that animals need air to breathe, and that candles need air to stay alight. But he never found out what air is made of.

It's actually a mixture of different gases, but most of them weren't discovered until the 20th century. Separating them out was just too difficult.

What's in air?

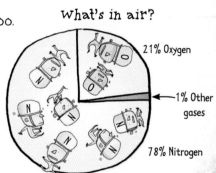

21% Oxygen

1% Other gases

78% Nitrogen

Know your properties

Two hundred years ago, scientists didn't know about different kinds of atoms, or even that atoms existed at all. But early chemists still knew an awful lot about how substances work, and what they can do. This is because they studied what are known as the physical and chemical properties of a substance.

What are physical properties?

Physical properties mostly describe what a substance is like on its own. The most basic example is what it looks like. Many physical properties are easy to find out, such as what colour a substance is, what it smells like, or what state it's in at room temperature.

Other physical properties can be found using simple tests. For example, you can heat a liquid to find its **boiling point** (the temperature at which it boils and changes state to become a gas). Or, if it's a solid, you can hit it, to see if it breaks into pieces or buckles, or if it's too strong even to dent.

What are chemical properties?

Chemical properties mostly describe what a substance can do, such as what happens when you heat it up, or mix it with other substances. For example, some things turn a different colour as they burn, or dissolve when mixed with water, or explode when mixed with acid.

The only way to test a chemical property is to make a chemical reaction happen. Creating a reaction is a bit like cooking – chemists do it by mixing together different substances, and often heating them up as well.

Salt facts

White solid; made up of little crystals.

Compound made of the elements sodium and chlorine.

No smell; tastes salty.

Boiling point: 1465°C

Melting point: 801°C

Flaming salt

1. Light a candle.

2. Put a few grains of salt onto a spoon.

3. Pour the salt onto the candle and watch...

...you should see tiny orange sparks appear. This is because sodium, one of the elements in salt, makes an orange flame.

Dissolving things

If you stir sugar into warm water, the sugar disappears.
Chemists call this **dissolving**. The sugar and water
molecules have mixed together. You might think
they've bonded to make a compound, but they haven't.
They've become a liquid mixture called a **solution**. The
ability to do this is a property of both sugar *and* water.

The molecules in
water and sugar
mix together to
make a solution.

Another property of water is that the hotter it
gets, the easier it becomes to dissolve things in it. This
explains why you sometimes find a sticky layer at
the bottom of a cup of cold tea. This is sugar that has
'dropped out' of solution as the tea cooled.

Oil doesn't dissolve in
water. Even if you stir
it, it soon floats to
the top.

Pure and simple

When a substance contains only one kind of atom
or molecule, and is not contaminated by other stuff,
chemists describe it as **pure**. One way to see if a
sample is pure is by looking at its physical properties.

For example, one physical property of pure water
is that it boils at 100°C. If a substance *looks* like water
but doesn't boil at this temperature, then either it's
not water, or it's not pure. The substances that make a
sample *impure* are often called **contaminants** and they
change the boiling point.

Tap water is never pure, so if you could measure
the temperature of boiling tap water (you'd need a
special thermometer from a lab to do this accurately),
you'd find it boils at just *over* 100°C. This is because it
contains small amounts of chlorine, which has been
added to kill any harmful bugs.

Don't forget about pressure!

On top of high mountains,
there is less air pressure
than on the ground. This
means that water can boil
at a cooler temperature
than normal. But tea made
with 'cold' boiled water isn't
very tasty...

Yuck!

Sorting out substances

Chemists can use their knowledge of properties to extract pure substances from impure samples. Here are some examples:

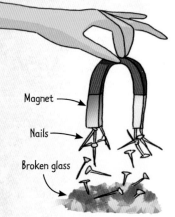

Magnet

Nails

Broken glass

How can you separate steel nails from broken glass?

Use a magnet. The nails will be attracted to the magnet and stick to it, but the glass will not.

How can you separate salt from oil?

Pour the salty oil into a jug of water. The salt will dissolve in the water, but the oil will not. The oil will float on top of the water and can be carefully poured off (or removed using a separating funnel, like the one on the left). The water can then be boiled away to leave behind pure salt.

How can you separate a mixture of sand and salt?

Add water to the mixture. This dissolves the salt but not the sand. If you pour this through a sheet of **filter paper**, the sand will collect on it, and the salt solution will flow through. This is called **filtration**. Finally, the water can be boiled off, leaving the salt behind.

Special equipment

Separating mixtures is easy with the right equipment. Chemists often make their own glass tubes and bottles to make sure they have exactly what they need.

Separating funnel

Oil

Tap

This separating funnel makes it easy to see and separate two liquids by draining one away from the other.

Flask

Water

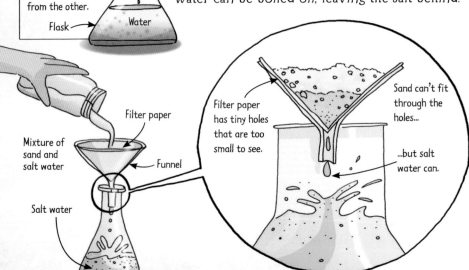

Mixture of sand and salt water

Filter paper

Funnel

Salt water

Filter paper has tiny holes that are too small to see.

Sand can't fit through the holes...

...but salt water can.

How can you separate a solution?

Solutions can appear tricky to separate because the molecules inside are so mixed up. But a chemist just needs to know the different properties of the substance that's dissolved – called the **solute** – and the liquid it's dissolved in, called the **solvent**.

Distilling fuels

Crude oil is a mixture of fuels and other useful substances. They can all be separated by a technique called fractional distillation, which uses chemists' knowledge of substances' boiling points.

The substances in crude oil have very different boiling points. Natural gas boils off first at 36°C, then petrol at 71°C and finally tar at about 515°C.

Separation technique No. 1: Distillation

Distillation is a method of purifying solutions by using boiling points. Usually, the aim is to boil off the solvent, and collect it as a pure liquid.

Heating a solution makes the solvent boil, forming a gas. This leaves behind the solute that was mixed into it. Meanwhile, the hot gas can flow into a long tube. Cold water is passed around the tube. This cools down the gas, until it becomes a liquid again. This liquid is pure and can now be collected.

This is an example of distillation apparatus.

Do-it-yourself distillation

This experiment shows how to distill pure water from sugar water.

 **WARNING**
Watch out: steam is very hot and can burn.

1. Pour a glass of water into a saucepan, and stir in a spoonful of sugar. It will now taste sugary.

2. Heat the sugar water until it boils. Wearing an oven glove, catch the steam on a metal tray.

3. On the tray, the steam condenses into drops of water. Taste it – it won't be sugary any more.

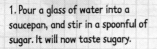
Oven glove
Sugar water

Separation technique No. 2: Chromatography

Chromatography is used to separate mixtures of many substances. There are two types: paper and gas.

Paper chromatography tells scientists what all the different parts of a mixture are. But it doesn't purify them. The mixture to be separated is dissolved in a solvent. The solution is then absorbed along the length of a piece of paper.

The different solutes spread out along the paper. Some spread further than others, depending on how strongly they stick to the paper (that's one of their properties). This piece of paper is known as a **chromatogram**. By studying it, chemists can identify the different substances spread across it.

Gas chromatography is used to help to identify tiny amounts of substances in a mixture. It even works on just a few molecules. Chemists turn the test substance into a gas and feed it into a machine. A computer records how the molecules spread out inside the machine and creates a chromatogram.

Chemists can compare this to chromatograms of known substances, in order to identify the molecules.

A gas chromatography machine uses a liquid or gas (instead of paper) to separate the sample. This means the separated parts can be collected once they've been through the machine. So this method can be used to purify substances as well as to identify them.

who developed it?

Me! Mikhail Tsvet. I developed chromatography in 1901 to find out what makes plants green.

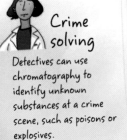

Crime solving

Detectives can use chromatography to identify unknown substances at a crime scene, such as poisons or explosives.

A chromatogram from a computer looks like a huge graph. Chemists can find out lots of information from it.

Do-it-yourself chromatography

Most felt-tip pens contain a mixture of dyes to make up their colour.
You can separate the dyes yourself, using paper chromatography.

1. Cut a strip of coffee filter paper. Dab ink from some felt-tip pens onto it, just above the bottom.

2. Wind the top of the paper around a pencil, stick it in place, and hang it inside a glass with a little water.

3. Leave it for a few minutes. Each ink should spread up the paper, separating into its different dyes.

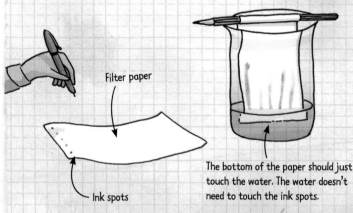

Filter paper

Ink spots

The bottom of the paper should just touch the water. The water doesn't need to touch the ink spots.

A chromatogram of inks

Separation technique No. 3: Centrifugation

Centrifugation uses a machine called a **centrifuge** to separate solutions into liquids that have different densities. **Density** is the amount of **mass**, or stuff, in a certain **volume**, or space. Things that aren't very dense will float on top of denser things. For example, oil is less dense than water, so oil floats on water.

The solution is placed in a set of test tubes and clipped to the centrifuge. It spins around really, really fast, forcing the denser parts to settle at the bottom of each tube. If the solution also contains any solid bits, they will sink to the very bottom.

Blood science

Sports officials often use centrifugation to check blood samples. It can reveal if an athlete has taken any illegal drugs.

Sorting out compounds

Compounds are trickier to separate than mixtures. To get at the elements in them doesn't just mean separating one kind of molecule from another – it means splitting each molecule into separate atoms.

Compounds are created by chemical reactions, so one way to split them is to trigger another reaction. For example, chemists can get copper out of the rocky compound copper oxide by heating the rock with carbon. The carbon swaps places with the copper, leaving behind carbon dioxide and pure copper.

Separation technique No.4: Electrolysis

Some compounds can be split apart using electricity. The compound is either melted or dissolved in a solvent to make something called an **electrolyte**. Then an electric current is passed through it, making the compound break apart. This is called **electrolysis**.

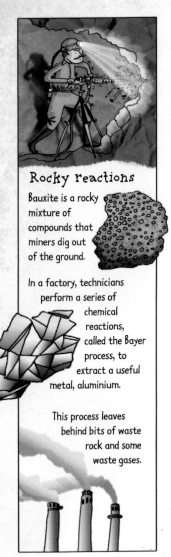

Rocky reactions

Bauxite is a rocky mixture of compounds that miners dig out of the ground.

In a factory, technicians perform a series of chemical reactions, called the Bayer process, to extract a useful metal, aluminium.

This process leaves behind bits of waste rock and some waste gases.

What's electrolysis useful for?

Electrolysis can be used to coat things in metal. It is commonly used to cover iron objects, such as nails, in zinc to stop them from rusting. This process is called **galvanization**.

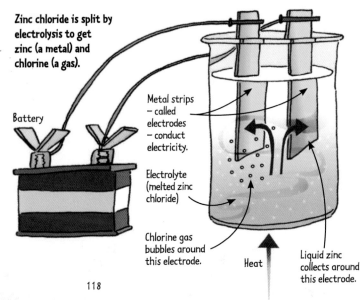

Zinc chloride is split by electrolysis to get zinc (a metal) and chlorine (a gas).

Battery

Metal strips – called electrodes – conduct electricity.

Electrolyte (melted zinc chloride)

Chlorine gas bubbles around this electrode.

Heat

Liquid zinc collects around this electrode.

The story so far

What is the world made of? Here are some of the ways a chemist might answer that question...

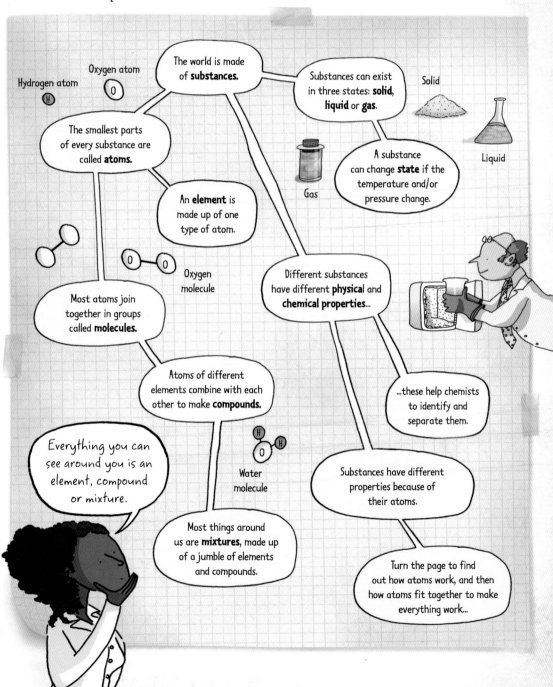

Hydrogen atom

Oxygen atom

The world is made of **substances.**

Substances can exist in three states: **solid, liquid** or **gas**.

Solid

Liquid

Gas

The smallest parts of every substance are called **atoms.**

A substance can change **state** if the temperature and/or pressure change.

An **element** is made up of one type of atom.

Oxygen molecule

Different substances have different **physical** and **chemical properties**...

Most atoms join together in groups called **molecules.**

Atoms of different elements combine with each other to make **compounds.**

...these help chemists to identify and separate them.

Everything you can see around you is an element, compound or mixture.

Water molecule

Substances have different properties because of their atoms.

Most things around us are **mixtures**, made up of a jumble of elements and compounds.

Turn the page to find out how atoms work, and then how atoms fit together to make everything work...

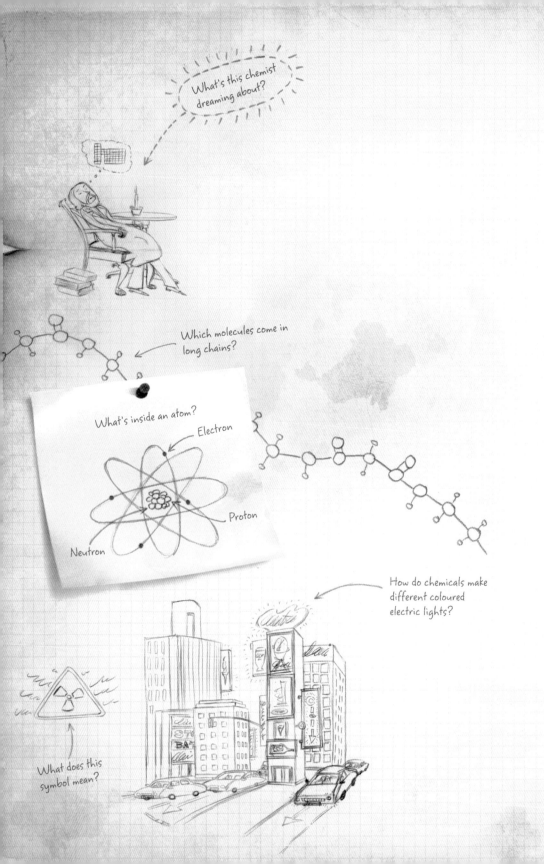

Part 2:
How does it all work?

The big secret behind chemistry is atoms. The reason
substances look different and have different properties is
all to do with the atoms they're made of. And the reason
that chemical reactions happen between substances is to
do with the bits inside each of those atoms.

What's inside an atom?

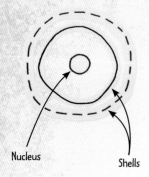

Nucleus   Shells

In the middle of every atom is a central part called the **nucleus**. It contains unimaginably tiny particles called **protons** and **neutrons**, which are all the same size as each other. Most of the rest of an atom is empty space – but at the edge there are even tinier particles called **electrons**, which whizz around the nucleus in layers. These layers are called **shells**. Small atoms only have one shell, but larger atoms can have several.

Protons and electrons both have an **electrical charge**, and it's this charge which holds an atom together. Protons have a positive charge, while electrons have a negative one. (Neutrons have no charge.) When the charges are balanced, they cancel each other out. Atoms have the same number of protons as electrons so, overall, atoms have no charge.

Feeling electrons

Step 1. Blow up a balloon and rub it on a carpet.

Step 2. Hold the balloon up to your head, and you should find that it'll stick to your hair.

What's going on?
Rubbing the balloon brings lots of electrons to the surface. This gives it a tiny negative electrical charge, which makes the balloon stick to your hair. This is called 'static electricity'.

How to identify an atom

Scientists can identify each element by looking for one simple clue: the number of protons in its atoms. For example, an atom with just one proton is a hydrogen atom. An atom with six protons is a carbon atom.

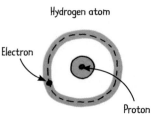

Hydrogen atom

Electron

Proton

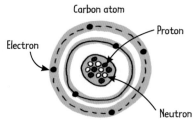

Carbon atom

Electron

Proton

Neutron

Hydrogen atoms are unusual – they don't have any neutrons. All other atoms do – usually around the same number as they have protons.

Carbon atoms have six protons and six neutrons inside the nucleus. They also have six electrons in two shells.

Build your own carbon atom

Chemists often make models of atoms to understand how they are put together. You can make your own simple models using grapes, peas, food wrap and cocktail sticks. Here's a model of a carbon atom:

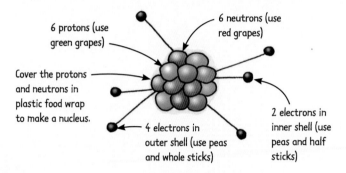

6 protons (use green grapes)

6 neutrons (use red grapes)

Cover the protons and neutrons in plastic food wrap to make a nucleus.

4 electrons in outer shell (use peas and whole sticks)

2 electrons in inner shell (use peas and half sticks)

Naming substances

Scientists often use symbols to describe substances. Oxygen, for example, is O_2. The 'O' is the chemical symbol for oxygen. The '2' (which is always written lower down and a bit smaller) means that one oxygen molecule contains two oxygen atoms.

Compounds get their names by combining the names of the elements in them. For example, carbon dioxide is CO_2. This means it's made of one carbon atom (C) and two oxygen atoms (O_2). $CaCl_2$ is calcium chloride – one atom of calcium (Ca) and two of chlorine (Cl_2).

Luckily, you don't have to memorize the name and symbol of every element. You can look them up – and find out many other things – on a chart called the **Periodic Table**. Turn the page to find out more...

All the atoms

The chart on the next page shows how many protons, neutrons and electrons every atom has.

You can make a model of any atom on the chart – as long as you can find enough fruit.

Symbols

The symbol for many elements is just the first letter of their name:

O = oxygen; **C** = carbon

Some use two letters (the first letter is always a capital):

Mn = manganese; **He** = helium

And some use letters from their name in Latin or Arabic:

K = potassium (Arabic: kalium)

Fe = iron (Latin: ferrum)

All chemicals have formal, scientific names, but lots of them have common names, too. For example, 'dihydrogen oxide' is better known as plain old 'water'.

Ah, nice cool dihydrogen oxide!

The Periodic Table

The Periodic Table lists all the elements in order of their **atomic number** (the number of protons in one atom). The table is divided into rows, called **periods,** and columns. Eight of the columns are called **groups**.

Elements in the same group have the same number of electrons in their outermost shell. Elements in the same period have the same number of shells. You can find out why shells are so important on page 129.

What's in each box?

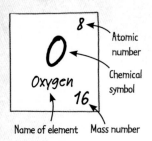

	8	← Atomic number
O		← Chemical symbol
Oxygen	16	

Name of element   Mass number

The **atomic number** is the number of protons.

The **mass number** is the number of protons plus the number of neutrons.

It's called the 'mass' number because it also shows the amount of stuff (or mass) in each atom. Electrons are so small – they have just 1/1800th the mass of a proton or neutron – that they hardly have any mass at all.

Who came up with the Periodic Table?

Lots of people tried to draw up a table of elements, but the first person to make it work was Russian chemist Dmitri Mendeleev in 1869. He said the idea for it came to him in a dream.

Types of elements

Hydrogen is a type all on its own.	Poor metals (see page 126)
Very reactive metals (see page 126)	Metalloids (see page 127)
Quite reactive metals (see page 126)	Non metals (see page 127)
Transition metals (see page 126)	Noble gases (see page 127)

Group I

1							
H Hydrogen 1							

Group II

3 **Li** Lithium 7	4 **Be** Beryllium 9						
11 **Na** Sodium 23	12 **Mg** Magnesium 24						
19 **K** Potassium 39	20 **Ca** Calcium 40	21 **Sc** Scandium 45	22 **Ti** Titanium 48	23 **V** Vanadium 51	24 **Cr** Chromium 52	25 **Mn** Manganese 55	26 **Fe** Iron 56
37 **Rb** Rubidium 85	38 **Sr** Strontium 88	39 **Y** Yttrium 89	40 **Zr** Zirconium 91	41 **Nb** Niobium 93	42 **Mo** Molybdenum 96	43 **Tc** Technetium 99	44 **Ru** Ruthenium 101
55 **Cs** Caesium 133	56 **Ba** Barium 137		72 **Hf** Hafnium 178.5	73 **Ta** Tantalum 181	74 **W** Tungsten 184	75 **Re** Rhenium 186	76 **Os** Osmium 190
87 **Fr** Francium 223	88 **Ra** Radium 226		104 **Rf** Rutherfordium 261	105 **Da** Dubnium 262	106 **Sg** Seaborgium 266	107 **Bh** Bohrium 264	108 **Hs** Hassium 269

These two rows of metals don't fit neatly into the table, so they're normally shown at the bottom, like this. Most of the elements in the bottom row are radioactive (see page 135).

57 **La** Lanthanum 139	58 **Ce** Cerium 140	59 **Pr** Praseodymium 141	60 **Nd** Neodymium 144	61 **Pm** Promethium 145
89 **Ac** Actinium 227	90 **Th** Thorium 232	91 **Pa** Proactinium 231	92 **U** Uranium 238	93 **Np** Neptunium 237

If you know a bit about the properties of just a few elements you can use this table to work out what properties other elements nearby might have, and which elements they're likely to react with.

The table is still growing. Only the elements up to number 93 are naturally occuring; all the higher elements have been artificially created in labs. So far no one has managed to make any of element number 117 – that's why there's a gap on the table.

Periods

Going across the periods from left to right, atoms increase in mass, because they contain more bits.

Surprisingly, they also get smaller, because the increasing electrical charge pulls the bits closer together.

Groups

Elements in the same group usually have similar properties. Going down the groups from top to bottom, atoms get bigger. They also tend to have lower melting points and are generally easier to break apart.

				Group III	Group IV	Group V	Group VI	Group VII	Group VIII
									2 He Helium 4
				5 B Boron 11	6 C Carbon 12	7 N Nitrogen 14	8 O Oxygen 16	9 F Fluorine 19	10 Ne Neon 20
				13 Al Aluminium 27	14 Si Silicon 28	15 P Phosphorus 31	16 S Sulphur 32	17 Cl Chlorine 35.5	18 Ar Argon 40
27 Co Cobalt 59	28 Ni Nickel 59	29 Cu Copper 64	30 Zn Zinc 65	31 Ga Gallium 70	32 Ge Germanium 73	33 As Arsenic 75	34 Se Selenium 79	35 Br Bromine 79	36 Kr Krypton 84
45 Rh Rhodium 103	46 Pd Palladium 106	47 Ag Silver 108	48 Cd Cadmium 112	49 In Indium 115	50 Sn Tin 119	51 Sb Antimony 122	52 Te Tellurium 128	53 I Iodine 127	54 Xe Xenon 131
77 Ir Iridium 192	78 Pt Platinum 195	79 Au Gold 197	80 Hg Mercury 201	81 Tl Thallium 204	82 Pb Lead 207	83 Bi Bismuth 209	Po	At	86 Rn Radon 222
109 Mt Meitnerium 268	110 Ds Darmstadtium 271	111 Rg Roentgenium 272	112 Uub Ununbium 277	113 Uut Ununtrium 284	114 Uuq Ununquadium 289	115 Uup Ununpentium 288	116 Uuh Ununhexium 293		Uuo Ununoctium 294

62 Sm Samarium 150	63 Eu Europium 152	64 Gd Gadolinium 157	65 Tb Terbium 159	66 Dy Dysprosium 163	67 Ho Holmium 165	68 Er Erbium 167	69 Tm Thulium 169	70 Yb Ytterbium 173	71 Lu Lutetium 268
94 Pu Plutonium 244	95 Am Americium 243	96 Cm Curium 247	97 Bk Berkelium 247	98 Cf Californium 251	99 Es Einsteinium 252	100 Fm Fermium 257	101 Md Meitnerium 258	102 No Nobelium 259	103 Lr Lawrencium 262

Metals

Most elements are **metals**. The easiest way to identify a metal is how it looks. All pure metals are shiny, and they share many other properties, too. Here are some of them...

Metals can be drawn out into wires, and are good at conducting electricity (see page 132).

PIIIING!!!

When solid, metals make a pinging sound if they're hit.

Metals can be bent without breaking.

Reactive metals

The elements in Groups I and II are all reactive metals. Because of this, they can be hard to find in their pure forms.

Two of the reactive metals in Group I, sodium and potassium, are so reactive that they catch fire when they come into contact with water.

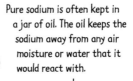

Pure sodium is often kept in a jar of oil. The oil keeps the sodium away from any air moisture or water that it would react with.

Transition metals

Transition metals make up a large block of elements. Many can be found in pure form, but they can also be combined to create metallic mixtures called alloys (see page 161). Transition metals include iron, copper, zinc, cobalt and mercury.

Poor metals

Most of the elements in Groups III-VI are metals, but many are softer and easier to melt than other metals. This makes them useful for different things. Common examples include aluminium, tin and lead.

Most drinks cans are made of aluminium. It's a soft metal that's easy to crush.

Elements, such as zinc and cobalt, are used to make the colours in stained glass.

Metalloids

Seven elements in Groups III-VI share some properties with metals, and some with non-metals. These in-betweeners are known as **metalloids**.

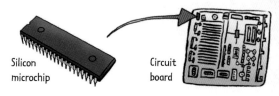

Silicon microchip

Circuit board

The metalloid silicon can conduct electricity, but only when it's heated up. Substances that do this are called **semi-conductors**.

Microchips are often made of silicon and are used on circuit boards. They turn on a circuit when heated up, and turn it off again when they're cooled down.

Non metals

Unlike metals, all **non metals** don't conduct heat or electricity very well at all. Many of them are gases at room temperature.

There are only 16 non metals, but they make up much of the world around us – including the atmosphere, the oceans and much of the Earth's crust.

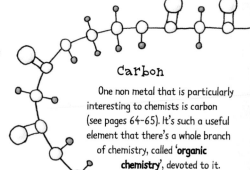

Carbon

One non metal that is particularly interesting to chemists is carbon (see pages 64-65). It's such a useful element that there's a whole branch of chemistry, called **'organic chemistry'**, devoted to it.

This diagram shows a carbon-based, chain-like molecule which is used to make plastics.

Sulphur

At room temperature, sulphur is a brittle yellow block that crumbles easily. It's used to make gunpowder and match heads.

Noble gases

Noble gases are incredibly unreactive non metals. Four of them share one very useful property – they produce a coloured light when an electric current passes through them.

Noble gases are used to light up cities at night.

What colour?

Neon makes red or orange lights.

Argon with mercury makes blue lights.

Krypton lights are pale pink.

Xenon lights are purple.

Pure elements

Only a few elements are found and used in their pure forms. For example, very unreactive elements such as gold, or the noble gases, almost always occur as pure elements. Some elements, such as copper, are often found in their pure forms because they are only reactive under certain conditions. Others, such as carbon, react quite easily, but they can exist on their own, too.

Other substances are found as elements because they're in plentiful supply. Oxygen and nitrogen are both reactive gases, but there's so much of them in the air that they couldn't possibly find enough other substances to react with.

People and animals inhale oxygen all day, every day, but more is constantly being produced by plants. So the supply of fresh oxygen never runs out.

Safe storage
Nitrogen is often used inside food packets. It keeps out oxygen, which would make the food go stale.

Pure krypton is used as part of really powerful lasers, for example in eye surgery.

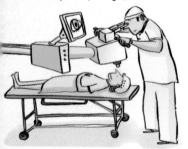

How are compounds made?

Most substances aren't elements – they're compounds or mixtures. The reason compounds exist is all to do with the electrons in a substance's atoms.

When two or more atoms collide, they may just bounce off each other. But sometimes, a few electrons are transferred from one atom to another. This changes the atoms, and makes them bond together. That's how compounds are made.

Complex compounds
Some compounds are made up of lots and lots of different atoms. In 1945, British chemist Dorothy Crowfoot Hodgkin worked out the complex structure of the compound that makes the drug penicillin.

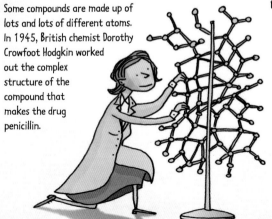

This process is called a chemical reaction, and it happens because of the number of electrons the atoms have in their outer shells.

How do shells work?

The first shell around a nucleus only has room for two electrons. The second and higher shells each have room for eight. When the first shell is full, a second shell forms. When the second shell is full, a third forms – and so on. The outer shells of the biggest atoms can fit as many as 32 electrons.

The key to chemical reactions is that atoms are much less likely to react if their outer shell is full. Or, to put it another way, most atoms want to be stable, so they try to find ways to have full outer shells.

For example, a hydrogen atom has one electron in its outer shell; but a helium atom has two. Helium is a stable element that hardly ever reacts. But hydrogen is very reactive, because it's always trying to fill its shell.

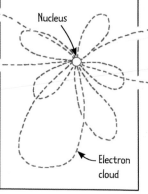

Going around

Electrons don't really travel around in neat, round shells. It's just easier to draw them that way.

In reality, chemists think electrons probably move in cloud shapes, a bit like this:

Nucleus

Electron cloud

A hydrogen atom has room for another electron in its shell.

A helium atom has a full outer shell.

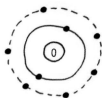

An oxygen atom has six electrons in its outer shell – so it 'wants' two more.

Gaining and losing

Not all atoms want to *add* more electrons to fill their shells. Some have nearly empty outer shells with one, two or three 'spare' electrons that they want to *lose*.

An atom of lithium, for example, has three electrons: two in its inner shell, and one in its outer shell. Instead of trying to find seven extra electrons, it's easier to lose one electron – leaving it with a single, full shell.

Half full

Transition metals have outer shells that are half full (or half empty). They are happy to add *or* give away electrons.

This means their properties are less predictable than other groups of elements. Some of them are really reactive and others can be very stable and unreactive.

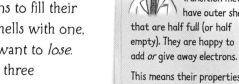

No reactions

Helium   Neon   Argon

Krypton   Xenon   Radon

Remember it's very difficult to make noble gases react with anything. That's because their outer shells are already full and they aren't interested in gaining or losing any electrons.

How do atoms fill up their shells?

In a chemical reaction, atoms can either give or take electrons, or they can share them.

    This works in three different ways...

1. Giving and taking electrons

Some atoms need to get rid of just one or two electrons to get a full outer shell. But they can't simply release their electrons into thin air – they have to find other atoms that need electrons. Then there's a bit of give and take, which chemists call **ionic bonding**.

    Here's how it works when an atom of sodium meets an atom of chlorine...

What happens: **How it looks as a diagram:**

Step 1. An atom of sodium (Na) meets an atom of chlorine (Cl).

The sodium atom needs to lose one electron to get a full outer shell.

The chlorine atom needs to gain one electron to get a full outer shell.

The sodium atom has 1 electron in its outer shell...

... and the chlorine atom has 7.

Step 2. The sodium atom gives its electron to the chlorine atom.

Step 3. The sodium atom loses its empty third shell. Both atoms now have full outer shells....

But that's not the end of the story...

After giving or taking electrons, an atom has an unequal number of electrons and protons. This gives it an electrical charge. Atoms with a charge are called **ions**. Electrons have a negative charge, so an atom that has gained electrons becomes a **negative ion**. An atom that has lost electrons becomes a **positive ion**.

Ions with opposite charges attract each other. After sodium and chlorine atoms have reacted and become ions, millions of them stick together to make structures that are big enough to see with your naked eye – chemists call these **crystals**.

2. Sharing electrons

Some atoms bond by sharing electrons. They do this by overlapping their outer shells. The shared electrons sit between the atoms, giving them both full outer shells. Chemists call this **covalent bonding**.

Here's how it works for two hydrogen atoms...

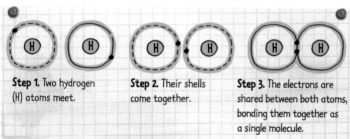

Step 1. Two hydrogen (H) atoms meet.

Step 2. Their shells come together.

Step 3. The electrons are shared between both atoms, bonding them together as a single molecule.

Atoms that have formed covalent bonds usually make small molecules. These molecules don't attract each other very much, because they have no charge. Instead they're free to spread out. That's why many elements and compounds made of covalent bonds, including hydrogen, are gases at room temperature.

Ionic bonds

Na^+ is the symbol for a sodium ion (positive charge).

Cl^- is the symbol for a chlorine ion (negative charge).

Millions of ions of sodium and chlorine bond to make crystals of a stable compound called sodium chloride – better known as table salt.

Covalent bonds

In a hydrogen molecule, two hydrogen atoms share one pair of electrons. This forms a bond called a single bond.

Some molecules, such as carbon monoxide, share two pairs of electrons. This makes a double bond, drawn like this:

Methyl-acrylonitirile is a compound made of 10 atoms. Each molecule contains seven single bonds, one double bond and one triple bond.

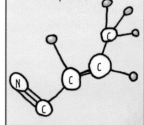

Making magnets
The way that electrons pool in some metals, such as iron, gives them a special property – it makes them magnetic.

3. Pooling electrons

Metal atoms have another way of sharing electrons: they cluster together and pool some of their outer electrons into a sort of sea that floats around them.

Electrons in this sea can flow around any of the atoms that are nearby, so every atom feels as if it has a full outer shell. Because all the metal atoms release some electrons, they all become positive ions.

Electron

Metal ion

The electrons in the 'sea' are free to move around and join up with different shells.

Heat race

Here's a quick experiment you can try to test how well metals can conduct heat compared to non metals:

First, make a nice, hot cup of tea. Then, take two spoons made of different material – one metal, the other plastic.

Stick them into the hot tea. Then stick both spoons into a glass full of ice cubes.

You will find that the metal spoon gets hot and cools down much quicker than the plastic spoon.

Explaining metals

Metal atoms cluster together in a regular pattern which chemists call a **giant metallic lattice**. In a metallic lattice, the atoms are packed together very tightly. This makes them extremely hard and is why they have very high boiling points and are solid at room temperature.

The sea of electrons around the lattice creates some useful effects. Electrons can carry heat and electrical energy. Because each electron can move around freely, it's easy for it to knock into and transfer energy to the other electrons next to it. This means heat or an electric current can flow through a metal very quickly. Because of this ability, chemists describe metals as being good **conductors**.

Sticking together

Most individual molecules and ions are too small to see. But the way they stick together affects how different substances look and behave.

Crystals of magnesium sulphate (epsom salt)

How do ions stick together?

Ions nearly always stick together to make crystals. These always have a regular pattern – imagine it as a bit like a climbing frame. The ions are the joints, and the bonds are the bars. The more ions that cluster together, the larger the crystal. Individual crystals can grow quite big. On the next page, you can find out how to grow your own.

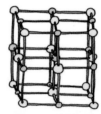

Inside sodium chloride, ions of sodium and chlorine bond together in a regular pattern.

It's usually very difficult to pull ions apart physically – even if you heat them up – so most **ionic compounds** are solid even at very high temperatures. But you can break whole *layers* of crystals apart from each other. This is how you can crumble salt into your food. You're not breaking apart the ions in the salt, but you're breaking apart salt crystals.

How do molecules stick together?

Molecules with covalent bonds form **covalent compounds**. There is still an attraction between the individual molecules, but it's weak. So weak, in fact, that these compounds are usually liquids or gases.

For example, water molecules only stick together quite loosely, which is why water is liquid at room temperature. Many gases, including oxygen and nitrogen, are made of covalent molecules, too.

Dissolving ions

Ionic bonds can be broken apart chemically, just by mixing them with the right substance.

For example, salt (sodium chloride) ions will separate when they mix with water. That's what's happening when salt dissolves. But no reaction has happened, so salt water is a mixture, not a compound.

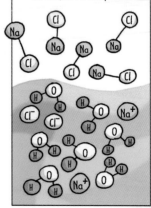

Do-it-yourself crystals

You can grow your own crystals using bicarbonate of soda (NaHCO$_3$). This experiment shows you how.

1. Fill two jars with hot water. Stir about six teaspoons of bicarbonate of soda into each jar. Keep adding more soda until no more will dissolve.

2. Put the jars in a warm place with a plate in between them. Make sure they won't get moved.

3. Cut a piece of wool as long as your arm. Tie a paperclip to each end of it, and place one end in each jar.

4. Leave the jars for at least a week. Crystals should grow gradually along the wool, and hang down over the plate.

What's happening?

Bicarbonate of soda is usually sold as a powder made up of tiny crystals. The powder dissolves in water. The mixture of water and soda is soaked up by the wool. The water then evaporates slowly, leaving behind pure bicarbonate of soda — which reforms into big crystals.

Nuclear reactions

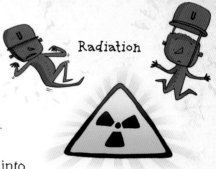

Radiation

Not all reactions happen because of electrons. Sometimes, the nucleus of an atom can split apart by itself, or fuse with the nucleus of another atom. These are both called **nuclear reactions**.

Nuclear reactions change one kind of element into another, because protons are lost or added. But they're pretty rare because they need lots of energy. They usually only happen inside stars, or power generators called nuclear reactors.

This symbol means a substance is radioactive (see below) and will emit radiation. Radiation is dangerous because it can cause serious illnesses, including cancer.

Unstable elements

A few elements have an unstable mix of protons and neutrons in their atoms. Because of this, the nucleus in any of these atoms can suddenly break down and emit (send out) some of its bits. Scientists call these unstable elements **radioactive**. The stuff they emit is called **radiation**.

Uranium is one of the few radioactive elements that can be dug out of the ground. It's found in lumps of rock called pitchblende. Inside pitchblende, single atoms of uranium emit two protons and two neutrons. These fuse to make something called an **alpha particle**. Losing these particles converts the uranium atom into a thorium atom.

Who discovered radioactivity?

I did - Henri Becquerel. I found that uranium salts have strange properties.

What about me - Marie Curie? My husband and I discovered radioactive elements in pitchblende. We invented the word 'radioactivity'.

The Curies and Becquerel shared a Nobel Prize for their work in 1903.

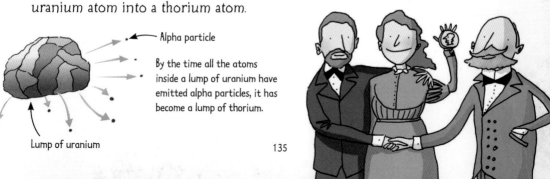

Alpha particle

By the time all the atoms inside a lump of uranium have emitted alpha particles, it has become a lump of thorium.

Lump of uranium

135

A brief history of atoms

Some of the first people to hit on the idea of atom-like particles were scholars in India about 2,700 years ago.

An Ancient Greek philosopher called Democritus invented the word 'atom' about 2,500 years ago. He had the idea that substances could be divided into smaller and smaller parts, until you found a particle so tiny it couldn't be divided any more. He called these particles 'atoms', which means 'uncuttable' in Ancient Greek.

The idea of atoms was ignored for centuries, because scientists were more interested in studying whole substances. Then, in the 18th century, Amedeo Avogadro in Italy began to study the way gases take up more or less space when temperature and pressure change. He guessed this happens because gases are made of tiny moving parts.

Amedeo Avogadro

In 1803, English chemist John Dalton was investigating how reactions work. He suggested that every element and compound must be made of minuscule particles, and he reused Democritus's word – atom. Over the next hundred years, scientists came to believe that atoms must really exist.

Ernest Rutherford won a Nobel prize in 1908 for his study of radioactivity.

After the discovery of radiation in the 19th century, scientists began to realize that supposedly 'uncuttable' atoms were actually made up of even smaller parts. In 1909, New Zealander Ernest Rutherford used radiation to detect the nucleus of a gold atom*.

In 1913, Danish scientist Niels Bohr suggested a way that electrons could fit around an atom's nucleus. This finally explained how atoms react with each other.

* To find out more about Ernest Rutherford's experiment, turn to page 195.

Niels Bohr

Atoms and bonds: need to know

An atom

Atoms are made of protons, neutrons and electrons.

Nucleus   Shell

Protons and neutrons stick together in the atom's nucleus.

Electrons orbit around the atom in layers called shells.

Protons and electrons have opposite charges, so they attract each other. Atoms have the same number of electrons as protons.

This diagram shows four electron shells circling the nucleus from different angles.

The number of protons tells you what element an atom belongs to.

Proton (+)

Electron (–)

Neutron (no charge)

Atoms are more stable if their outer shell is full of electrons. If they don't have a full shell, they will react with other atoms until they do. They can do this in three ways:

3. Metal atoms join together in a giant metallic lattice, pooling their electrons in a sea that flows all around them.

1. Some atoms give or take electrons to become ions.

Ions have a positive or negative charge. Opposite ions attract each other and make ionic compounds.

2. Some atoms overlap their shells, and share their electrons to become molecules.

What did these men invent?

What makes a firefly glow?

What happens to atoms and molecules during a reaction?

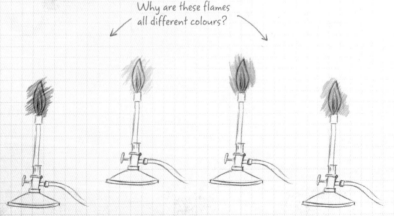

Why are these flames all different colours?

Part 3:
Let's make things happen!

Chemistry can sometimes seem like magic.
After all, how on earth does a firework explode into
different coloured lights when you set it off? And how
can a dangerous acid turn into harmless and tasty table
salt? What's really going on (in both cases) is just a
chemical reaction. But the effects of any reaction can be
spectacular, surprising – and often very useful...

Reactions: the basics

Reactions happen between the *atoms* of different substances but the results affect the *whole* substances.

Substances that react are called **reactants**, and any new substances formed by the reaction are called **products**. Reactions also take in and give out **energy** – usually as heat or light (for example, as a flame). But this energy doesn't count as a reactant or a product.

When reactants are mixed together, most of their molecules or ions will react, if part of one reactant is attracted to part of another. Their molecules break down, and rearrange to form new products. But there can be some molecules of each reactant that don't react, so they're left over at the end.

Reactions all around

Chemical reactions are happening all around us, all the time. They're even happening inside your body right now. When you breathe in air, the oxygen it contains reacts with chemicals from your food, producing carbon dioxide and water vapour (which you breathe out). This reaction also gives out energy, providing power for your cells, organs, muscles and brain.

By-products

Chemists often use a reaction to get a specific product. Any other products are then described as **by-products**. Many by-products are useful, but some are dangerous – such as polluting smoke that comes from coal-burning power stations.

A simple reaction

When hydrogen chloride (HCl) meets sodium hydroxide (NaOH)...

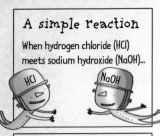

...the molecules knock together, and their bonds break.

This splits up the compounds into ions.

New bonds form...

...making two new compounds:
Sodium chloride (table salt)...   ...and water

This reaction also gives out a tiny bit of heat energy.

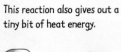

How do reactions start?

No matter how keen a substance is to react, a certain amount of energy is needed to kick-start any reaction. That's because energy is needed to help break the existing bonds inside the reactants.

Energy to start a reaction can come in different forms. Most often it's heat, but it could also be light or electricity. And some energy (again, usually heat) is given out at the end when the products are formed.

Heat in, heat out

Some reactions take in more heat at the start than they give out at the end. These are called **endothermic** reactions. For example, when you eat sherbet, it takes heat from your body to react with water in your mouth. This makes your tongue tingle (it's really feeling cold).

Exothermic reactions are the opposite – they give out more than they take in. If you drop an indigestion tablet into a bowl of vinegar, it will fizz. The bowl becomes warm, because the reaction gives out heat.

Food chemistry

Baking and cooking are just chemical reactions in a kitchen. Heating food speeds up the reaction between the ingredients. Stirring helps the ingredients (or reactants) to mix together properly, so they react more swiftly.

Yum!

Lunching on light

Plants use the green stuff in their leaves (called chlorophyll) to capture light energy from sunshine. This kick-starts a reaction between water and carbon dioxide to make glucose (food). This whole process is called photosynthesis.

Natural torch

Inside a firefly, there's a substance that reacts with oxygen to give out light. This is what makes the firefly glow.

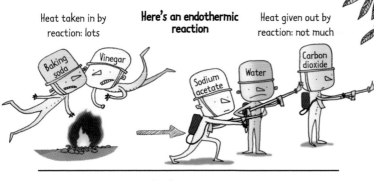

Heat taken in by reaction: lots

Here's an endothermic reaction

Heat given out by reaction: not much

Baking soda · Vinegar

Sodium acetate · Water · Carbon dioxide

Heat taken in by reaction: not much

Here's an exothermic reaction

Heat given out by reaction: lots

Methane · Oxygen

Carbon dioxide · Water

BANG!

Gunpowder is made of reactants that react so quickly they cause an explosion.

Silver objects react with air to form a layer of tarnish. It can be removed by polishing.

Ready, steady, react!

The amount of energy a reaction needs to get going is called its **activation energy**. Some reactions need a lot of activation energy, but others only need a little.

Once they get going, some reactions happen in seconds, such as exploding gunpowder. Others, such as silver turning black (tarnishing), can take many weeks. The rate of a reaction depends on the **reactivity** of the reactants – which means how keen they are to break up and form new products.

Speeding up and slowing down

Many reactions will happen more quickly if you add an extra substance called a **catalyst**. The catalyst isn't a reactant – it just lowers the activation energy. At the end of the reaction, the catalyst is unchanged and can even be used again. Different substances can be catalysts for different reactions. For example, platinum speeds up a reaction in car exhaust pipes to get rid of poisonous gas.

You can slow down or even stop a reaction from happening by adding another susbtance called an **inhibitor**. For example, galvanized iron is coated in a layer of zinc, which is an inhibitor. It slows the reaction between iron and air that forms rust.

Reactions can also be speeded up or slowed down by changing the temperature. Heat makes molecules rush around and collide more often, so they react faster.

But if reactants are cooled down, they have less energy to move around and bash into each other, so they react more slowly.

Life savers

Your body is brimming with biological catalysts called enzymes. They speed up vital processes that keep you alive.

But sometimes an enzyme can speed up a reaction so much it makes you feel ill or in pain. Many medicines, for example aspirin, work by inhibiting these reactions.

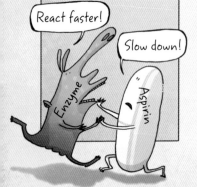

React faster!

Slow down!

Enzyme

"Aspirin"

What's the point of catalysts?

Chemists often do experiments to work out a
reaction's activation energy, and which catalysts
can help. This is so that they can change the reaction
conditions in factories, to manufacture products more
quickly and efficiently.

For example, in 1909, German chemist Fritz
Haber worked out how to make nitrogen react with
hydrogen to produce ammonia (NH_3). This is a key
ingredient in many fertilizers, used to help grow crops.
Haber found he could produce lots of ammonia by
raising the temperature and pressure to the right levels,
and adding iron as a catalyst.

Feed the world
Over one third of the world's
population relies on food
grown with the help of
ammonia fertilizers.

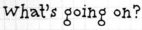

Do-it-yourself reaction race
In this simple experiment, you can see for yourself how heat changes the speed
of a reaction. You will need some tap water and two soluble indigestion tablets.

1. Take two glasses. Put cold water in the
first and hot water in the second.

2. Drop one tablet into each of the
glasses at the same time. If you don't
drop them in at the same time, it won't
be a fair experiment.

Cold water
(from the
fridge)

Hand-hot
water (from
the hot tap)

What's going on?
The reaction between the tablets and the water needs
a little heat to start. Cold water won't start to fizz
until it warms to room temperature. But the hot water
kick-starts the reaction right away. This reaction is
also exothermic — so when the reactants do start to
fizz, they make the water even hotter.

3. Watch the two glasses closely.
You should find that the glass
with warm water starts to fizz
up after a few seconds, before
the glass with cold water.

writing down reactions

Chemists write down reactions using **equations** that look a bit like maths. They add the reactants together on the left, then draw an arrow, and finally show what the products are on the right.

Here's a simple chemical equation in words:

Sodium hydroxide + Hydrochloric acid $\longrightarrow$ Table salt + Water

And here's how it looks using chemical symbols:

$$NaOH \ + \ HCl \longrightarrow NaCl \ + \ H_2O$$

Balancing equations

One of the most important things to know about reactions is that, overall, nothing is destroyed or made. This is called the **Law of Conservation of Mass**.

It means the total number of atoms of each element has to be the same on both sides of the arrow. This is called balancing the equation.

This equation shows the reaction plants use to make glucose (food)*:

$$\text{Water} \ + \ \text{Carbon dioxide} \xrightarrow{\text{+ sunlight}} \text{Glucose} \ + \ \text{Oxygen}$$

Here's how it looks when balanced, using chemical symbols:

$$6H_2O \ + \ 6CO_2 \longrightarrow C_6H_{12}O_6 \ + \ 6O_2$$

On the left:

There are six molecules of water and six molecules of carbon dioxide.

$6 \times H_2 = 12$ hydrogen atoms

$(6 \times 0) + (6 \times O_2) = 18$ oxygen atoms

$6 \times C = 6$ carbon atoms

On the right:

The reaction produces one molecule of glucose and six molecules of oxygen.

$H_{12} = 12$ hydrogen atoms

$O_6 + (6 \times O_2) = 18$ oxygen atoms

$C_6 = 6$ carbon atoms

* See pages 62-63 to find out more about how plants make food.

Science symbols

Some equations use symbols to give extra information:

↯ means light energy.

Δ means heat energy.

(s), (l) or (g) means a substance is solid, liquid or gas. (aq) means a substance is 'aqueous' – dissolved in water.

I'll give this plant sunlight and water so it can make food.

There are the same number of carbon, hydrogen and oxygen atoms on both sides of the equation.

Weird and wonderful reactions

Chemists have discovered all sorts of chemical reactions – some useful and some not so useful. Here are a few examples...

Down on the farm

Dairy farmers often add certain bacteria to cows' milk. The bacteria cause a reaction in the milk that produces a delicious-tasting acid. This is how yoghurt and cheese are made.

Hmm, shall I try propionibacterium or lactobacillus today?

Scorching sunburn

Sunshine contains an invisible energy called ultraviolet light. It causes a reaction in your skin which gives you a tan. But too much leads to sunburn. Sunscreens block the ultraviolet light and prevent the reaction from happening.

Sharp sauce

Soy sauce is made from soy beans and wheat boiled in water. Bacteria in the water 'ferment' (or cause a reaction in) the mixture, breaking it down into alcohols and acids. The acid is what gives soy sauce its sharp taste.

Airy cakes

Baking soda is a sodium compound that produces carbon dioxide when it's heated. It's bubbles of this gas that make a cake rise in the oven.

Catching your breath

Potassium chlorate, lithium chlorate and sodium chlorate all give off oxygen when heated. They are used to provide people in space stations or submarines with oxygen to breathe.

Crippling cramp

Lactic acid is a product of a reaction in your muscles. You use the reaction to get energy when you're doing a lot of exercise. But too much lactic acid can make your muscles ache, and sometimes gives you a cramp.

All kinds of reactions

There are many different ways for substances to react and exchange atoms or ions. Here are just six common types of reaction...

Reaction type 1: trading places

Sometimes, a substance reacts with a compound by kicking out part of that compound. This is called a **displacement reaction**.

For example, zinc metal reacts with hydrochloric acid to displace hydrogen gas. This happens because there's a stronger attraction between zinc and chlorine than between hydrogen and chlorine.

A zinc atom can give an electron to each of two chlorine atoms. The zinc and chlorine become ions and bond with each other. Loose hydrogen atoms are kicked out. They bond in covalent pairs and float away.

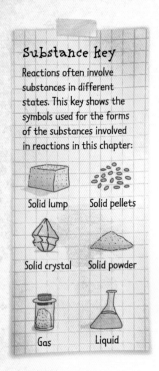

Substance key

Reactions often involve substances in different states. This key shows the symbols used for the forms of the substances involved in reactions in this chapter:

Solid lump   Solid pellets

Solid crystal   Solid powder

Gas   Liquid

How it happens...

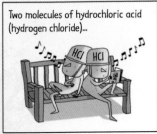

Two molecules of hydrochloric acid (hydrogen chloride)...

...meet an atom of zinc.

A-HA! JUST WHAT I NEED TO GET RID OF SOME ELECTRONS.

The zinc atom splits each molecule apart...

I AM ZINC – REACT WITH ME!

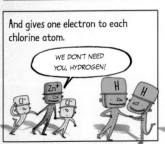

And gives one electron to each chlorine atom.

WE DON'T NEED YOU, HYDROGEN!

At the end of the reaction, there's a molecule of zinc chloride, and a molecule of hydrogen.

WELL WE DON'T NEED YOU EITHER!

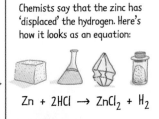

Chemists say that the zinc has 'displaced' the hydrogen. Here's how it looks as an equation:

$$Zn + 2HCl \rightarrow ZnCl_2 + H_2$$

Reaction type 2: breakdown

If a compound has enough energy, it can sometimes break apart to make new products all by itself. A chemical change has taken place, so this still counts as a chemical reaction. It's called **decomposition**.

For example, when calcium carbonate is heated it breaks apart to form calcium oxide and carbon dioxide gas. Here's the equation:

When a lump of calcium carbonate is heated, it decomposes and releases carbon dioxide gas.

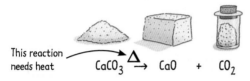

This reaction needs heat

$$CaCO_3 \xrightarrow{\Delta} CaO + CO_2$$

Reaction type 3: back and forth

Sometimes, reactants form new products, only for the products to react together and turn back into the original substances. These are called **reversible reactions**. Because they can keep going back and forth, the reactions never quite finish happening.

For example, if you heat nitrogen dioxide, it splits into nitrogen monoxide and oxygen. This is a decomposition reaction – but it's also reversible. When the products cool down, they react with each other to form nitrogen dioxide again. Heat is the key. If the products stay warm enough, the reverse reaction can't happen.

This equation has an arrow pointing both ways to show that the reaction is reversible:

The break-up

When two molecules of nitrogen dioxide are heated up...

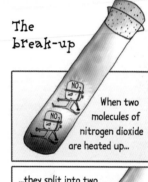

...they split into two molecules of nitrogen oxide and one molecule of oxygen.

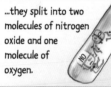

But when they cool down, the molecules recombine...

...fusing back into two molecules of nitrogen dioxide.

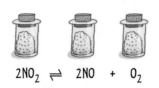

$$2NO_2 \rightleftharpoons 2NO + O_2$$

147

Reaction type 4: two-in-one

Some reactions are made up of two 'half' reactions in which reactants lose and gain electrons.

One reactant loses electrons – this is called **oxidation**. The other reactant gains those electrons – this is called **reduction**. Together, oxidation and reduction make lots of ions – which are then attracted to each other and bond, forming products. The whole process is called a **redox reaction** (short for reduction/oxidation reaction).

One common redox reaction happens between calcium and chlorine. The reaction can be shown as two half equations or one whole equation...

What's in a name?

When oxidation reactions were first discovered, chemists thought they were all about substances gaining oxygen.

Since the discovery of electrons, chemists now know that oxidation is really all about electrons. But the name has stuck.

Oxidation half reaction:
A calcium atom loses two electrons and becomes an ion, written as Ca^{2+}. The calcium is 'oxidized'.

$$Ca \rightarrow Ca^{2+} + 2e^-$$

Overall redox reaction:
The calcium ions (Ca^{2+}) bond with the chloride ions (Cl^-), to form the final product: calcium chloride.

Reduction half reaction:
A molecule of chlorine gains these two electrons and becomes two ions, written as $2Cl^-$. The chlorine is 'reduced'.

$$Cl_2 + 2e^- \rightarrow 2Cl^-$$

$$Ca + Cl_2 \rightarrow CaCl_2$$

Calcium chloride is an unreactive powder, which is good at absorbing water. It's sometimes used as a food preservative. Chemists use it in labs to protect reactive substances from moisture in the air.

Danger!

This symbol is put on labels to show that a substance is an 'oxidizing agent'.

Most oxidizing agents, such as potassium nitrate, can cause nasty burns. They must be handled with care.

Don't worry - I'll protect you from any mischievous moisture!

Blast off!

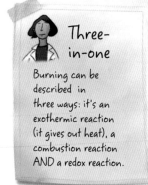

Burning, or **combustion** as chemists like to call it, is the most famous redox reaction of all. For example, in a rocket engine, hydrogen gas burns with oxygen. A spark activates the reaction between the two gases, and they keep burning until one runs out. This reaction gives out a massive amount of heat and power that pushes the rocket up into space.

Oxidation half reaction:

$$2H_2 \rightarrow 4H^+ + 4e^-$$

Reduction half reaction:

$$O_2 + 4e^- \rightarrow 2O^{2-}$$

Overall redox reaction:

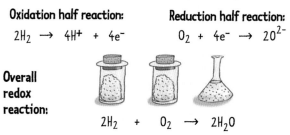

$$2H_2 + O_2 \rightarrow 2H_2O$$

The hydrogen is oxidized and the oxygen is reduced.

Three-in-one

Burning can be described in three ways: it's an exothermic reaction (it gives out heat), a combustion reaction AND a redox reaction.

What a firecracker!

Redox reactions are also the secret behind fireworks. Fireworks contain a mixture of metal and other compounds that produce oxygen after they are lit. The oxygen reacts with the metal, making it burn with a coloured flame.

Here's the equation for a reaction inside a blue firework, made using copper chloride:

Oxidation half reaction:

$$4Cl^- \rightarrow 2Cl_2 + 4e^-$$

Reduction half reaction:

$$O_2 + 4e^- \rightarrow 2O^{2-}$$

Overall redox reaction:

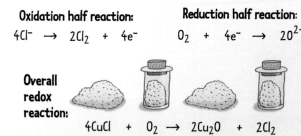

$$4CuCl + O_2 \rightarrow 2Cu_2O + 2Cl_2$$

The chlorine is oxidized and the oxygen is reduced. The copper starts out bonded to chlorine and ends up bonded to oxygen – so it has changed – but it hasn't been oxidized or reduced.

Testing, testing

Different metal compounds burn different colours. Chemists use the colours as a simple check to see what metal a substance contains. This check is known as a **flame test**.

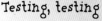

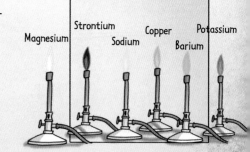

Magnesium   Strontium   Sodium   Copper   Barium   Potassium

Reaction type 5: meet in the middle

Yet another kind of reaction happens when a compound called an **acid** is mixed with a compound called a **base**.

What's an acid?

Acids vary from weak acids — like the sour-tasting citric acid in lemon juice — to strong acids, like the sulphuric acid used in car batteries. Many weak acids are used as flavourings. Strong acids are usually poisonous and are also **corrosive**, meaning they can cause burns.

Chemists define an acid as a substance that makes positive ions of hydrogen (H+) when dissolved in water. How strong the acid is depends on how many of its molecules break up into ions.

What's a base?

A base is the opposite of an acid. In water, it makes negative ions of hydroxide (OH-). Like acids, bases can be strong or weak. Weak bases, such as baking soda, are edible, although they don't taste of much. Strong bases, such as oven cleaner, are as corrosive as strong acids. When a base is dissolved in water, it's called an **alkali**.

A happy medium

When an acid and a base are mixed in the right quantity, they react to form water and a **salt**. Table salt (sodium chloride) is just one kind of salt. Salts aren't acids or bases: they're **neutral**. So this kind of reaction is called a **neutralization reaction**.

Strong and weak

Most acids come dissolved in water. If there is a lot of water, they're said to be **diluted**. If there's hardly any water, they're **concentrated**.

CORROSIVE

Hydrochloric acid is very corrosive, but it's safe to handle when it's diluted in lots and lots of water.

There's dilute hydrochloric acid in your stomach that helps digest food. It's dilute enough so it doesn't burn your tough stomach lining (but it's still strong enough to give you heartburn).

Citric acid is weak. But in a lab, it's possible to make it so concentrated that it could cause burns.

Lemons contain dilute citric acid. It's just strong enough to give pancakes a bit of zing.

This equation shows the neutralization reaction between sodium hydroxide (a base) and hydrochloric acid, which produces table salt and water:

$$NaOH \;+\; HCl \;\rightarrow\; NaCl \;+\; H_2O$$

Water test

Copper sulphate is one of many kinds of salt. When it's dry, it's white, but if it touches even a tiny amount of water, it turns blue. So chemists often use it to test if another substance contains water.

The pH scale

The strength of an acid or a base is measured on a scale called the **pH scale**, which goes from 0 to 14.

A really powerful acid has a pH of 0. The strongest base has a pH of 14. A neutral substance has a pH of 7.

How can you tell them apart?

Luckily for chemists, there's a simple way to tell acids from bases – they use a substance called an **indicator**. One of the simplest indicators is called litmus paper. There are two kinds of litmus paper:
- Blue litmus paper turns red in an acid.
- Red litmus paper turns blue in a base.

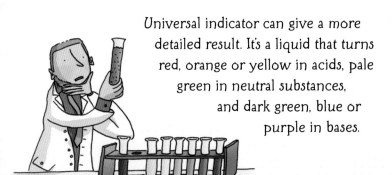

Universal indicator can give a more detailed result. It's a liquid that turns red, orange or yellow in acids, pale green in neutral substances, and dark green, blue or purple in bases.

Know your acids from your bases

Acids:	pH
Sulphuric acid	0
Hydrochloric acid	1
Ethanoic acid (in vinegar)	4
Bee sting	5
Citric acid	5
Carbonic acid (in fizzy drinks)	6

Neutral:	
Water	7

Bases:	
Baking soda	8
Soap	8
Wasp sting	9
Magnesium hydroxide (in indigestion tablets)	10
Sodium hydroxide (in drain cleaner)	14

This table shows the colours that universal indicator can turn, depending on the pH of the substance it's mixed with.

Do—it—yourself indicator

You can make your own indicator by following these instructions.

You will need: a red cabbage, a saucepan, some empty glass jars and a variety of household substances to test. You could try: vinegar, mouthwash, orange juice, baking soda, indigestion tablets, peppermint extract — or anything else you like.

1. Chop the red cabbage up into little bits.

2. Boil the cabbage in water for about 10 minutes, until the water turns a pink-purple colour.

3. You don't need the cabbage now. Strain it, and keep the purple liquid. This is your indicator.

4. Allow the indicator to cool, then pour some into a few empty jars.

5. Try adding different substances to the jars, to see which ones make the indicator change colour.

Acids will turn the indicator red.

Bases will turn it blue.

Indicator tip

If a substance is a very weak acid or base you might have to add lots to see a colour change.

You can also make the indicator change colour back and forth by adding an acid first and then lots of a base (or the other way around).

Not quite neutral

When acids and bases mix, they don't always form a neutral product. For example, if you mix a strong base like sodium hydroxide with a weak acid like hydrogen carbonate, it makes a weak base: sodium hydrogen carbonate, more commonly known as baking soda.

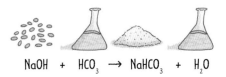

$$NaOH + HCO_3 \rightarrow NaHCO_3 + H_2O$$

In the same way, adding a strong acid to a weak base creates a weak acid. For example, hydrochloric acid and ammonia make ammonium chloride – a weak acid used in shampoo to help prevent split ends in hair.

What's going on?

When a weak acid reacts with a strong base...

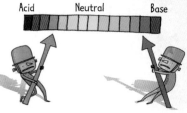

Acid   Neutral   Base

...they don't balance out neutrally. Instead, they make a weak base.

Soap story

Mixing the right kind of weak acid with the right kind of base makes one very useful product – soap.

Soap contains lots of long chain-like molecules. One end of the chain likes water. That's why a gloopy, soapy mixture forms when you mix soap with water.

The rest of the chain hates water, but loves grease. When you dip greasy hands in soapy water, these ends gather around the grease particles, trapping them. Rinsing with water then allows you to wash away the soap *and* the grease. That's how soap gets things clean.

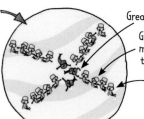

Bowl of soapy water

Grease particles

Grease-loving parts of soap molecules gather together, trapping the grease particles.

Water-loving end of soap molecule

Hands off

Hundreds of years ago, people used to make soap by hand, by mixing animal fat with a base called lye.

But pure lye is so strong that many people burned their hands while making soap. Nowadays people who make soap wear protective clothing.

Reaction type 6: fantastic plastics

Yet another kind of reaction is used in factories that make **plastics**. The reactants are small molecules found in crude oil. Heat, pressure and, sometimes, catalysts make these molecules react to form really long chains, called **polymers**. Chemists call this a **polymerization reaction**.

All plastics are made of polymers. Some polymers exist in nature, too. They're found in things such as wool, cotton and the hairs on your head.

Different plastics have very different properties, making them useful for all sorts of things. Some are hard and strong, others are stretchy and light, and most can be pulled around to make different shapes, from plastic cutlery to toys.

Plastic geniuses

Most plastics that people use today were only invented in the 20th century:

1908 Leo Baekeland created bakelite, used in old-fashioned radios and telephones.

1933 Eric Fawcett and Reginald Gibson invented polythene, great for making plastic bags.

1935 Wallace Carothers invented nylon fibre, used in clothing.

1965 Stephanie Kwolek invented Kevlar®, now used in bulletproof vests.

Bulletproof vest

Kevlar® plastic is stitched together to make the vest.

The molecules in Kevlar® are very tightly packed. The structure absorbs and spreads out the impact of a bullet.

Plastic fabrics

Plastic is so versatile that it can even be pulled out into thin threads, and woven together to make fabrics that are light, warm and hard-wearing. Lycra® is a plastic used in underwear and sports clothing.

Polyester, another plastic, can be used in pillows, and acrylic plastic is often mixed with wool to weave into warm fleeces.

Plastic pollution

Many plastics don't break down naturally in rubbish dumps. But some, such as polyester and PET plastic, can easily be recycled.

Reactions: the lowdown

Chemical reactions are happening all the time, everywhere.

A reaction is when the bonds between atoms break and the atoms rearrange themselves into new substances.

Bonds are strong – it takes energy to break them, and energy is released when new ones form. The amount of energy needed to start a reaction is called the activation energy.

1. Two molecules meet.

2. They break apart for a split second.

3. They give, take or share electrons.

4. They form new molecules, called products.

There's always the same amount of matter at the start and end of a reaction.

If more energy is taken in, it's an endothermic reaction.

If more energy is given out, it's an exothermic reaction.

Reactions can be written down as equations using symbols, numbers and arrows.

$$NaOH + HCl \longrightarrow H_2O + NaCl$$
$$\longrightarrow \Delta$$

The triangle means this reaction gives out heat.

Acids and bases are chemical opposites. Their strength is measured in pH units.

There are six common types of reaction:
- displacement
- decomposition
- reversible
- redox
- neutralization
- polymerization

When they react together, they produce neutral salts.

Some reactions involve more than one of these types.

Plastics are made of long chain molecules called polymers.

What is this and what can it do?

What chemical gives cinnamon its flavour?

Which non metals help plants to grow?

Which metals can be mixed together and used to make nuts and bolts?

Which halogen is used to power pacemakers?

Part 4:
How is chemistry useful?

Even before chemists knew anything about molecules, atoms and electron shells, they did experiments to find new ways of using substances – from common carbon and oxygen to rarer stuff such as phosphorus and molybdenum. Along the way, they've worked out how to make all sorts of useful things, some rather unusual and some quite ordinary. In this chapter, you can discover how chemistry plays a role in almost every part of our lives.

Carbon chemistry

Carbon is one of the most useful elements on Earth both as an element and in compounds. Confusingly, pure carbon comes in two main forms which have very different properties: **graphite** and **diamond**.

Graphite is black and crumbly. It's the bit of a pencil that you write with. In graphite, each carbon atom is joined to three others in layers. Each layer can easily slide over the others. That's why the graphite in a pencil rubs off onto paper when you write.

Diamond is the opposite. It's clear and hard – in fact, it's the hardest natural material on Earth. Each carbon atom is bonded to four others in a large, interlocking crystal. This gives diamond its strength. As well as making jewels, it's used in industrial drills.

Carbon for life

Deep inside you – and every living thing – there are molecules of your very own personal carbon compound, known as **DNA**. It contains hydrogen, nitrogen and some other things, but it's mostly carbon.

The chemicals in your DNA are linked in an order that's unique to you. The order is like a code that tells your body what to do. Your DNA affects everything – from the colour of your eyes to the shape of your nose, and even how good you are at solving puzzles. You inherit half of the code from each of your parents. That's why children and parents share many similar features.

Bucky balls

'Bucky balls' (short for buckminster fullerenes) are a special form of carbon first discovered in a lab. They look like microscopic footballs, made up of sixty carbon atoms linked together.

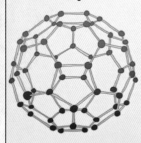

They're really strong and good conductors of electricity. Chemists are exploring ways of using them like incredibly tiny machines, for example to carry molecules of medicine to specific areas of the human body.

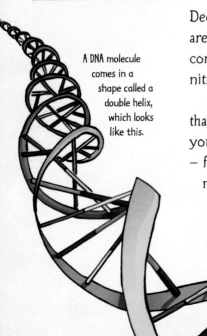

A DNA molecule comes in a shape called a double helix, which looks like this.

Carbon and oxygen

Carbon can bond with another common element, oxygen, in different ways.

Carbon monoxide (CO) is a colourless, odourless, and extremely poisonous gas. It's formed whenever carbon compounds burn in a limited amount of oxygen, for example in car engines. Car exhaust fumes contain a lot of carbon monoxide.

Carbon dioxide (CO_2) is what we breathe out. Plants absorb it from the air to use in photosynthesis. It's also used in some kinds of fire extinguisher. Fires need oxygen to burn, so smothering a flame with carbon dioxide means that oxygen can't get to it.

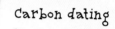

Carbon dating

Scientists can use carbon to date very old remains, such as this sabretooth tiger skull, which is over 11,000 years old.

And how does it work? Well, all living things contain small amounts of a radioactive type of carbon called carbon-14 (^{14}C). After they die, the amount of ^{14}C gradually decreases. Scientists can measure how much is left to work out how long ago they lived.

Mineral carbon

Many common minerals contain carbon compounds known as carbonates (CO_3). For example, limestone rock is mostly calcium carbonate. Lithium carbonate can be found in anything from glass to glue to pills.

Chemists use carbonates to make carbon dioxide. If any kind of carbonate is mixed with a strong acid, it will fizz up and give off carbon dioxide (CO_2) gas.

Testing, testing

Chemists can check if a reaction produces carbon dioxide by using a solution of calcium hydroxide, also known as limewater.

Limewater is clear. But if it mixes with carbon dioxide, it turns cloudy. This is because it reacts with the gas to make calcium carbonate – a powder that doesn't dissolve.

When calcium carbonate is mixed with hydrochloric acid, it produces carbon dioxide.

The bubbles of gas are collected in water.

There's pure carbon dioxide in this tube.

The reaction also produces water and calcium chloride (a solid that dissolves in the water).

All about metals

Metals all have similar properties, but some are tougher than others, or better at conducting heat. Here are a few examples of ways people use metals...

Taking the heat

Molybdenum doesn't melt until it reaches an astonishing 2,623°C. It's used on the outside of spacecraft, because it can withstand the intense heat that builds up on re-entry into the Earth's atmosphere.

Hard and soft

Aluminium is the most common metal in the Earth's surface. It's tough but also very light. Thick aluminium makes sturdy frames for cars and trains. Thin sheets of it make crushable drinks cans.

Copper top

Copper conducts electricity well and is often used for electrical wiring. It's also decorative and so is used to make roofs for fancy buildings. It reacts slowly with air to form a protective layer of attractive green copper carbonate.

Body metals

Many reactive metals are found in compounds inside living things. Calcium forms bones and teeth. Potassium makes muscles work. Sodium helps carry signals across nerve cells in the brain.

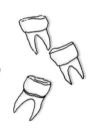

Do-it-yourself: green copper

You can see for yourself how copper turns green in this simple experiment.

You should find that the unrinsed coin starts to turn green after a few hours. But the other coin will stay shiny a while longer.

Step 1. Place two copper coins in a cup of vinegar with a little salt for a few minutes until they are shiny.

Step 2. Rinse one of the coins in water. Leave both coins on a windowsill to dry.

What's happening? The unrinsed coin reacts with the vinegar and salt solution to form a layer of green copper acetate. The rinsed coin reacts with air to form a layer of green copper oxide (this reaction normally takes longer).

Alloy, alloy, alloy!

Different metals can be combined to make metal-based mixtures known as **alloys**. Alloys are useful because they combine properties of all the elements in them.

The earliest man-made alloy was so useful that it spread around the world and gave its name to a whole period of history – the Bronze Age. Bronze is made by melting and mixing together copper and tin. It's strong (like copper) and resists corrosion (like tin).

Brass tacks

Brass is an alloy of copper and zinc. It's used to make all sorts of bits and pieces, such as nuts, bolts and tacks because it's tough.

Bronze is often used to make statues.

Inside bronze, atoms of copper and tin jumble together. Most bronze contains a lot more copper than tin.

Soldering on

Solder is made of tin and silver or lead. It melts at low temperatures, and is useful for sealing metal joints and building electronic circuits.

The secret of steel

Special alloys can also be made by mixing metals with non metals. The most famous is steel, an alloy of iron and carbon. A small amount of carbon keeps the iron atoms in a rigid structure, making steel super tough.

Steel is harder to make than bronze, because iron needs very high temperatures to melt. But it's easier to find iron because there's lots of it in the ground. Today steel is used to make things that need to be really strong, such as the frames of skyscrapers. Steel can also be mixed with chromium to stop it from rusting. This 'stainless' steel is used to make cutlery.

The perfect sword

Some of the first steel-makers were swordsmiths in Japan. They melted and re-forged their blades many times over. This made the carbon and iron atoms spread out more evenly, making the blades extra tough.

wrestling with reactions

Some metals are more willing to react than others. All metals can be listed in order of their willingness to react – this is called the **reactivity series**.

One way of picturing the series is to imagine all the metals are taking part in a wrestling competition. The metals that win the most fights are the most reactive.

For example, when zinc chloride is mixed with magnesium, zinc and magnesium 'compete' to form a bond with chlorine. Magnesium is more reactive than zinc, so it 'wins' the competition, and bonds with chlorine to form magnesium chloride.

Here's how some of the most useful metals stack up against each other in the reactivity series:

Metal reactions

All metals share some chemical properties as well as physical ones. These three reactions will produce the same kind of product with any metal.

Any metal + oxygen
⟶ a metal oxide

Any metal + a strong acid
⟶ a salt + hydrogen

Any metal + superhot steam
⟶ a metal oxide + hydrogen

Just face it, I'm more reactive than you!

Zn   Pb

I may not be a metal, but I'll take you all on!

C

Carbon and hydrogen aren't metals, but they often compete with metals to react with substances, such as oxygen. So, chemists usually include them in the reactivity series.

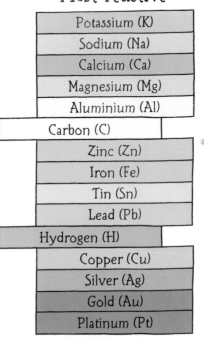

Most reactive

Potassium (K)
Sodium (Na)
Calcium (Ca)
Magnesium (Mg)
Aluminium (Al)
Carbon (C)
Zinc (Zn)
Iron (Fe)
Tin (Sn)
Lead (Pb)
Hydrogen (H)
Copper (Cu)
Silver (Ag)
Gold (Au)
Platinum (Pt)

Least reactive

You'll never beat me!

Ca   K

I always lose.

Pt

Using gases

Hydrogen and helium are the two most common elements in the Universe. They're both colourless and odourless gases.

If you've ever seen party balloons that float up to the ceiling, they were full of helium. Helium is less dense than air, so a helium balloon will rise until it hits something. Outside, it will drift up until the air pressure gets so weak that the pressure of the helium pushing outwards inside the balloon makes it burst.

Hydrogen is also less dense than air. Some of the first 'airships' were filled with a mixture of air and hydrogen, to make them rise. But, because hydrogen burns very easily, many accidents happened. Modern airships use helium instead, because it's much safer, even though it's harder to get than hydrogen.

Oxygen is the third most common element in the Universe. Pure oxygen is one of the gases found in air. People need to breathe it to survive. It's also needed for things to combust, or burn.

Oxygen is very reactive and forms many compounds called oxides. The most common of these is water. Another is hydrogen peroxide (H_2O_2), a pale blue liquid also known as bleach. It has lots of uses – killing bacteria, making hair dyes, and even as a fuel for prototype space rockets.

DIY voicechanger

Step 1. Open the end of a helium balloon and carefully suck in a mouthful of gas.

Step 2. Say something...

Eeeeeee!

...You should find that your voice sounds really squeaky.

What's going on?
Because helium is lighter than air, it makes the vocal cords in your throat vibrate faster. This makes your voice sound high and squeaky.

Burning question

For a long time, even the cleverest scientists weren't sure what made things burn.

In the 1770s, three chemists – Frenchman Antoine Lavoisier, Englishman Joseph Priestley and German Carl Scheele, all found the answer independently...

It's oxygen!

what about non metals?

There aren't very many non metals, but they're found in some of the most useful substances on Earth.

Explosive nitrogen

TNT is a well-known explosive. It's named after the nitrogen compound it contains: tri-nitro-toluene. Chemist Joseph Wilbrand invented TNT as a yellow dye in 1863. Its explosive properties weren't discovered until decades later.

No flies on phosphorus

The compound phosphorus trihydride is a poisonous gas. It's used to kill pests which eat grain. Farmers only use a mild form of it, so the grain isn't poisoned as well.

Fertilizers

Nitrogen and phosphorus are both major ingredients in fertilizers. They help farmers to grow more plants in places with poor soil.

Using the halogens

The halogens are very reactive non metals. Some of them are quite dangerous, but chemists have still found uses for them.

Boring bromine

In the past, doctors used bromine compounds, called bromides, to help people to sleep. For many years, the word 'bromide' just meant anything really boring.

Medical iodine

When solid iodine is dissolved in alcohol, it's a strong antiseptic which can be used to treat wounds.

Lithium iodide is used in the batteries of pacemakers. These are tiny machines that help steady a person's heartbeat.

Choking on chlorine

Chlorine is used in carefully controlled amounts to disinfect swimming pools and drinking water.

Pure chlorine gas is so poisonous, it was used as a weapon in the First World War. Soldiers had to protect themselves from it by wearing gas masks.

Pacemakers can be seen by an X-ray.

What a stink!

Chemistry labs can be full of strange and terrible smells. One of the smelliest chemicals is sulphur, but it's not the only culprit...

WARNING

Never sniff or inhale any strange chemicals. They might make you very sick.

Smelly food

Sulphur is found in rotten eggs, which have a really unpleasant smell. It's also what gives garlic its strong taste, in a compound called allicin.

Smelling salts

When a person faints, one way to revive them can be to release a strong smell. Smelling salts react with air to release a tiny amount of ammonia gas, which can sometimes do the trick.

Skunk spray

Skunks spray a horrible smell that sends any attackers running. It's full of sulphur compounds called thiols. The smell is so strong it can spread for over a mile. The spray can even cause temporary blindness if aimed at the eyes.

Dead smelly

Some nitrogen compounds have very strong smells, with names that match! Putrescine and cadaverine are the compounds that make rotting (or 'putrescent') things and dead bodies (or 'cadavers') smell awful.

Butyric acid

One common smell is very hard to forget. Butyric acid wafts up from parmesan cheese, rancid butter, vomit and even from people who don't wash.

Fume cupboard

Some chemical reactions create very smelly and even dangerous gases. Chemists do these reactions inside a fume cupboard. A fan in the top of the cupboard whisks the gases safely away.

Chemical curiosities

Every day, clever chemists around the world are unlocking the chemistry of substances and finding out how things work. All sorts of things happen because of chemistry – some that you might never have thought of...

Why do I like chocolate?

Chocolate contains two delightful compounds – tryptophan and theobromine – which react with the body to produce hormones that make people feel happy and relaxed.

Detective work

It's not always easy to tell dried blood from dried ketchup or other red substances. Detectives spray a compound called luminol onto suspicious red stains. If there's any blood, the luminol will glow blue.

Flavourings

Cinnamaldehyde is the chemical that gives natural cinnamon its flavour. The same chemical can be made in labs and factories, and used as an artifical flavouring.

Lawn lovers

Hexenal is the substance that gives freshly cut grass its particular smell. Some insects also produce it as a scent to attract their mates.

Preserving specimens

Formaldehyde is a strong-smelling liquid used to preserve animal specimens and human organs. It soaks into them and stops them from decaying.

A brain preserved in formaldehyde

Mad hatters

In the 19th century, mercury was used to make hats shiny. But inhaling the fumes made some hat-makers rant, rave and shake. This is where the phrase 'as mad as a hatter' comes from.

How to tell what's what

Identifying different elements and compounds can be a tricky business. Big labs often have an incredibly useful machine called a mass spectrometer to do that.

What happens inside a mass spectrometer?

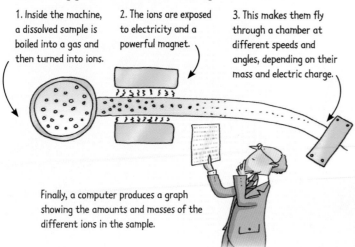

1. Inside the machine, a dissolved sample is boiled into a gas and then turned into ions.

2. The ions are exposed to electricity and a powerful magnet.

3. This makes them fly through a chamber at different speeds and angles, depending on their mass and electric charge.

Finally, a computer produces a graph showing the amounts and masses of the different ions in the sample.

Walk-in testing

Some airports have giant pods that passengers step into. A mass spectrometer is attached to the pod.

The pod quickly sucks in particles on the passengers' clothes and the mass spectrometer checks these particles for any traces of illegal drugs or explosives.

Micro-investigations

One way to find out about a substance is to get a really good look at it. Here are two methods that can help chemists do this...

X-tra special

The way X-rays shine through or bounce off the surface of crystals gives clues about how the molecules hold together.

Rosalind Franklin used a technique called X-ray crystallography on crystals of DNA. Her work was vital to understanding its structure.

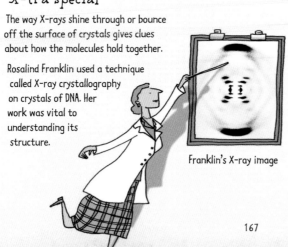

Franklin's X-ray image

Copper oxide crystals seen by SEM

Mighty microscopes

A scanning electron microscope (SEM) can see tiny details that a normal microscope cannot. It fires a stream of electrons at the surface of a substance, and records where other electrons are knocked off it. The machine uses this data to create a computer image of the surface.

Is there a simple way to find out what a substance is?

In a high-tech lab, professional chemists would use a mass spectrometer to identify a mysterious substance. But you don't always need big machines to identify substances. There are simple tests that you can try out in a school lab. This two-stage chemical sorter will help you to work out what kind of substance a mystery solid is.

Sorter stage one

First, you need to make sure you've got a pure element or compound, and not a mixture. You could try a few separation techniques (see pages 114-117). Here are some of the questions you can ask and tests you can do to help you identify a substance. It's not always possible to get a precise answer.

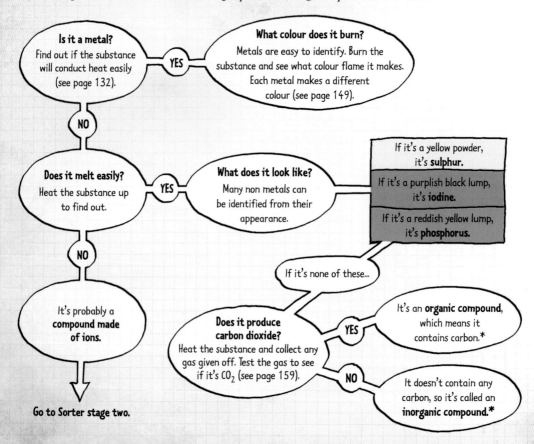

Is it a metal?
Find out if the substance will conduct heat easily (see page 132).

YES → **What colour does it burn?**
Metals are easy to identify. Burn the substance and see what colour flame it makes. Each metal makes a different colour (see page 149).

NO

Does it melt easily?
Heat the substance up to find out.

YES → **What does it look like?**
Many non metals can be identified from their appearance.

If it's a yellow powder, it's **sulphur**.

If it's a purplish black lump, it's **iodine**.

If it's a reddish yellow lump, it's **phosphorus**.

If it's none of these...

NO

It's probably a **compound made of ions**.

Does it produce carbon dioxide?
Heat the substance and collect any gas given off. Test the gas to see if it's CO_2 (see page 159).

YES → It's an **organic compound**, which means it contains carbon.*

NO → It doesn't contain any carbon, so it's called an **inorganic compound**.*

Go to Sorter stage two.

Sorter stage two

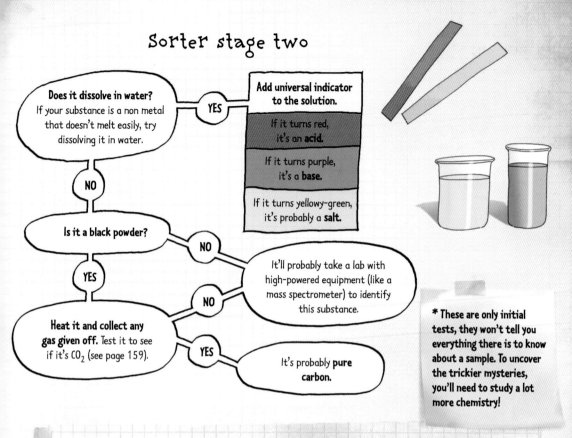

Does it dissolve in water?
If your substance is a non metal that doesn't melt easily, try dissolving it in water.

YES

Add universal indicator to the solution.

If it turns red, it's an **acid.**

If it turns purple, it's a **base.**

If it turns yellowy-green, it's probably a **salt.**

NO

Is it a black powder?

NO

YES

It'll probably take a lab with high-powered equipment (like a mass spectrometer) to identify this substance.

NO

Heat it and collect any gas given off. Test it to see if it's CO_2 (see page 159).

YES

It's probably **pure carbon.**

* These are only initial tests, they won't tell you everything there is to know about a sample. To uncover the trickier mysteries, you'll need to study a lot more chemistry!

Can I identify colourless gases?

When chemists do reactions, they usually have an idea of what products will form. Many reactions produce oxygen or hydrogen as by-products. So, to check a reaction has worked, chemists can test for these gases.
Here are two tests you can try in a school lab:

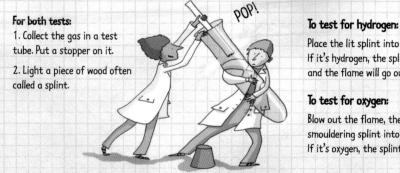

POP!

For both tests:
1. Collect the gas in a test tube. Put a stopper on it.

2. Light a piece of wood often called a splint.

To test for hydrogen:
Place the lit splint into the test tube. If it's hydrogen, the splint will go pop and the flame will go out.

To test for oxygen:
Blow out the flame, then stick the smouldering splint into the test tube. If it's oxygen, the splint will re-light.

Part 5:
Our chemical Universe

Cross-section of planet Earth

Space

Upper atmosphere

Lower atmosphere

Mantle

Outer core

Inner core

← Earth's crust

The Universe and all the stars and planets in it – including our own planet, the Earth – were formed by chemical processes billions of years ago. Ever since then, chemistry has been making changes all day, every day, to the land, sea and sky.
Chemistry is also involved in the life and death of all living things, including human beings. Read on to find out how elements are formed, what rocks and air are made of, and what chemicals your body needs to survive.

Where did the elements come from?

Most scientists think that the Universe exploded into existence about $14\frac{1}{2}$ billion years ago. At first, there was only one element – hydrogen. There were billions and billions and billions of hydrogen atoms, all squashed up into baby stars.

AT THE DAWN OF TIME, ATOMS OF HYDROGEN FLOATED AROUND IN A HUDDLE.

AS TIME WENT BY, GRAVITY AND PRESSURE PULLED THEM CLOSER TOGETHER, AND THEY GOT HOTTER AND HOTTER UNTIL...

...THEY EXPLODED. THAT'S HOW THE FIRST STARS WERE BORN.

THE INSIDE OF A STAR WORKS A BIT LIKE A PRODUCTION LINE...

WHEN TWO HYDROGEN ATOMS ARE SQUASHED TOGETHER, A NUCLEAR REACTION HAPPENS. THEY FUSE AND MAKE A HELIUM ATOM.

THE REACTION RELEASES MASSIVE AMOUNTS OF ENERGY. THIS POURS OUT AS HEAT, LIGHT AND RADIATION.

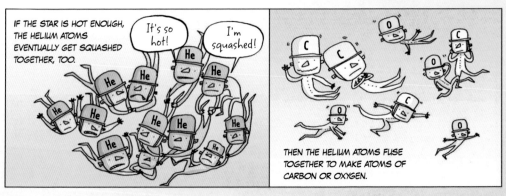

IF THE STAR IS HOT ENOUGH, THE HELIUM ATOMS EVENTUALLY GET SQUASHED TOGETHER, TOO.

It's so hot!

I'm squashed!

THEN THE HELIUM ATOMS FUSE TOGETHER TO MAKE ATOMS OF CARBON OR OXYGEN.

AS NEW, HEAVIER ELEMENTS ARE MADE, THE STAR BECOMES DENSER...

...AND MUCH, MUCH HOTTER.

INSIDE A REALLY BIG, HOT, DENSE STAR, EVEN HEAVIER ELEMENTS CAN BE MADE...

...AND MORE HEAT, LIGHT AND RADIATION ARE GIVEN OUT.

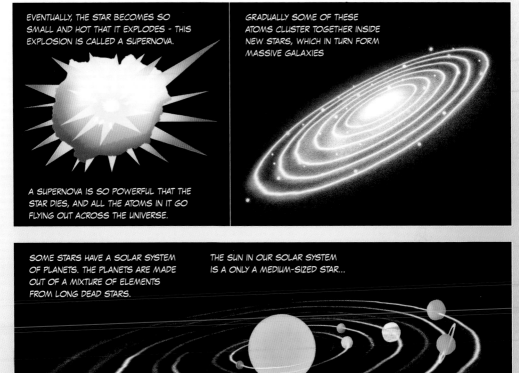

EVENTUALLY, THE STAR BECOMES SO SMALL AND HOT THAT IT EXPLODES - THIS EXPLOSION IS CALLED A SUPERNOVA.

A SUPERNOVA IS SO POWERFUL THAT THE STAR DIES, AND ALL THE ATOMS IN IT GO FLYING OUT ACROSS THE UNIVERSE.

GRADUALLY SOME OF THESE ATOMS CLUSTER TOGETHER INSIDE NEW STARS, WHICH IN TURN FORM MASSIVE GALAXIES

SOME STARS HAVE A SOLAR SYSTEM OF PLANETS. THE PLANETS ARE MADE OUT OF A MIXTURE OF ELEMENTS FROM LONG DEAD STARS.

THE SUN IN OUR SOLAR SYSTEM IS A ONLY A MEDIUM-SIZED STAR...

...INSIDE IT, HYDROGEN IS TURNED INTO HELIUM. BUT IT'S NOT HOT ENOUGH TO MAKE HEAVIER ELEMENTS.

Rocks are chemicals too

The surface of the Earth is made of rock – both on land and under the sea. Rocks might look like lumps that never do anything. But, like everything else, they're actually taking part in chemical reactions.

Cave chemistry

Inside limestone caves, extraordinary natural sculptures are built very slowly.

Step 1. When it rains, water trickles into the cave, dissolving tiny bits of limestone.

Step 2. The water drips down from the roof and lands on the floor of the cave.

Step 3. The water evaporates and leaves little bits of limestone behind.

Over thousands of years, these tiny deposits build up to create rock formations.

Stalagmites rise up from the cave floor; stalactites hang down from the ceiling.

Breaking mountains

Most mountains have tiny cracks in their rock faces. Rainwater flows into these cracks, and often freezes into ice. Ice takes up more space than water, forcing the crack to widen.

After many thousands of years of rain and ice, the crack gets so wide that part of the mountain simply falls off.

There are three main types of rock...

1. Igneous

The inside of the Earth contains molten (melted) rock, called **magma**. This gradually cools to form **igneous** rocks, such as granite or pumice.

Mt. Rushmore, USA is made of granite, an igneous rock.

2. Sedimentary

Sedimentary rocks are formed when tiny bits of rocks, bones and shells get squashed together, often underwater, making one gigantic new rock, such as chalk or sandstone.

The white horse of Kilburn, UK, is carved from sandstone and covered in a layer of chalk.

3. Metamorphic

Metamorphic rocks form when other rocks are heated and squashed underground. A chemical reaction creates a new type of hard, shiny rock, such as marble or slate.

A Roman tomb sculpted out of metamorphic marble.

The rock cycle

The rocks on Earth are all constantly changing, very, very slowly. So if you could travel far into the future, you'd see quite a different landscape. Mountains would have moved and changed shape, and rocks of one kind would have changed into another.

Wind and rain **erode** (wear away) surface rocks, grinding large rocks into tiny pieces of sediment. Over millions of years, this sediment builds up and gets squashed, creating new sedimentary rocks. Deep underground, intense pressures and high temperatures convert igneous and sedimentary rocks into new, metamorphic types. Eventually, these rocks can get squished down into the Earth's superhot interior, where they melt back into magma. This is called the **rock cycle**.

Moving Earth

Deep underground it's hot enough to melt rocks into a liquid. This molten rock sits in a layer called the **mantle**, below the Earth's surface.

On top of the mantle, the surface – or **crust** – is divided into sections called plates. These plates are constantly moving – but normally very, very slowly.

The rock cycle is happening around us all the time. But each stage of the cycle takes thousands of years.

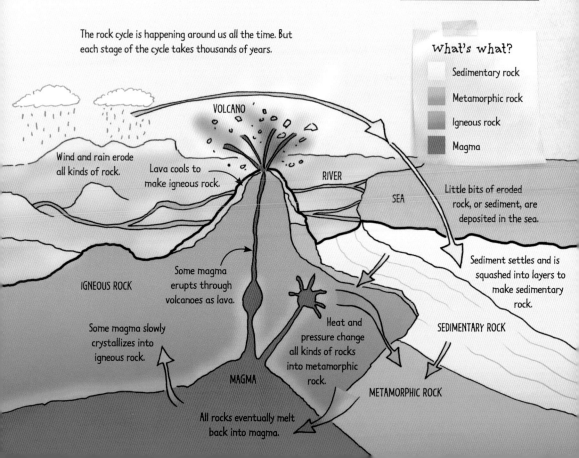

What's what?

Sedimentary rock

Metamorphic rock

Igneous rock

Magma

VOLCANO

Wind and rain erode all kinds of rock.

Lava cools to make igneous rock.

RIVER

SEA

Little bits of eroded rock, or sediment, are deposited in the sea.

IGNEOUS ROCK

Some magma erupts through volcanoes as lava.

Sediment settles and is squashed into layers to make sedimentary rock.

Some magma slowly crystallizes into igneous rock.

Heat and pressure change all kinds of rocks into metamorphic rock.

SEDIMENTARY ROCK

MAGMA

METAMORPHIC ROCK

All rocks eventually melt back into magma.

What's up in the air?

The Earth comes equipped with its own air protection system – called the **atmosphere**. The atmosphere is a mixture of gases that blankets the Earth and it's responsible for the weather, and the air you breathe.

High up in the Earth's atmosphere, a layer of gas called ozone (O_3) protects the Earth from some harmful rays from the Sun. Below this layer, gases such as carbon dioxide keep the Earth warm by trapping heat.

Since the invention of power stations, factories and cars, people have been releasing a lot of harmful gases into the atmosphere. These pollute the air, making it harder to breathe. Some create acid rain, which poisons plants and corrodes buildings. And some of these gases react with ozone, making holes in the ozone layer.

The greenhouse effect

Carbon dioxide is sometimes described as a greenhouse gas, because it acts like an insulating blanket around the planet, stopping heat from escaping. Without any greenhouse gases, the Earth would be too cold for people to survive. But many scientists worry that we are pumping too much carbon dioxide into the air and over-heating the Earth. This process is known as the **greenhouse effect**.

Fossil fuels, such as oil and coal, contain many carbon compounds. As these are burned, they react with oxygen to produce lots of carbon dioxide. Other greenhouse gases include methane and the gases in aerosol sprays. Scientists are working to find ways to generate energy without releasing harmful gases.

Lightning gas

When a bolt of lightning strikes, it leaves behind a strange smell. This is the smell of ozone gas. At ground level too much ozone is an air pollutant and can cause breathing problems.

What's up there?

The atmosphere is made up of four main layers...

Thermosphere – this is full of ions that block some harmful rays from the Sun.

Mesosphere – it's very cold here.

The **ozone layer** is in the upper stratosphere.

Stratosphere – this is where planes fly.

Troposphere – this is where weather happens.

Living chemistry

Plants and animals are brimming with chemical secrets. Some of them are deadly poisons, but many others are sources of wonderful medicines.

Frog of doom

Poison-dart frogs from South America excrete a poison called batrachotoxin through their skin. The poison causes heart failure in small animals that attack the frog. Some rainforest peoples extract the poison to use on the tips of their hunting darts.

Fish of doom

Pufferfish have a deadly poison called tetrodotoxin in their skin, spikes and organs. This kills any predator that tries to bite or squash them.

A puffer fish shows its deadly spikes.

Death to Socrates!

In Ancient Greece, the philosopher Socrates was sentenced to death for teaching dangerous ideas. He was poisoned with the plant hemlock, which contains a deadly chemical called coniine.

Natural medicines

In the past, people all over the world have turned to plants to help fight pain or cure diseases. Nowadays, chemists can identify the active ingredients of many plants and copy them in labs to make medicines.

The Qincocha Indians chewed the bark from willow trees to cure fever. It contains acetylsalicylic acid, which is now used to make aspirin. It blocks pain and reduces fevers.

Nearly 2,500 years ago, the Sumerians used mint leaves to cure stomach aches. The leaves contain a compound called menthol, which has soothing properties.

The Romans used feverfew plants to treat headaches. The active ingredient is a compound called parthenolide, which eases aches and swelling.

How does your body work?

Your body depends on chemistry to keep it going. It uses thousands of compounds to stay alive and well.

People and most other animals have an iron-based compound called hemoglobin in their blood. It helps transport oxygen from the lungs to the rest of the body. This form of iron is the reason your blood is red. Some sea creatures, such as horseshoe crabs, have another compound called hemocyanin – it's made of copper instead of iron, which makes their blood blue.

Blood test

Blue blood extracted from horseshoe crabs reacts with bacteria. Doctors can use it to test that new medicines are bacteria-free.

A horseshoe crab

You are what you eat

Most food contains carbon, hydrogen and oxygen, which your body uses for energy.

You also need to eat tiny amounts of some metals and other elements. Your body uses these for things like growing, repairing damage and fighting disease.

Cabbage leaves are full of phosphorus, which strengthens the immune system.

Blue cheese has lots of sodium, for a healthy brain and nerves.

Spinach contains iron, for healthy blood.

Beef contains potassium and phosphorous, for healthy nerves and bones.

Shellfish contain selenium, which helps to control chemical signals in the body.

178

A lifetime of chemistry

Some chemical reactions happen inside your body every minute of every day. But there are some important reactions that only happen at certain stages of life...

Starting out

A new mother has lots of the hormone oxytocin in her system. It helps her bond with her baby.

Virus killer

When people catch a virus, such as chicken pox, the body activates a protein named interferon. Interferon generates chemicals called antibodies that fight off the virus. It also stops people getting ill from the same virus twice.

Sleeping late

Melatonin is a hormone which tells your body to sleep. Usually the brain releases it in the evening. But many teenagers stay up late because their melatonin is released later at night. It keeps them in bed for longer in the morning, too.

Loved up

Falling in love sends two hormones called dopamine and serotonin racing around the body and brain. They make people feel warm, cuddly emotions.

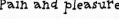

Pain and pleasure

When a person does a lot of exercise, the brain releases hormones called endorphins. They pump around the body, blocking pain and making the person feel good.

Turning grey

Hair colour comes from a compound called melanin. As some people get older, their hair produces less melanin. Eventually, there's no colour left and their hair turns white.

Death swell

After a person dies, the bacteria in the body start to break it down. This produces gases underneath the skin that make the body bulge and turn green.

Chemistry through the ages

People have been studying substances for thousands of years. In about 750, Arab scholars named this work *al quemia*, meaning 'the chemistry'. This term was translated into English as 'alchemy'. This early science gradually evolved into what we know today as 'chemistry'...

about 800,000 years ago

Early people work out how to create fire. They experiment with it to use for heat, light and cooking.

about 5,300 years ago

Ancient Egyptians and Sumerians discover that a reaction inside a mixture of grain and water makes beer.

about 5,000 years ago

Metal workers in the Middle East melt copper and tin. Mixing them together, they create the alloy bronze, which is strong and good for making cooking pots.

about 750 – 1400

Great Persian scholars such as Jabir, Al-Razi and Nasir Al-Tusi study *al quemia*. They develop strict scientific methods and equipment, and discover many acids and metals.

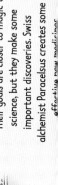

1661

Robert Boyle publishes his book *The Sceptical Chymist*. He complains that alchemists don't conduct their experiments properly.

He also puts forward the theory that substances are composed of millions of tiny parts.

1770s

Antoine Lavoisier proves that matter can't be created or destroyed – it can only be changed from one form to another. This is now called the 'Law of Conservation of Mass'.

about 1430 – 1530

European 'alchemists' borrow the work of the Arab experimenters and do their own experiments. They try to turn lead into gold, and brew potions they hope will grant them eternal life.

Their goals are closer to magic than science, but they make some important discoveries. Swiss alchemist Paracelsus creates some effective new medicines.

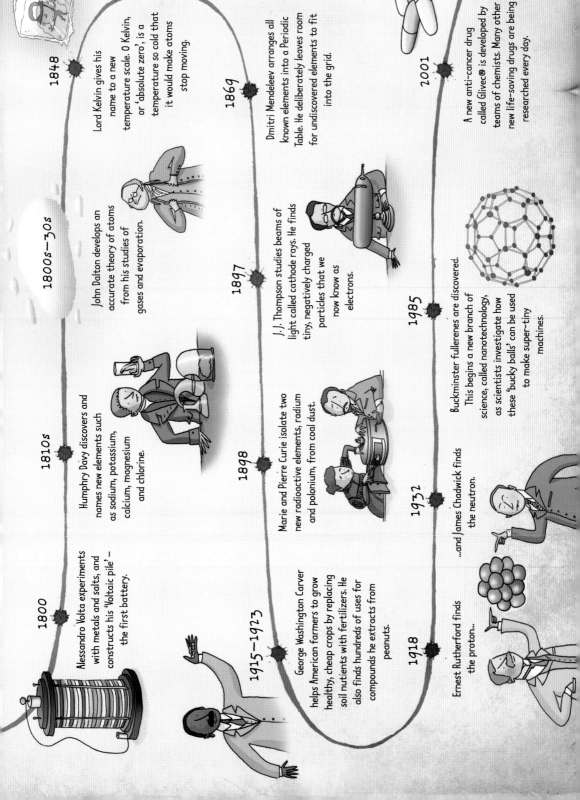

1800
Alessandro Volta experiments with metals and salts, and constructs his 'Voltaic pile' – the first battery.

1810s
Humphry Davy discovers and names new elements such as sodium, potassium, calcium, magnesium and chlorine.

1800s–30s
John Dalton develops an accurate theory of atoms from his studies of gases and evaporation.

1848
Lord Kelvin gives his name to a new temperature scale. 0 Kelvin, or 'absolute zero', is a temperature so cold that it would make atoms stop moving.

1869
Dmitri Mendeleev arranges all known elements into a Periodic Table. He deliberately leaves room for undiscovered elements to fit into the grid.

1897
J. J. Thompson studies beams of light called cathode rays. He finds tiny, negatively charged particles that we now know as electrons.

1898
Marie and Pierre Curie isolate two new radioactive elements, radium and polonium, from coal dust.

1915–1923
George Washington Carver helps American farmers to grow healthy, cheap crops by replacing soil nutrients with fertilizers. He also finds hundreds of uses for compounds he extracts from peanuts.

1918
Ernest Rutherford finds the proton...

1932
...and James Chadwick finds the neutron.

1985
Buckminster fullerenes are discovered. This begins a new branch of science, called nanotechnology, as scientists investigate how these 'bucky balls' can be used to make super-tiny machines.

2001
A new anti-cancer drug called Glivec® is developed by teams of chemists. Many other new life-saving drugs are being researched every day.

What's Physics all about?

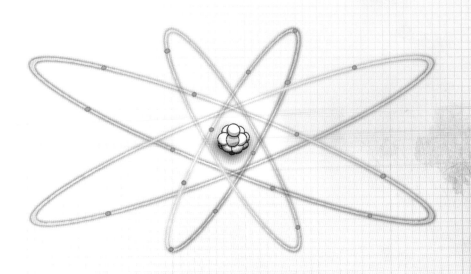

Contents

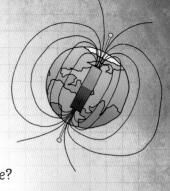

Part 4: It's electrifying!

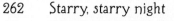

Part 5: Lost in space

Internet links

You can find out all sorts of things about physics on the internet. You can find experiments to do at home, design your own theme park using the laws of physics, read all about life as an astronaut, and ask a physicist a question. For links to these websites, and many more, go to **www.usborne.com/quicklinks** and type in the keywords "what is physics".

Please follow the internet safety guidelines displayed on the Usborne Quicklinks website.
The links are regularly reviewed and updated, but Usborne Publishing cannot be responsible for any website other than its own.

what's physics all about?

Physics is about how things work, and why things happen the way they do. Physicists ask all sorts of questions about life, the Universe and everything, from why a teaspoon gets hot when it's in a cup of coffee, to what happens to your body when you dive to the bottom of the sea.

They also ask some really big questions...

what is the Universe made of?

Deep down, every single thing in the Universe is made from the same tiny bits of stuff called atoms.

But is an atom the smallest thing there is? And where did all this stuff come from in the first place? Physicists don't have *all* the answers, but they have lots of ideas.

How does the Universe work?

Physicists can't explain how the whole Universe works – at least, not yet. But they can explain how all the things in it work the way they do.

If you've ever wondered why there are different seasons in a year, or why things fall to the ground, the chances are physics has the answers.

what is energy?

Energy is what makes things happen. It makes atoms move, light shine and electricity flow. If there was no energy, the Universe would be a really quiet, cold and boring place to live.

Physicists study all kinds of energy. And they try to find new energy sources so that our power supplies will never run out.

Lightning is electrical energy that flashes through the sky.

What's out in space?

Physics is about everything in our world and beyond – so physicists want to know what it's like in space.

Do things in space work in the same way that things work on Earth? Does time change if you travel through space? Physicists who try to answer questions like this are called astrophysicists. Astronomers, who study the night sky, are physicists too.

When you look at the stars, you're seeing all the way into outer space...

A journey into the unknown...

The really exciting thing about physics is that there is so much still to discover. Physicists argue about things such as whether using a mobile phone can give you cancer, and if there is life on other planets. Perhaps no one will ever know all the answers for certain, but physics can help scientists get closer to the truth.

Just a matter of time?

One day, an over-enthusiastic physicist in a lab somewhere might create a completely new universe in a beaker.

Physics all around

People have been studying physics – without calling it that – for thousands of years, and using their discoveries to make life easier along the way. The first people who invented the wheel, or built canoes, were using the rules of physics. Without physics there would be no...

...parachutes

In 1617, Croatian inventor Faust Vrancic made an early kind of parachute by strapping a curved canopy to his back. It slowed his fall when he jumped off a tall tower in Venice.

...telephones

The telephone was invented by Scotsman Alexander Graham Bell in 1876. Bell spent years investigating the way sounds are created and how they move.

...light bulbs

In 1878, Englishman Sir Joseph Swan and Thomas Edison from the USA invented the light bulb almost simultaneously. Instead of fighting, the pair went into business together.

...motorbikes

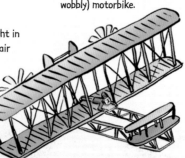

In 1885, German engineer Gottlieb Daimler attached an engine to a wooden bicycle to make the first (rather wobbly) motorbike.

...planes

The Wright brothers made the first powered flight in America in 1903. Their plane only stayed in the air for 12 seconds and, when it landed, the wind blew it away – so they had to build a new one.

...computers

One of the first computers, the ENIAC, was designed by two American scientists, John Mauchly and J. Presper Eckert. It took them three years to build it. When they finished, in 1946, it took up the space of about five classrooms. The first home computer wasn't invented until 1975 – until then, computers were too big to have at home.

...televisions

The first television was built in 1925 by Scottish inventor John Logie Baird. He made it in his attic out of household objects. By 1929, the British Broadcasting Corporation was using his television system to broadcast tv shows.

...microwave ovens

In 1945, American scientist Percy Spencer was walking past a machine called a magnetron when the chocolate bar in his pocket suddenly melted. He worked out that a kind of energy called microwave energy, emitted by the magnetron, was responsible. He used the magnetron to invent the microwave oven.

...World Wide Web.

In 1989, British scientist Tim Berners-Lee invented a way of sharing information between computers quickly and easily. It's called the World Wide Web, and today it links computers all over the world.

WWW.USBORNE.CO.UK

...MP3 players

The MP3 data storage file was developed by a team of German and US engineers. An MP3 is a type of computer file that contains a digital version of a song or a video.

The first MP3s were released on the internet in 1994, but the first MP3 players weren't sold until 1998.

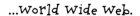

Who knows what could be next?

As physicists make new discoveries, things that seem impossible today might one day become reality. In the future we might zoom through the air on rocket-propelled skateboards, or take a trip to the Moon for a holiday, in our own personal spaceships. Whenever you hear about an amazing new gadget, just think – it's probably thanks to physics.

Is the Universe growing or shrinking?

What's an atom and why is it so important?

What are the tiniest things in the Universe?

In what way are these people the same age?

How did an exploding star turn into our Solar System?

Part 1:
The beginning of everything

Physics starts at the very beginning – of everything. Before the Universe, nothing existed. At all. There was no sound, or light, or dark. Time and space didn't exist either. So how did everything come to be – and what's it all made of?

Read on to find out about the birth of our Universe, and the tiny bits of stuff that make up *everything* in it...

How did the Universe begin?

Scientists are still struggling to understand how the Universe began. No one knows exactly when or why it started. But in the 1940s physicists came up with a theory known as the **Big Bang**. It goes a bit like this:

The Big Bang

Up until about 13.7 billion years ago, there was nothing. Then suddenly – BANG – there was something. Scientists still don't know how something came out of nothing, but it did. And that something was an incredibly tiny speck.

This speck was really, amazingly small – thousands of times smaller than the head of a pin – but it contained all the matter and energy that has ever existed. The speck exploded, and expanded at an incredible speed.

Within a second it had become a huge, blisteringly hot fireball, and it grew bigger with every moment.

As the fireball spread out, it cooled down and lumps of matter started to form. After about a billion years, these lumps joined together to form the first stars.

Creation ideas

Over the centuries, non-physicists have come up with other ideas for how the Universe might have begun...

An ancient Chinese myth says it all started when a giant hatched from a huge egg. The egg became the heavens and the Earth, and the giant's eyes turned into the Sun and Moon.

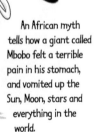

An African myth tells how a giant called Mbobo felt a terrible pain in his stomach, and vomited up the Sun, Moon, stars and everything in the world.

In 1975, a French racing car driver called Claude Vorilhon founded a religious cult called Raëlism. His followers believe that aliens used their superior technology to create life on Earth – including humans.

The Big Silence

Although scientists call this event the Big Bang, the beginning of the Universe would actually have been completely silent – because sound can't travel through empty space.

How will it all end?

The Universe is still expanding. Some physicists believe it will go on getting bigger and bigger forever. Others think that, eventually, it will collapse back in on itself in a 'Big Crunch' – and disappear completely – until another Big Bang happens.

Another universe, another you

Who's to say ours is the only universe? Some physicists think there are an infinite number of universes, each one slightly different from the others, which are all expanding towards each other.

Eventually, billions of years from now, they might join together to form a single super-universe. If humans are still around, they might even be able to meet their twins from some of those parallel worlds.

You're a star!
(Well, you used to be...)

Our Solar System – the Sun, and the planets which orbit around it – formed almost 10 billion years after the Universe began, when a huge star exploded...

...leaving a cloud of dust and gas.

Gradually, the dust and gas joined together to create the Sun and the planets. And, eventually...

...us.

What does the Universe look like?

The shape of the Universe is still a mystery. Some scientists believe it's round like a ball, but others think it might look more like a tube, or a giant doughnut.

What's everything made of?

Everything in the Universe, from faraway stars to the ground under your feet, is made from stupendously tiny pieces called **atoms**. Atoms are all so tiny, it's impossible to see them without powerful equipment. The full stop at the end of this sentence contains about 200 million atoms.

If you could zoom in on the tip of a pencil a few million times, you would see rows and rows of carbon atoms. There are about 5 million at the tip of a really sharp pencil.

Sticking together

Atoms hardly ever float about on their own. They usually join together in clusters to make **molecules**. Every substance there is is made up of atoms or, more often, molecules.

Substances which are made of just one kind of atom, and can't be broken down into simpler substances, are called **elements**. 118 different kinds of atoms have been discovered so far, which means there are 118 elements. Carbon, iron, aluminium and gold are just a few examples.

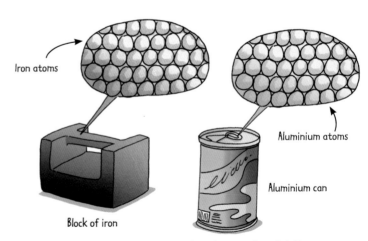

Iron atoms

Aluminium atoms

Aluminium can

Block of iron

You're as old as your Dad...

Physicists believe all the atoms in the Universe were created at the same instant, in the Big Bang. That means that your atoms are the same age as dinosaur bones – and a new-born baby, and anything else you can think of.

But *most* substances contain molecules made of different types of atoms. For example, water molecules are made of hydrogen and oxygen atoms joined together.

Smaller and smaller

By the end of the 19th century, physicists realised that atoms weren't the smallest things in existence – they're made of even tinier particles. They imagined these scattered randomly throughout an atom like fruit in a cake. This was known as the 'plum pudding model'.

In 1909, a scientist named Ernest Rutherford decided to test this model by firing tiny helium atoms, also known as alpha particles, at a thin sheet of gold foil. He expected them to pass through the gold foil in a straight line, or to veer sideways slightly, as if they had hit some 'fruit' (smaller particles).

What Rutherford expected to happen...

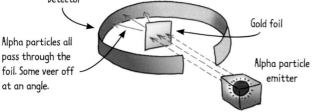

Detector

Gold foil

Alpha particles all pass through the foil. Some veer off at an angle.

Alpha particle emitter

But, in fact, a few of the alpha particles *bounced back*. It was as if they'd hit one tightly-packed area of matter in the middle of the atom.

What actually happened...

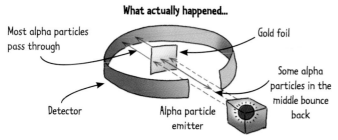

Most alpha particles pass through

Gold foil

Detector

Alpha particle emitter

Some alpha particles in the middle bounce back

Rutherford was astonished. He said it was as incredible as if he'd fired a bullet at a piece of tissue paper and it had come back to hit him. Turn the page to find out what he discovered...

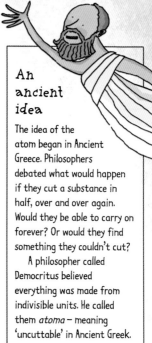

Fantastic physicist: Ernest Rutherford 1871-1937

Ernest Rutherford's work earned him a Nobel Prize in 1908 – for chemistry. He was rather taken aback as he was a physicist, not a chemist.

But he decided it didn't matter. He thought that chemistry was just a branch of physics, which he described as "the only real science".

What's inside an atom?

The structure of an atom is a bit like a miniature solar system. In the middle is a solid part that Rutherford detected, which is now called the **nucleus**.

The nucleus is made from tiny particles known as **protons** and **neutrons**, squashed together in a ball. Even smaller particles called **electrons** zoom around the nucleus – like speeded-up planets orbiting a sun.

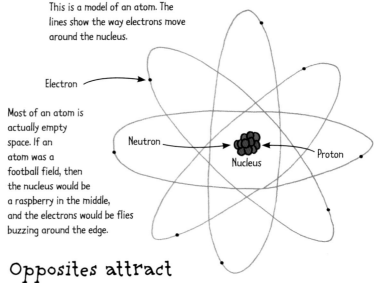

This is a model of an atom. The lines show the way electrons move around the nucleus.

Electron

Neutron

Nucleus

Proton

Most of an atom is actually empty space. If an atom was a football field, then the nucleus would be a raspberry in the middle, and the electrons would be flies buzzing around the edge.

Little and large

All atoms are tiny, but some are tinier than others, because they don't have as many bits.

The very smallest atom is hydrogen, which has just one electron orbiting its nucleus. The biggest atoms have over 100 electrons.

Why can't we walk through things?

If everything is mostly empty space, you might wonder why we can't walk through lamp posts and other things.

While protons and electrons attract each other, two sets of electrons repel each other.

So, when the electrons on the edge of your forehead meet the electrons on the edge of a lamp post, they push each other away.

Stupid electrons!

Opposites attract

Atoms hold together because the different particles are attracted to each other. Have you ever heard the phrase 'opposites attract'? That's definitely true of atomic particles. Protons have a **positive charge** and electrons have a **negative charge**. The reason atoms don't fall apart is because opposite charges attract.

An atom of any element has the same number of protons and electrons, and neutrons don't have any charge of their own. So, overall, the atom is **neutral** – it has neither a positive nor a negative charge.

The smallest things of all?

Until about 50 years ago, scientists thought protons, neutrons and electrons were the smallest bits of matter in existence. But then physicists found a way to break protons and neutrons into even tinier pieces. They did this by smashing them together at incredibly high speeds, inside a machine called a particle accelerator.

Scientists now know that protons and neutrons are made from mind-bogglingly mini specks called **quarks**, which are glued together by even tinier specks called **gluons**.

Inside a particle accelerator

Protons hurtle towards each other...

...and after they've collided, quarks fly out.

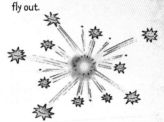

To be continued...

The quest to find the smallest particle is still going on. Physicists spent twenty years building a particle accelerator in Switzerland, the Large Hadron Collider (LHC), to look for one tiny piece of matter they weren't even sure existed. They named it anyway, though: the Higgs boson.

Inside the LHC

Scientists think the Higgs boson existed for a fraction of a second after the Big Bang, so they're using the LHC to recreate the Big Bang in miniature, to try to find it.

About the Large Hadron Collider

• Building the LHC to recreate the Big Bang was the largest scientific endeavour ever conducted.

• If it weren't for the LHC, the World Wide Web might not exist. Tim Berners-Lee created the Web so scientists all over the world could share information more quickly, to help with the design of the LHC.

• The Higgs boson – if it really exists – is so important that some scientists have nicknamed it the 'God particle'.

• Some scientists feared the LHC would create giant black holes which would swallow up the Earth when it was first switched on in 2008 – but that didn't happen.

• The LHC was only switched on for 10 days – not long enough to find the Higgs boson.

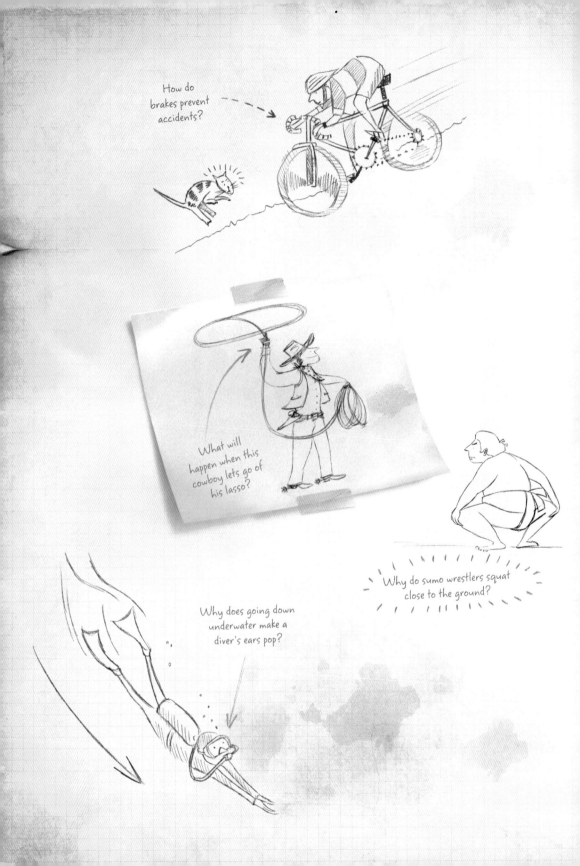

Part 2:
Feel the force

A force is a push or a pull. You can't see a force, but you can see what it does. Forces can get things moving, or make them change direction. They can speed things up and slow them down, too. Forces can squeeze things, or change their shape. But, whatever they do, forces always act in a straight line.

Forces act on all of us all the time. Often forces balance and cancel each other out, so you don't notice them. But when they don't balance, they become more obvious. Read on to find out about different kinds of forces and what they do.

Speed triangle

Physics is full of word equations that describe how to calculate one measurement if you know two others. Most of them can be drawn up in a 'magic triangle':

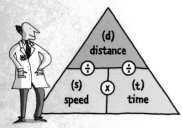

If you cover up the measurement you're trying to work out, you'll be left with the equation you need.

To find out the quantity at the top, you multiply the two at the bottom. So:

$$d = s \times t$$

If you need to work out either of the quantities at the bottom, you divide the top by the other bottom quantity. So:

$$s = \frac{d}{t} \quad \text{and} \quad t = \frac{d}{s}$$

Speed and motion

Imagine you're pushing a trolley in a supermarket. That push is a force. The result of the force is that the trolley moves. If you push harder – in other words, apply a greater force – the trolley will move faster. Its **speed** will increase. But exactly how fast is the trolley moving? And how fast are you moving yourself?

Speed is a measure of the *distance* something travels in a certain *time*. Physicists measure speed in metres per second (m/s) – how many metres something travels in a second. You can work speed out using this formula:

$$\text{speed (s)} = \frac{\text{distance (d)}}{\text{time (t)}}$$

These people in a supermarket are all moving at different speeds:

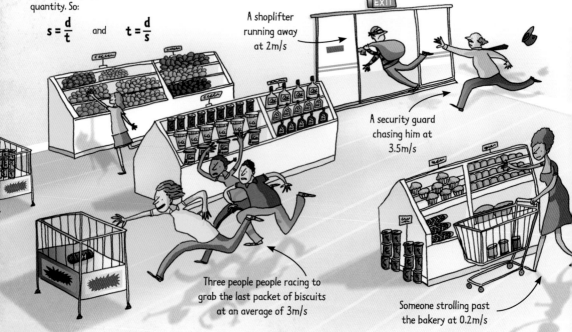

A shoplifter running away at 2m/s

A security guard chasing him at 3.5m/s

Three people people racing to grab the last packet of biscuits at an average of 3m/s

Someone strolling past the bakery at 0.2m/s

Now imagine you're in the supermarket too and YOU want the last packet of biscuits. You skid 12 metres down the aisle and reach it in 3 seconds. To work out your speed, you divide the distance you travelled by the time it took:

$$\text{speed} = \frac{\text{distance}}{\text{time}} = \frac{12 \text{ metres}}{3 \text{ seconds}} = 4\text{m/s}$$

This means you were travelling at 4 metres per second. That's faster than anyone else in the supermarket.

Which way?

The thing about forces is that they always act in a straight line. Physicists use the word **velocity (v)** to describe how fast something is moving in a particular direction. Like speed, it's measured in m/s.

Something can change velocity by changing direction, even if it doesn't change speed. It can also change velocity by speeding up (or accelerating) or slowing down (or decelerating).

Acceleration and **deceleration** are measured in metres per second *per second*, which is written m/s^2 (how much velocity changes in a second).

You can work out acceleration using this formula:

$$\text{acceleration} = \frac{\text{end velocity - start velocity}}{\text{time}}$$

Suppose, trying to outrun the security guard, the shoplifter runs faster, increasing his velocity from 0 m/s to 4 m/s in 5 seconds (without changing direction).

$$\text{Acceleration} = \frac{4-0 \text{ metres/second}}{5 \text{ seconds}} = \frac{4}{5} = 0.8\text{m/s}^2$$

So the shoplifter's acceleration is 0.8 metres per second per second in the direction of the exit.

m/s or km/h?

On a motorway, a car can easily travel about 33 metres in a second. But because a car can travel very fast for a long time, people usually talk about how many *kilometres* (km) it can travel in an *hour* (h).

Divide by 1,000 to convert metres into kilometres:
33m = 0.033km

Multiply by 60 to convert seconds into minutes, and by 60 again to convert minutes into hours.
0.033 x 60 x 60 = 118.8

33m/s is the same as 118.8km/h.

Slowing down

You can work out deceleration in almost the same way as acceleration.
This is the formula:

deceleration =
$$\frac{\text{start velocity - end velocity}}{\text{time}}$$

When the security guard catches him, the shoplifter slows down from 4m/s to 0m/s in 10 seconds. What's his deceleration?

$$\text{Deceleration} = \frac{4-0}{10} = \frac{4}{10}$$

$$\text{Deceleration} = 0.4\text{m/s}^2$$

Mass matters

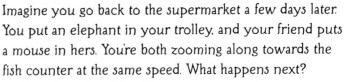

Why roads have speed limits

When a car is driving really fast, it has a lot of momentum. This makes it hard to slow down and stop, even if the car has really good brakes.

A car that's driving above the speed limit will take longer to stop, and will do much more damage if it crashes, than a car driving at the limit.

Massively different

Because a mouse has so much less mass than an elephant, the only way they could have the same *momentum* is if the elephant was walking really slowly, and the mouse was zooming along almost as fast as light – which is the fastest thing in the Universe.

LIGHT SPEED ROCKET

Imagine you go back to the supermarket a few days later. You put an elephant in your trolley, and your friend puts a mouse in hers. You're both zooming along towards the fish counter at the same speed. What happens next?

Your friend will be able to stop her trolley neatly at the counter. But you will find it incredibly hard to steer and stop – so your trolley will smash into the counter, showering seafood everywhere.

But *why*? Well, it's because the elephant in your trolley is so *massive*. The original meaning of 'massive' is something that has a lot of **mass** – or in other words, contains a lot of **matter**, or stuff. When something with a lot of mass is moving at a high velocity, it also has a lot of something called momentum.

What's momentum?

Momentum is a measure of how *forcefully* something is moving in a particular direction. If something has a lot of mass (such as an elephant), it's hard to start it moving, because the amount of mass weighs it down.

But once it *is* moving, that mass and the velocity it's moving at make it even harder to slow down, or steer, than it was to get it going in the first place.

The greater the mass of an object, and the higher its velocity, the more momentum it has. Of course, physicists like to know *exactly* how much momentum an object has.

202

Mass is measured in kilograms, and velocity in metres per second, so momentum is measured in kilogram metres per second (kg m/s).

momentum (p) = mass (m) x velocity (v)

Where does force come into it?

It takes force to make the trolley (and the elephant) move in the first place. And it takes force to make it stop. You might be strong enough to get the trolley going, but it would probably take a weightlifter to stop the trolley crashing. The trolley's momentum would be so great, only a weightlifter could exert a big enough force to stop it.

Force (F) is measured in kg m/s^2, more simply called **newtons (N)**, and can be calculated using this formula:

Force (F) = mass (m) x acceleration (a)

If the elephant in the trolley had a mass of 6,000kg, and was accelerating towards the fish counter at $0.2m/s^2$, what would be the force exerted on the counter?

Force = mass x acceleration

= 6,000kg x $0.2m/s^2$ = 1200N

So to stop the crash, the weightlifter would have to pull on the trolley with an equivalent force of 1200 newtons.

Momentum triangle

Here's another magic triangle you can use to work out momentum, mass and velocity. It looks like this:

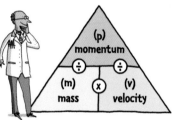

Measuring force

The strength of a force can be measured with a **force meter**.

This device contains a spring attached to a hook. When you apply a force to the hook, the spring stretches. You can read the size of the force in newtons down the side.

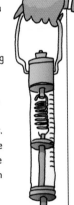

Force triangle

Force, mass and acceleration can be worked out using this magic triangle:

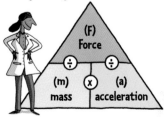

Different kinds of forces

The force you use to get a trolley going is an example of a 'push' force.

If you wanted to open a cupboard door, you'd use a pull force.

Here are some of the main kinds of forces...

...push & pull

Most forces are pushes or pulls of some kind.

...elastic

Elastic force makes something bounce back when you've stretched it – like elastic.

SQUEAK!!!

...compression

Compression is the force you exert when you squash something.

...twist

When you turn a door handle or twist the lid of a jar, you're using a twisting force.

...electrical

Electrical force is caused by charged particles attracting or repelling each other. Static electricity is an example of electrical force. This is what makes your hair stand on end when it's rubbed by a balloon.

...magnetic

This is the force that makes magnets attract or repel each other.

...tension

Tension is the force that things have when they're pulled tight, like a rope in a tug-of-war.

Friction — there's the rub

Now imagine you're back in the supermarket. You give the trolley a big push and let it go, sending it wheeling along the aisle. Eventually, the trolley will naturally slow down and stop. This is because of friction.

Friction is a force which happens when two things rub together, like the wheels and the floor. It opposes motion and makes things slow down.

If you took the trolley outside and tried to wheel it across grass, you would have to push much harder. The rough grass would catch against the wheels more than the smooth floor, increasing friction and slowing down the trolley.

Sometimes friction can be a real hindrance, but it can be a great help, too...

Defeating friction

Friction between two things can be reduced if they are separated with a thin layer of liquid, or lubricant.

If you've ever seen anyone fixing a car engine, you'll know they often end up with grease all over their hands. The grease helps the engine parts to move over each other smoothly.

AHHHH!

Brakes wouldn't work without friction, so there would be a lot more accidents.

Without friction, you wouldn't be able to tie your shoelaces. They'd be so slippery, they'd slide off each other.

If there wasn't any friction, you'd slide all over the place and wouldn't be able to stand up...

Have you ever been annoyed by a creaky door or a squeaky wheel? It's friction between the moving parts that causes the sound.

...but you'd never graze your knees when you fell over.

SQUEAK

It's the law!

Over 300 years ago, Isaac Newton studied forces and came up with a set of laws to explain how things move. These laws apply just as much to the latest sports car as to the first ball that was ever kicked across the ground. They're known as **Newton's Laws of Motion**.

Don't change — the first law

Newton's first observation was that *an object which isn't moving won't start moving unless a force is applied to it.* A football lying on the ground won't score a goal on its own — someone has to kick it.

Egg-nertia

Liquids have inertia (see right) too. Spin a raw egg on a plate. Stop it spinning with your fingers, then let go almost immediately. It should start spinning again, because the runny egg inside the shell won't have stopped moving.

She kicked it!

I never touched it!

Ah, but you must have. An object at rest will stay at rest unless an unbalanced force acts on it.

This seems pretty obvious. But the first law also states that, *once an object is moving, it won't stop unless another force makes it stop.*

So the football will carry on sailing through the air unless it hits the back of the net, or the goalkeeper catches it, or the Earth's gravity drags it down (see page 212) and friction stops it rolling across the grass.

In other words, *objects resist changing velocity* — they won't speed up, slow down or change direction on their own. This is called **inertia**.

Defining a force — the second law

Newton's second law defines what a force is, and says that *the force needed to change something's velocity depends on its mass.* That's really just another way of saying **force = mass x acceleration**.

If you give a shopping trolley with a mouse in it a little push, it will move across the floor. But it will get moving much faster if you give it a bigger push. *Things accelerate more quickly if the force pushing them is greater.*

You'd have to give the trolley with the elephant a much bigger push to get it moving at the same speed. In other words, *the larger an object is, the greater the force needed to make it accelerate the same amount.*

> The bigger the force, the more something will accelerate. The more mass something has, the bigger the force needed to make it accelerate.

Unscary equation

This is how to work out the force needed to make an elephant with a mass of 700kg accelerate at 5m/s^2:

F = m x a   F = 700 x 5
F = 3500N

So what force would you need to make a 0.05kg mouse accelerate at the same speed?

A push and a pull — the third law

Newton's third law states that *whenever there is a force acting on something in one direction, another force of the same size is acting on it in the opposite direction.*

The first two laws are pretty obvious, but this one can seem surprising. After all, when you push a trolley, it doesn't push you back — or does it?

Imagine you're getting out of a boat. As you step out, the force from your legs pushes the boat down into the water and away from you. It's the boat *pushing back* that gives you the force to step up onto dry land. Of course, if you don't tie the boat to the dock first, your legs will push the boat too far away and you might fall in...

> I keep telling you: for every action there is an equal and opposite reaction.

work harder!

work triangle

Here's a magic triangle to show how to calculate work, force and distance from each other:

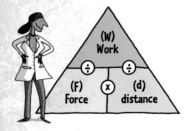

Unscary equations

How much work do you do when you use a force of 0.5N to lift a pen 40cm (0.4m) to scratch your head?

See if you were right below.

According to the laws of physics, when you use a force to move something you're doing **work**. The bigger the force, or the further you move an object, the more work you do.

So in physics, you actually do more work when you pick up a chocolate bar and eat it than when you solve a problem in a physics book.

As well as defining what work is, physicists have also come up with a way to measure amounts of work. They use **joules (J)**, which are also called newton metres (Nm). You can calculate the amount of work done using this formula:

Work (W) = Force (F) x distance (d)

Imagine you've had enough of that massive elephant you've been carting around. You want him to go back to the zoo, but he doesn't want to leave, so you have to push him all the way.

You'd need to use a force of 400N and the zoo is 100m away.

How much work would you have to do?

Work = force x distance = 400N x 100m = 40,000J

You'd need to do 40,000 joules of work – which is very difficult, even for the world's strongest weightlifter. But do not despair! Read on to find out how physics can help...

ZOO

Physics makes work easier

Since it's too hard to *push* your elephant to the zoo, you could try *wheeling* him there in a shopping trolley. It would be easier than just pushing him, because a trolley is a kind of machine.

In physics, a **machine** is something that makes it easier to do work. Most people use lots of machines every day without realizing it.

Here are some very simple machines. You'll see machines everywhere once you start to look.

Fulcrum

Lever

A lever is something that has a fixed point, called a **fulcrum**, which stays still while other parts move. It converts a weak force you exert over a long distance into a strong force over a short distance on the other side of the fulcrum.

Pliers, bottle-openers and shoehorns are all kinds of lever.

Inclined plane

An inclined plane is a sloped surface. It's much easier to move something up an inclined plane than lifting it straight up, just as it's easier to wander along a sloping path than drag yourself up a cliff face.

Wheel

The wheel is one of the simplest machines of all. It's easier to transport things using wheels because they turn, rather than just dragging across the ground. This reduces the impact of friction.

Pulley

A pulley is a wheel with a rope attached. It turns a weak force over a long distance into a strong force over a short distance, a bit like a lever. But unlike a lever, a pulley changes the direction of your force. A set of pulleys would help you hoist an elephant *up*, even though you're pulling the rope *down*.

Wedge

A wedge is a kind of inclined plane. Some wedges, like axes and shovels, are used to break things apart. Others, like doorstops, stop things moving.

Screw

A screw is a curved inclined plane. Screws are useful for holding things together. If you screw a shelf to a wall, it's unlikely to fall off.

Gravity — it makes you more attractive

Newton and the apple

Isaac Newton didn't discover the force of gravity – but he was the first person to explain what it is.

The story goes that an apple fell from a tree and hit him on the head, and he guessed a force was pulling it towards the Earth.

Gravity is a force which pulls objects together. If you drop something, gravity makes it fall to the ground. Without gravity, it would just hang in the air.

Everything that has mass has gravity too, but you only notice the gravity of *really* massive objects, like the Sun, the Earth or other planets, which pull everything towards them.

Gravity in space is almost non-existent. You might have seen videos of astronauts in spaceships spinning around and chasing after floating objects. If it wasn't for the Earth's gravity pulling us down, we'd float around all the time, too.

Gravity

No gravity

Space to grow

Astronauts grow taller in space because there is almost no gravity pushing the discs in their spines together.

But they shrink down to normal when they get back to Earth.

Likewise, if the Moon wasn't attracted by the Earth's gravity, it would drift off into space instead of circling the Earth. The Moon's gravity also affects the Earth – it pulls the seas and oceans, causing the tides.

How much do you weigh?

On the Earth's surface, the pull of gravity makes everything accelerate downwards at about $10m/s^2$. This is what gives you your **weight** – weight is actually the force Earth's gravity exerts on you. In physics, weight is measured in newtons. A set of 'weighing' scales is really measuring mass (in kg).

To work out your weight on Earth, you need to multiply your mass by the amount Earth's gravity makes you accelerate ($10m/s^2$).

A mass-ive difference

Mass is the amount of matter in an object. It is constant (doesn't ever change).

Weight measures how strongly gravity pulls on an object. It is a force that changes depending on where the object is.

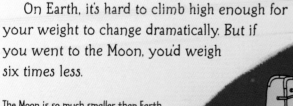

If you have a mass of 50kg, what's your weight?

Force (or weight) =

mass (kg) x acceleration due to pull of gravity (m/s^2)

= 50 X 10 = 500N

So, your weight on Earth is 500 newtons

How to lose weight quickly

If you climbed to the top of a really tall building you'd weigh a tiny bit less than you did at ground level – but you wouldn't be any thinner. Your *mass* wouldn't change, but your *weight* would, because gravity gets weaker with distance. It pulls on you less as you move further away from the centre of the Earth.

On Earth, it's hard to climb high enough for your weight to change dramatically. But if you went to the Moon, you'd weigh six times less.

The Moon is so much smaller than Earth, it only has one sixth of the Earth's gravity. So you'd be able to jump six times as high – and kick a ball much further, too.

What would you weigh on different planets?

If you weighed 500N on earth, you'd weigh...

...89N on Mars (a small planet, with low gravity)...

...and 1182N on Jupiter (a huge planet, with high gravity).

Forces: a matter of life and death

The further things fall, the more chance the force of gravity has to make them accelerate. If someone next to you dropped a penny on your head, it wouldn't hurt very much. But if he dropped it from the top of a skyscraper, by the time it hit you it'd be moving about as fast as a speeding bullet, and might badly injure you.

Falling things don't keep getting faster forever. As the penny falls, air rubs against it and slows it down. This is called **air resistance**, and it's a form of friction.

Eventually, the air resistance would be equal to the falling force (or weight) of the penny, so it would stop accelerating and fall at a constant speed. This natural speed limit is called **terminal velocity**.

If you jumped out of an aeroplane without a parachute, you'd accelerate downwards until you reached a terminal velocity of about 59m/s – so fast, you'd die when you hit the ground. But if you had a parachute, the air would have a greater area to push against. This extra air resistance would slow your terminal velocity to about 5.4m/s, so you'd land gently.

What if there's no air?

Without air resistance, everything would fall at exactly the same rate of acceleration, regardless of size or mass.

In 1971, an astronaut decided to test this by dropping a hammer and a feather on the Moon. Because the Moon has no air resistance, they fell at the same rate and landed at the same time.

Resisting resistance

Air resistance can be really useful, as parachutes prove. But sometimes, people don't want air to slow them down.

Fast-moving jet planes are smooth and streamlined, with pointy tips, so the air doesn't have much area to push against.

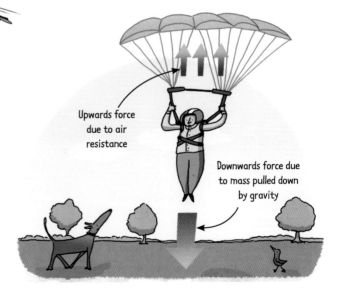

Upwards force due to air resistance

Downwards force due to mass pulled down by gravity

Going around in circles

If things move because of forces, and forces always act in a straight line, how can things move in *circles*? Well, they can do this because of **centripetal force**, a force which pulls all spinning things towards the middle of a circle.

Imagine you're a cowboy spinning a lasso. Your hand is exerting a centripetal force on it, pulling it inwards. As the lasso spins, its velocity is constantly changing direction, making the lasso move in a circle, even though the force itself is acting in a straight line. Without a centripetal force, it wouldn't go around in a circle. So when you let go (to catch a cow, or a bandit), the lasso flies off in a straight line.

See for yourself: centripetal force

Try spinning a scarf like a lasso. Your hand provides a centripetal force, which pulls the scarf in towards your hand.

If you let go of it, the scarf will carry on moving in a straight line, until gravity pulls it down.

Spinning the lasso...

...and letting it go.

If you've ridden on a fast-spinning funfair ride, you might have felt as if you were being pulled outwards, away from the middle of the ride. What you're actually feeling is inertia — your body resisting the constant centripetal force that the ride is exerting on you.

Because you're moving around in a circle, you feel the effects of inertia constantly — because you're always changing direction. This inertia is described as **centrifugal 'force'**, although it isn't really a force at all.

See for yourself: centrifugal force

Hold hands with a friend and spin around in a circle. You might notice that your hair flies out behind you and you feel as if you're being pulled outwards.

A balancing act

Because gravity is always pulling us down, staying upright isn't always easy. Just try balancing on one leg and see how long you can stay like that.

Balancing is all about something physicists call the **centre of gravity**.

What's the centre of gravity?

The Earth's gravity pulls down on every particle in an object (such as your body) with a force related to that object's mass. Although the force pulls on every particle, the combined effect of all the forces appears to pull down on just one imaginary point, which physicists have named 'the centre of gravity'.

Every object that has weight has a centre of gravity. As long as that centre is over the base of the object, it will be stable. But sometimes, the centre of gravity can end up hanging away from the base.

Imagine a (mean) person gave you a push. If you were standing firmly on two legs, you wouldn't budge. But now imagine you're wearing a backpack full of camping gear. Your centre of gravity would be behind you, and you probably *would* fall over.

Balletic balancing

Ballet dancers spend quite a lot of time standing on one foot. They also make a lot of beautiful shapes with their arms.

These arm movements aren't just decorative – they help the dancers to balance, by altering their centre of gravity.

Lifting a ladder

If you tried to pick up a ladder at one end, you'd be really far away from its centre of gravity and it would be hard to lift the whole ladder off the ground.

But if you hold the ladder in the middle, it's much easier to pick it up.

Centre of gravity

Base

Centre of gravity

Base

214

Keeping upright

It's very hard to make something fall over if it has a low centre of gravity. That's because you'd have to tip it quite far to make its centre move away from its base. Here are some examples...

The Leaning Tower of Pisa

The Leaning Tower of Pisa famously leans quite a lot. Scientists were worried it might eventually fall over. So they added extra mass to the bottom of the tower to lower its centre of gravity.

They could have tried to straighten it – but then it would just have been an ordinary tower.

Sumo wrestlers usually squat when they're preparing to fight each other. This makes it harder for their opponents to push them over.

Racing cars are built low to the ground, to stop them tipping over when they drive around tight corners.

Surfers crouch low over their surfboards and wave their arms about a lot to keep their balance.

See for yourself: centre of gravity

Try pushing over an empty plastic bottle. It should be pretty easy to make it topple over.

Centre of gravity

Try again with the bottle half-full of water. It should be harder to topple because the water makes the bottle heavier at the bottom, so it has a lower centre of gravity.

Centre of gravity

Now fill the bottle to the top with water. It'll be easier to topple again. Because the water fills the whole bottle, the weight is spread out and its centre of gravity will be higher again.

Centre of gravity

Under pressure

A force can be applied to a small area or a large area with different effects. Try pushing your thumb into a piece of wood. You probably won't even make a dent. But if you push down with the same force on a drawing pin, it will go deep into the wood.

That's because your push is now concentrated over a smaller area (the end of the pin), which means the *pressure* applied to the wood is greater.

Pressure is the amount of force there is on something over a certain area. It's measured in newtons per square metre (N/m^2), sometimes known as pascals (Pa). The formula for working it out is:

$$\text{Pressure (P)} = \frac{\text{Force (F)}}{\text{Area (A)}}$$

How much pressure do you apply with your thumb, if you push with a force of 2N, and the area of your thumb is 2cm^2 (0.0002m^2)?

$$\text{Pressure} = \frac{\text{force}}{\text{area}} = \frac{2N}{0.0002m^2} = 10{,}000N/m^2$$

10,000N/m^2 is the same as just 10N/cm^2 – so your thumb isn't applying that much pressure.

Now, how much pressure do you apply with the drawing pin, if the force you use is still 2N, and the tip of the pin has an area of half a square millimetre (0.0000005m^2)?

$$\text{Pressure} = \frac{\text{force}}{\text{area}} = \frac{2N}{0.0000005m^2} = 4{,}000{,}000N/m^2$$

The pin applies four million newtons per square metre of pressure, or the same as 4,000N/cm^2 – 400 times as much pressure as you apply with your thumb.

Spread the pressure

In snowy places, people sometimes wear snow shoes with wide soles. These have a large surface area, so they stop people sinking into soft snow.

Camels have really wide feet, so that they don't sink into desert sand.

How can a magician lie on a bed of nails?

Some magicians wow their audiences by lying on a bed of nails. It might look painful, but it doesn't hurt that much, as long as there are enough nails to spread their weight.

If a magician only lay on one nail, his body would exert a lot of pressure on it – and he'd get a nasty nail-shaped hole in his back.

Why pressure makes you bleed

It's not just solids that apply pressure to other things. Liquids always push against the sides of whatever container they're in, trying to escape.

This includes the blood inside you. Your heart pumps blood around your body. The blood is constantly pushing outwards, but your veins and arteries hold it in. If you cut yourself, it can escape through the hole – and you bleed.

Gases exert pressure, too. The air in the atmosphere pushes on us with enormous pressure. Luckily, the liquid inside our bodies pushes back with equal pressure. Otherwise, we'd be squashed to death by the weight of the air.

See for yourself: pressure

Use a pair of scissors to make two holes in the side of an empty aluminium drinks can, one near the top and one near the bottom. Cover the holes with sticky tape, and fill the can with water.

Stand the can by a sink, and pull off the tape.

You should find water spurts out further from the lower hole because it's under more pressure, caused by the weight of the water above it.

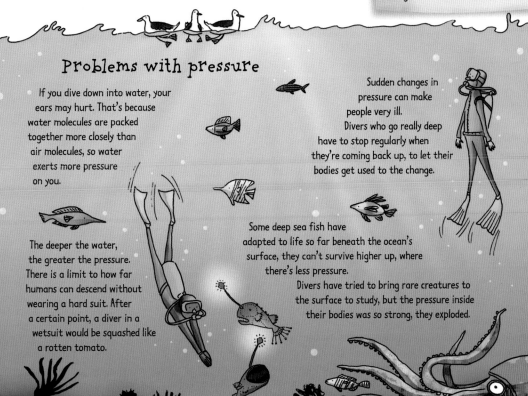

Problems with pressure

If you dive down into water, your ears may hurt. That's because water molecules are packed together more closely than air molecules, so water exerts more pressure on you.

The deeper the water, the greater the pressure. There is a limit to how far humans can descend without wearing a hard suit. After a certain point, a diver in a wetsuit would be squashed like a rotten tomato.

Some deep sea fish have adapted to life so far beneath the ocean's surface, they can't survive higher up, where there's less pressure.

Divers have tried to bring rare creatures to the surface to study, but the pressure inside their bodies was so strong, they exploded.

Sudden changes in pressure can make people very ill. Divers who go really deep have to stop regularly when they're coming back up, to let their bodies get used to the change.

Why does wood float?

Measuring volume

Volume is measured in cubic metres (m³). If you want to measure the volume of a box, for example, you multiply its length by its width by its height.

If you drop a stone into a river, it'll sink. If you drop a piece of wood, it'll float. The force of gravity acting on the wood and the stone is the same, so why does one thing float and not the other?

It's all because of something called **density**. Density describes how much mass is packed into an object. A stone is denser than water, so it sinks. Wood is less dense than water, so it floats.

You can work out the exact density of an object by comparing its mass to its **volume** (how much space it takes up). Volume is measured in cubic metres (m³), and density is measured in kilograms per cubic metre (kg/m³). Here's a handy formula for calculating density:

$$\text{density } (\varrho) = \frac{\text{mass (m)}}{\text{Volume (V)}}$$

Density triangle

Here's another magic triangle to help you work out density, mass and volume.

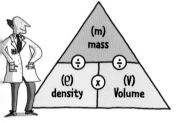

The symbol for 'density' might look a bit strange. It was tricky for physicists because 'd' already stands for distance. So they borrowed the Greek letter 'ϱ' (pronounced 'rho') instead.

Lighter than air

Imagine you have a dolphin-shaped helium balloon on the end of a string, exactly the same size and shape as a real dolphin. If you let it go, the balloon would float in the air – but there's no way that a real dolphin would.

It's all because of density:

Real dolphin's mass = 160kg   Real dolphin's volume = 2m³

$$\text{Real dolphin's density} = \frac{m}{V} = \frac{160\text{kg}}{2\text{m}^3} = 80\text{kg/m}^3$$

Balloon-dolphin's mass = 0.1kg   Balloon-dolphin's volume = 2m³

$$\text{Balloon-dolphin's density} = \frac{m}{V} = \frac{0.1\text{kg}}{2\text{m}^3} = 0.05\text{kg/m}^3$$

The density of air is about 1.2 kilograms per cubic metre. Helium balloons are much less dense than air, so they float. Dolphins are much more dense than air, so they don't float.

Why does a huge steel ship float?

Water has a density of 1,000kg/m³, but steel is much denser (about 9,000kg/m³), so a solid lump of steel will sink. But a ship made of steel isn't a solid lump. Inside there are lots of empty rooms filled with air, which has a low density (1.2kg/m³). Because there is so much air, the ship's *overall* density is less than water's, so it floats.

Submarines use density to dive or float. When the crew want to go underwater, they let sea water fill up empty tanks inside the submarine. This increases the submarine's density, so it sinks. To come up again, they pump air back into the tanks, so the submarine's density decreases.

A submarine floating on the surface.

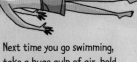

See for yourself: changing density

Next time you go swimming, take a huge gulp of air, hold your breath and let yourself float on the water. You should find it's quite easy.

Then blow the air out again. You should find you sink a little lower, and it gets harder to float. This is because you'll have less air in your lungs, so your average density becomes higher.

An elephant in the bath

Next time you have a bath, look at what happens to the water. Notice how it moves up the sides of the bath when you get in. This is called **displacement**.

The amount of water you push out of the way (or displace) is equal to the volume of your body. If a mouse got into your bath, it wouldn't displace much water. But if an elephant got in, so much water would be displaced there wouldn't be much left in the bath.

Displacement is a useful way of measuring the volume of an object which has an odd shape. You can drop it into a container filled to the brim with water, and collect the water it displaces. The volume of the water displaced will be the same as the volume of the object.

Fantastic physicist: Archimedes about 287–212BC

The first person to notice displacement was Ancient Greek scientist Archimedes. It's said he filled his bath too full, and water splashed out when he got in.

He was so excited by his new idea that he ran into the street naked, shouting "Eureka!" ("I've got it!").

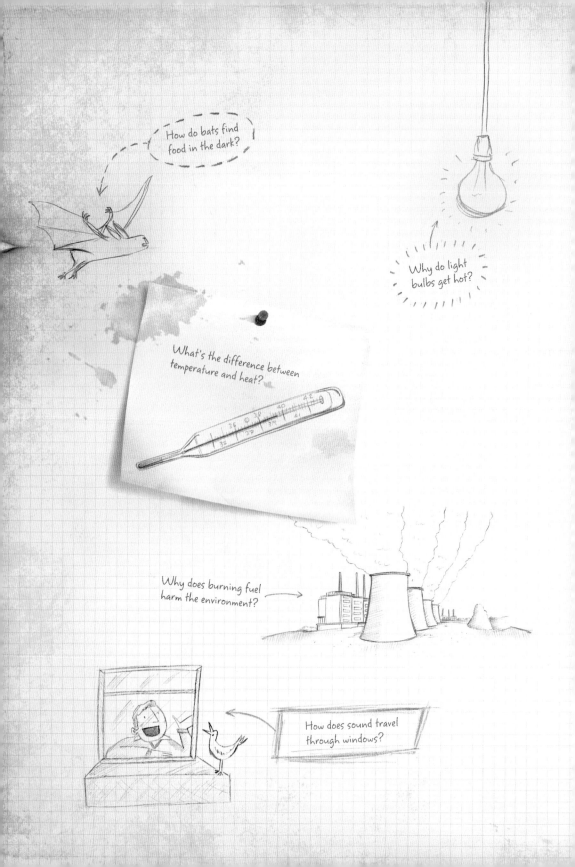

Part 3:
Energy everywhere

If there were no energy, nothing would ever happen.
Like everything else in the Universe, energy was created
in the Big Bang. And now it's everywhere, in everything.

Light energy is what allows you to see this book, and
if someone asks you a question, you can hear it because
of sound energy. If you decide to walk away, you use
movement or 'kinetic' energy. Read on to find out more
about these kinds of energy, and discover how one kind of
energy can change into another.

why is energy like a superhero?

Kinds of energy

Energy comes in many forms.

Sound energy – energy that you hear.

I'LL SAVE YOU!

Heat energy – energy you feel as heat.

Chemical energy – stored energy (e.g. in food, fuel or batteries).

Kinetic energy – movement energy.

Light energy – energy that allows us to see.

Potential energy – energy that something has because of its position (e.g. above the ground, because gravity is pulling on it), or if it's squashed or stretched.

Electrical energy – energy that comes from the movement of electrons. We use it to power our homes.

Magnetic energy – energy that makes magnetic objects, such as magnets, attract or repel each other.

Nuclear energy – energy stored in the nuclei of atoms.

To a physicist, **energy** is the ability to do work – it makes it possible to exert a force and move things.

Energy isn't a physical thing you can touch, in the way you can touch matter. But energy has all sorts of powers to affect things. In fact, you could see energy as the ultimate superhero...

 Energy is all-powerful: nothing could move without energy to exert a force.

 Energy is everywhere: everything that exists has energy of some kind.

 Energy can take many different forms, and change form as if by magic.

 Energy is immortal: it's impossible to destroy it. New energy can't be created – all the energy in the Universe has been around since the Big Bang, although it keeps changing from one form to another.

 Energy gets things done. The release of energy does work – for example, when you run down the road. And, when work is done on something (on a pencil, if you pick it up, for example), energy is *added* to it.

222

where do you get your energy from?

If anyone's ever asked you this question, now you can tell them the *real* answer. All the energy on Earth comes from heat and light from the Sun. When that energy is used, it doesn't disappear: it changes form.

This is known as **energy transfer**. It works like this:

1. THE SUN SENDS OUT HEAT AND LIGHT ENERGY.

2. SEEDS USE HEAT AND LIGHT TO GROW INTO HEALTHY PLANTS.

3. PLANTS PRODUCE FRUITS WHICH STORE THE ENERGY AS CHEMICAL ENERGY.

4. WHEN YOU EAT FRUITS, AND OTHER FOOD, THE CHEMICAL ENERGY IS TRANSFERRED TO YOUR BODY, WHERE IT'S STORED, UNTIL...

5. ...YOU GO OUT TO PLAY, CONVERTING CHEMICAL ENERGY INTO KINETIC ENERGY AND HEAT.

If energy can't be destroyed, why worry about 'saving energy'?

Like all superheroes, energy has a weakness. When it changes form – whether from chemical to kinetic, or electrical to light – some of it always turns into heat. That's why light bulbs, computers and televisions get warm when they're used, and why you get hot if you do a lot of exercise.

Heat is much harder to catch and recycle than other kinds of energy, so most of that heat escapes into the atmosphere. Heat can build up in the atmosphere, warming the whole planet.

The energy to drive

This is how energy changing form can make a car go:

A car is filled with petrol, which contains chemical energy.

Explosion happens in here

Inside the car engine, a spark makes a tiny amount of the petrol explode. The explosion pushes a piston, which turns an axle and makes the wheels spin. Chemical energy from the petrol is converted into kinetic energy. Some is also turned into sound and heat.

Piston

Axle

VROOOM

But where does petrol come from? Turn the page to find out...

Hot topic

Most of the energy we use to heat houses, run computers and make cars go comes from fuels such as oil, coal and natural gas.

These are called **fossil fuels** because they're formed from the fossilized remains of living things – things that died millions of years ago and were squashed together deep under the ground. Coal is made from dead plants, and oil and natural gas from dead sea creatures.

What's the problem with fossil fuels?

One problem is that the Earth is running out of fossil fuels – and it'll be millions of years before new ones form. But scientists have discovered a worse problem: burning fossil fuels is bad for the environment.

When they're burned, fossil fuels give off waste gases. Some of these pollute the air and water, and harm living things. And most of them, including carbon dioxide (CO_2), contribute to **global warming**: an increase in the temperature of the air and oceans.

What's wrong with global warming?

You might think global warming just means more summery weather. But even a tiny rise in temperature causes huge problems around the world. These include:

● Melting icecaps, which lead to colder seas, rising sea levels and flooding in some places.

● More extreme weather, such as hurricanes and droughts, which cause massive damage.

● Changing climates. Some parts of the world may become too hot for many animals, including humans, to live. Some types of animals may even die out entirely.

Power stations convert chemical energy in fossil fuels into electrical energy. But they pollute the environment at the same time.

Where else can we get energy from?

Scientists are still working hard to try to find sources of energy that are both safe *and* efficient. Until they succeed, it's best if everyone reduces the amount of energy they use, so that global warming will be reduced and existing energy sources will last longer.

Here are some of the best alternative energy sources that exist today:

Solar power

How it works: solar panels convert heat from the Sun into electrical energy people can use.

Advantage: doesn't pollute the environment.

Disadvantage: the panels are expensive to build. And they're not very effective on cloudy days.

Wind power

How it works: wind turns the blades of a turbine, which converts kinetic energy into electricity.

Advantage: doesn't pollute the environment with harmful gases.

Disadvantage: can't work if there's no wind, or if there's a really strong wind.

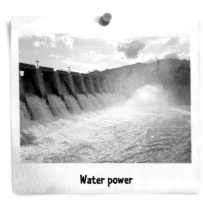

Water power

How it works: converts the kinetic energy from moving water (such as waves or waterfalls) into electricity.

Advantage: even a small water power station can produce lots of energy.

Disadvantage: building a station means building a dam to store the water. This can damage the local environment.

Nuclear power

How it works: produces energy by splitting atoms.

Advantage: produces a large amount of energy without making much CO_2.

Disadvantage: produces toxic nuclear waste, which has to be stored very carefully for thousands of years, until it becomes harmless.

You've got the power

Power triangle

You can use the magic triangle below to calculate power, work and time.

Cover up the value you want to know, and the equation you'll need to use will be in the two sections left.

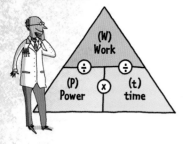

If you're sent upstairs to tidy your room, you might drag your feet, and take as long as possible. But if someone tells you there's a surprise waiting up there, you might rush upstairs pretty quickly. You'll have done the same amount of work, but in much less time – meaning you'll have used more *power* to do it.

Power is a measure of the amount of work done – or the amount of energy converted – in a particular time. Here's a formula to calculate power:

$$\text{Power (P)} = \frac{\text{Work (W)}}{\text{time (t)}}$$

Work is measured in joules, and so power is measured in joules per second (J/s) – the number of joules of energy that are converted every second.

Joules per second are also known as watts (W), so 1 J/s = 1 W.

Light bulb? Watt light bulb?

You might have noticed that the brightness of light bulbs is measured in watts. Usually, the higher the number of watts, the brighter the bulb.

But the brightness also depends on how efficient the bulb is. An efficient 20W bulb can be as bright as an inefficient 100W bulb, because it converts more electrical energy to light, and less to heat.

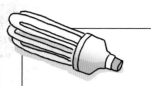

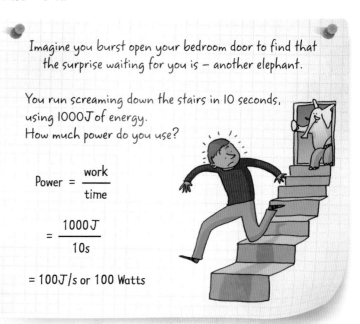

Imagine you burst open your bedroom door to find that the surprise waiting for you is – another elephant.

You run screaming down the stairs in 10 seconds, using 1000 J of energy.
How much power do you use?

$$\text{Power} = \frac{\text{work}}{\text{time}}$$

$$= \frac{1000\,J}{10s}$$

= 100 J/s or 100 Watts

The heat is on

Substances can exist in three different states: solid, liquid or gas. What state a substance is in depends on its **heat**, or 'thermal energy'.

Adding heat converts solids to liquids, and liquids to gases. That's why ice melts in warm drinks, and why steam rises from a boiling kettle. Removing heat, or cooling, reverses the process.

So how does heat melt ice?

Remember that all substances are made of atoms or molecules. Even in a solid, such as ice, all these molecules are vibrating slightly. If you warm the ice, the heat energy makes them vibrate more, and they move apart, so the ice becomes liquid water.

If you continue to heat the water, the molecules gain even more energy. This makes them move even faster and move further apart. Eventually, some of them break away, or **evaporate**, forming steam.

But if the steam hits a cool surface, like a window, it gives some of its heat energy to the window. This makes it **condense**, or become liquid again, forming water droplets.

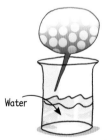

Ice

In ice, water molecules are arranged in a regular formation, touching each other.

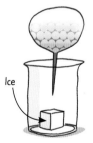

Water

In water, the molecules spread out a bit, and are free to move past each other.

Steam

In steam, water molecules are free to whizz around and occasionally bump into each other.

See for yourself: changing state

You can see what happens when something changes state by taking an empty jar and pouring a handful of peas in it.

Tap the jar. The peas will vibrate, but they'll stay together. This is what happens inside a solid.

Shake the jar gently. The peas will have more energy, so they'll flow over each other, like molecules in a liquid.

Now go outside and shake the jar as hard as you can. Some of the peas will fly out. That's what happens when a liquid boils and some of the molecules turn into gas.

Heating up

Different energies are converted into heat in all sorts of ways:

Electric radiators convert electricity into heat.

Friction converts kinetic energy into heat – just try rubbing your hands together and you'll feel them warm up.

In the Sun, atoms squeeze together incredibly tightly, releasing some of their nuclear energy, which is converted into (a lot of) heat.

Weird water

When water is cooled to 4°C, it contracts. But, unlike most substances, it doesn't continue to contract if it gets any colder.

Instead, when it turns to ice at 0°C, it expands again. The molecules spread out and the ice becomes less dense – which is why ice floats on top of water.

What's the difference between heat and temperature?

Temperature tells you how *hot* something is. It can be measured on three different scales – degrees Celsius (°C), degrees Fahrenheit (°F) and Kelvin (K). When something gains heat energy, its temperature rises. When it loses heat energy, its temperature falls.

Heat refers to *thermal energy*, which can be measured in joules. A warm bath is at a lower *temperature* than a steaming hot mug of tea. But because the bath is much bigger, it has more *heat energy* than the tea.

What happens to things when they're heated?

When a substance is heated, but not enough to change state, it will **expand**. This means it'll get a bit bigger and less dense. And when it's cooled, it'll **contract**, or get smaller and denser. Gases expand the most, followed by liquids. Solids expand the least.

You can see this effect for yourself. Find a jar with a really tight lid. Hold the lid under some hot water for a few moments. Then try twisting it, and it should come right off.

How does heat loosen the lid?

The jar lid loosens because of heat expansion. The heat energy passes from the hot water to the metal lid. This makes the lid expand, so it fits more loosely on the jar.

Heat expansion is what makes **thermometers** work. They contain liquids that expand or contract as they get hotter or colder. If you put a thermometer into something warm, the liquid inside it will get warm, too, and expand.

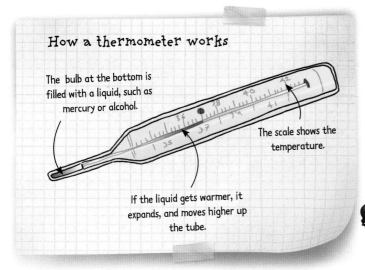

How a thermometer works

The bulb at the bottom is filled with a liquid, such as mercury or alcohol.

The scale shows the temperature.

If the liquid gets warmer, it expands, and moves higher up the tube.

Fantastic physicists

In 1724, Daniel Fahrenheit created a temperature scale based on a 'frigorific' mixture. This mixture, which combines different amounts of ice, water and ammonia salt, *always* settles at the same temperature: 0°F.

In 1742, Anders Celsius developed another scale, based on water's freezing point (0°C) and boiling point (100°C).

In 1848, William Thomson (who became Lord Kelvin) suggested a new scale, based on **absolute zero** – the temperature something would be if it had no heat energy at all. This is the scale physicists use today.

In reality, absolute zero, or 0 Kelvin, is impossible to reach. But Thomson worked out it would be equal to -273°C or -460°F.

Hot to trot

Heat loves to travel. It always moves from a hotter region to a cooler one – that's why an ice cream melts when you lick it. Heat energy moves from your tongue to the ice cream, so your tongue gets cooler and the ice cream gets warmer.

Heat energy moves around in three main ways. They're called **conduction**, **convection** and **radiation**. Turn the page to find out more.

Why do teaspoons get hot?

If you leave a cold spoon in a hot cup of tea, the spoon will get hot. This is because of conduction. **Conduction** is how heat moves through an object, or between objects that are touching. Things which are good at conducting heat, such as metal teaspoons, are called **conductors**.

Hot molecules inside the tea pass on their heat to cooler molecules on the edge of the spoon. Inside the spoon, the newly-hot molecules vibrate more than normal — making them hotter. In turn, these molecules pass on their vibrations (and heat) to any molecules they're touching, until the whole spoon is hot.

Cooking with conduction

Conduction is useful when you're cooking. You put a metal pan full of water on a hob. When you turn on the hob, heat hits the pan. The pan conducts the heat to the water – which boils and cooks your food.

How do radiators heat up rooms?

Hot water inside a radiator heats the radiator by conduction. The radiator makes the air around it warm by radiation. But it's convection that makes the warm air near the radiator spread around in a room.

Convection is how heat is transferred in a liquid or a gas. The molecules in warm air move further apart, making the air less dense. Because it's less dense, the warm air rises, while the cool air around it sinks. When this cool air warms up, it rises too, and more cool air takes its place. This creates a cycle called a **convection current**.

Convection on a global scale

The wind is an example of a convection current on a large scale. Hot places warm the air close to them. The warm air rises, and is replaced with cool air. We feel this movement of air as wind.

Convection happens in the world's oceans, too. Warm water moves to colder areas, and cold water moves to warmer ones, creating ocean currents (shown above).

Warm air rises

Cool air replaces it

How does the Sun send out heat?

All particles emit *some* heat by **radiation**, though often it's too small to notice. But very hot things such as bonfires, or incredibly hot things such as the Sun, radiate a lot of heat.

Radiated heat moves in waves emitted by the object. These waves can even travel through empty space. The energy caried in these waves is absorbed by the things they hit, making them hot.

Absorbing heat

Heat affects some objects more than others. Dark coloured or dull things absorb more heat than light coloured or shiny things. That's why tennis players often wear white – it helps them stay cool. And solar panels which harness heat and light from the Sun are black, so they absorb as much as possible.

How do sweaters keep you warm?

Things which are bad at conducting heat, such as wood, wool or plastics, are called **insulators**. Instead of losing heat energy, they trap it.

Woollen sweaters or plastic fleeces keep you warm on cold days. Buildings are insulated too, to reduce the amount of energy needed to keep them at a comfortable temperature.

Evaporation

Heat can also be transferred by **evaporation** – when a liquid changes state and becomes a gas. The evaporating molecules have lots of heat energy. When they turn into gas, they take that energy with them, so what's left behind has less heat energy and becomes cooler.

Your body uses evaporation to cool you down. When you get hot, you sweat. The sweat evaporates and takes some heat energy with it.

See for yourself – heat absorption

Take two aluminium drink cans, and paint one black and one white.

When they're dry, put them in the Sun. Leave them for about half an hour.

Touch the cans. Which feels the warmest? The black can will probably feel hotter, because dark objects absorb more heat.

What's a wave?

All **waves** transfer energy from place to place. If you drop a stone in a pond, you'll see waves of kinetic energy travelling outwards in ripples.

The Sun radiates waves of energy through empty space. But many other types of energy, such as sound and kinetic energy, need a substance, or **medium**, for their waves to travel through. They transfer energy by making the medium move up and down, or from side to side. This is called **oscillation**. But, although the *waves* travel, the *medium* doesn't. It oscillates and returns to its original position.

It's a bit like being part of a Mexican wave in a sports stadium. Imagine the people sitting on the opposite side of the stadium to you stand up, wave their arms about, and sit down again. Then the people to their left do the same. Soon it's your turn. Before you know it, you've stood up and sat down, and the *wave* has moved on – but *you* are exactly where you were before.

During a storm, huge waves of kinetic energy stir up the ocean, making it oscillate.

Waves to watch out for

Electromagnetic waves, and the waves you see on an ocean, are known as **transverse waves**. They wobble up and down in a shape like this:

Soundwaves are called **longitudinal waves**. They make the medium they're moving through move back and forth, squashing together and spreading apart, like this:

Peaks and troughs

This diagram shows the different parts of a transverse wave:

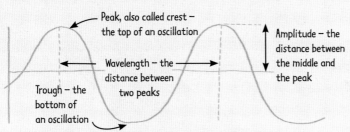

Peak, also called crest – the top of an oscillation

Amplitude – the distance between the middle and the peak

Wavelength – the distance between two peaks

Trough – the bottom of an oscillation

Wavelength (λ, or lambda) measures the distance between two peaks on the wave, and **amplitude** measures how high each peak is (both using metres). **Frequency (f)** tells you how many oscillations pass a point in one second. It's measured in **hertz (Hz)**.

Wave speed (c), measured in m/s, tells you how fast a wave is moving. You can work out wave speed with this equation:

Wave speed (c) = frequency (f) x wavelength (λ)

For example, the speed of a soundwave in air is about 340m/s.

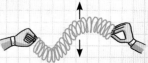
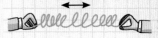
Wave triangle

You can work out wave speed, frequency and wavelength using this magic triangle:

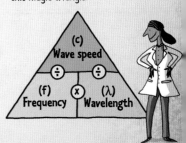

(c) Wave speed

(f) Frequency   (x)   (λ) Wavelength

The electromagnetic spectrum

The light you can see is part of a large range, or 'spectrum', of energy waves called the **electromagnetic spectrum**. Electromagnetic energy radiates like heat – it doesn't need a medium to travel through. Each wave in the spectrum has its own wavelength and frequency, and they all have different characteristics.

The fastest thing in the Universe

As far as scientists know, the waves in the electromagnetic spectrum are the fastest things that exist. They all travel at the same speed, known as the **speed of light,** or 'c' for short. This is about 300,000,000 m/s. Electromagnetic waves can travel about 7 times round the Earth in a single second.

The Earth is 150 million km (93 million miles) from the Sun. So it takes about 8 minutes for the Sun's light to reach us. If the Sun suddenly disappeared, it would take us 8 minutes to notice.

X-rays

X-rays were discovered by a German physicist called Röntgen in 1895. He named them "X" because he didn't know much about them.

X-rays pass through flesh but are absorbed by dense things such as bones or metal. So doctors use X-ray images to see if you've broken your arm, or swallowed something strange.

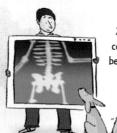

This diagram shows the main types of energy wave found across the electromagnetic spectrum.

Shortest wavelength, highest frequency

Time travel physics

It's impossible to travel at the speed of light. But one day people might be able to go *almost* as fast. Physicists predict that at this immense speed, *time would slow down.*

Imagine you could travel off into space at near-light speed for five years. When you got back home, all your friends would be five years older. You'd be five years older, too, but because time was moving so slowly for you, you'd look and feel the same age as the day you left.

Gamma rays

Gamma rays can travel through almost anything, even lead. If they pass through your body they can cause cancer, which can be deadly. Gamma rays are given off by substances that send out energy from the nuclei of their atoms. These are known as **radioactive** substances.

DANGER

This symbol means something is radioactive.

Ultraviolet waves

Ultraviolet waves come from the Sun and are the reason you get a suntan. But too many of them can damage your skin.

Really long, really short

The longest wavelengths are as big as the Universe. The shortest are as small as the tiniest particles inside atoms.

Microwaves

Microwaves don't just heat food up quickly. They're also used in radar, to locate distant objects. Radar transmitters fire out microwaves, which bounce back when they hit something. Radar operators can work out how far away that thing is from the amount of time it takes the waves to return.

Fantastic physicist: Albert Einstein 1879–1955

Albert Einstein was the first person to work out the strange things that happen at the speed of light. Because it's impossible to travel that fast, he conducted 'thought experiments' and imagined it instead.

Einstein loved maths and wanted to be a teacher when he left school. But he couldn't find a teaching job, so he became a clerk in a patents office, and studied physics in his spare time.

Visible light

This is the light our eyes can see. It's really made up of many different colours, all with different wavelengths.

Longest wavelength, lowest frequency

Infra-red radiation

Infra-red is a kind of heat – it's radiation produced by hot objects. If you were hiding in the dark, someone could use an infra-red detector to find you. That's because your body is warmer than your surroundings, so you'd give off more infra-red radiation.

Radiowaves

All sorts of messages are sent using radiowaves. They're used to broadcast radio programmes, and to transmit mobile phone and wireless internet signals.

Energy equals...

In 1905, Einstein published four theories which completely changed what scientists believe about light, space and time.

One of his theories included the equation: $E = mc^2$. In words, this says 'the amount of energy in an object (E) equals its mass (m) times the speed of light squared (c^2)'.

This means that even something with a tiny mass – such as an atom – contains loads of energy. This idea helped other scientists to invent the atomic bomb.

A photo of a dog taken with an infra-red camera

Let there be light!

If you're reading this book, there must be a light source near you — whether it's the Sun or an electric light or even a candle.

Without light you wouldn't be able to see anything at all. The reason you see things is because light waves shine out from a light source, bounce off different objects, and then go into your eyes.

Seeing the light

When some objects get really hot — above about 600°C — they glow.

This is how the Sun, fires and some kinds of light bulbs work. Physicists call them 'luminous bodies' because they send out light that we can see.

See-through science

You can't see someone through a brick wall, because bricks are **opaque**. That means light can't travel through them.

Windows, on the other hand, are see-through or **transparent** — meaning light can travel through them.

There are some objects, such as frosted glass, which are semi-see-through or **translucent**. Some light can travel through them, but the path is disrupted so you don't get a clear image of what's on the other side.

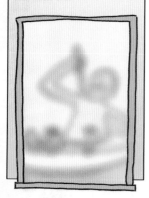

Why can't we see around corners?

Well, you *can* see around corners — but only if you use a mirror (and you can find out more about *that* over the page). Light waves travel in a straight line. You can see this if you stand in a dark room and shine a torch on the wall. Light waves can't turn corners or bend of their own accord — they have to hit something first.

Where do shadows come from?

Opaque objects (things you can't see through) cast shadows because light can't pass through them. Instead, they absorb or reflect light, leaving a black area behind them. The size and shape of the shadows depend on where the light is coming from.

When a light source, such as the Sun, is directly overhead, you only cast a tiny shadow, like this:

But when the Sun is low in the sky, your shadow looks really long and thin, like this:

What makes a rainbow?

Light is actually a mix of different colours. When you see a rainbow, you're seeing all the different colours, separated by droplets of water in the air.

Each colour of light has a slightly different wavelength, so they all behave a bit differently. When each colour hits a transparent object, such as a drop of rain, it moves through it at a slightly different speed. This makes the colours separate and spread out.

Newton's solar spectrum

Isaac Newton was the first person to show that white light is made up of different colours.

One sunny day, he covered up the windows in his room, all except for one tiny hole which let a beam of sunlight through. He put a prism in front of it, and it bent the light into a pattern of colours on his wall. He called this the **solar spectrum**.

The photograph on the right shows light being split into its different colours using a triangular chunk of glass called a prism.

There are seven colours, which always split up in the order of their wavelengths. Red (the longest) splits at the widest angle, followed by orange, yellow, green, blue, indigo and lastly, violet.

Lights hits a prism and is split into rays of different colours

Seeing colours

Just as objects absorb different amounts of heat, they also absorb different amounts – and colours – of light.

Shiny objects look bright and shiny because they bounce back lots of light. White objects are often bright because don't absorb *any* light. Instead, it all bounces off them and into your eyes. Black objects absorb *all* colours. Nothing bounces off, which is why they look black.

Other objects absorb all the colours *except* for the colour they appear to be. For example, grass absorbs most colours, but bounces green light back. That's why grass looks green. People who are colour-blind aren't able to see certain colours because their eyes can't detect that wavelength.

Colour mixing

Although there are seven colours of light in the rainbow, it's possible to use just three of them to make all the rest.

These three colours – red, blue and green – are known as the primary colours of light.

If you shine rays of red, blue and green light all in the same place, they'll produce white light.

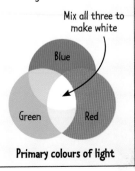

Mix all three to make white

Blue

Green   Red

Primary colours of light

Reflecting light

All surfaces reflect some light – if they didn't, we wouldn't be able to see them. But some surfaces are better at reflecting light than others. Smooth, shiny, light-coloured things reflect more light than dull, uneven, dark things. This is why you can see your face reflected in a flat, shiny mirror and not in a dark, bumpy tree.

The rule of reflection

If you throw a ball straight at a wall, it will bounce straight back at you. And if you throw it from one side, at an angle, it will bounce back at the same angle on the opposite side. This is called the **rule of reflection**, and it works for light, too.

Ball thrown straight at a wall   Ball thrown at an angle

You can try it yourself by shining a torch at a mirror. If you shine it straight at the mirror the light will bounce straight back at you. That's because you're shining it along the **normal** – an imaginary line at right angles to the surface of the mirror.

More about mirrors

Everything you see in a mirror is the wrong way around. That's why the writing on a book or newspaper always appears back to front in a mirror.

When you stand close to the mirror, and then walk away from it, your reflection moves exactly the same distance away in the mirror.

Meow, that's bright

'Catseyes' are road markings which light up when headlights shine on them. They're called catseyes because they appear to shine in the dark in the same way as real cats' eyes.

Artificial catseyes contain balls of glass with a reflective coating inside. When light hits them, it bounces back out again. The reflected light shows drivers where they are on the road.

But if you shine the torch at an angle, the light will bounce off the mirror at an equal and opposite angle on the other side of the normal.

The angle at which the light hits the mirror is called the **angle of incidence**. The angle the light makes when it bounces back is called the **angle of reflection**.

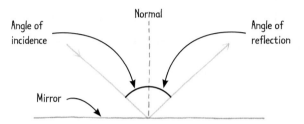

The rule of reflection

This is how your physics teacher might teach you the rule of reflection:

The angle of incidence = the angle of reflection

Scattering light

The rule of reflection only works for a completely flat, smooth mirror, known as a plane mirror. Uneven surfaces reflect light in all different directions. Physicists call this **scattering**. Curved or bumpy surfaces form wonky reflections, and some scatter light so much that you can't see any reflection at all.

If you look at yourself in a curved mirror, your reflection will look quite strange.

Why is the sky blue?

As light passes through the atmosphere, the colours with longer wavelengths (red and orange) pass straight through. Colours with shorter wavelengths (blue and violet) are scattered by the air. This makes the sky overhead look blue.

If you look into the distance, the sky will be a paler blue. That's because more distant light must pass through more air to reach you. Some of the blue light gets scattered away in other directions, so less of it reaches your eyes.

Nothing there... you must be hungry.

Flexible fibre optics

Fibre optic cables are very flexible. The fibres are thin and bendy, so they're often used in medical procedures.

When someone gets a really nasty tummy ache, a doctor might push a fibre optic cable with a tiny camera on it down their mouth, to see what's going on inside their stomach.

Total internal reflection

Sometimes light can be trapped inside a substance because it reflects again and again and again. This is called **total internal reflection (t.i.r.)**.

Usually, some light waves are absorbed by their surroundings. But in t.i.r. light is **totally** reflected (as the name suggests) – so none is absorbed as the light travels. This can be very useful.

Fibre optic cables use t.i.r. to carry light signals for telephones, the internet and televisions. Because no light is lost, they can transmit very clear, strong signals a really long way. It works like this:

A computer modem converts electricity into light signals.

These travel along a fibre-optic cable by total internal reflection.

The signals arrive at another computer which converts them back into electricity.

Why does a straw look bent when it's in a glass of water?

Sometimes, a straw in a glass of water looks bent or broken. But it's the light, not the straw, that's bent.

Light travels at different speeds in different mediums. It slows down as it enters water – just as you'd slow down if you ran into a pond – and it speeds up again when it re-enters the air. As it slows down or speeds up, it bends. This is known as **refraction**.

Light bends when it enters water, making this straw look bent.

How can refraction help you see?

Glasses, telescopes, microscopes and cameras all contain **lenses** – specially cut pieces of plastic or glass that curve inwards (concave) or outwards (convex).

Lenses **focus** light waves by refracting the light entering the lens. Combinations of lenses in magnifying glasses and telescopes help to form a clear image of an object that's too tiny or far away to see with the naked eye. There are two main types of lens:

Why do some people need glasses?

Lenses aren't just manmade objects. They also occur in nature – in your eyes, for example.

The lenses in your eyes are very sophisticated. They can change shape to help your eyes focus on objects that are either nearby or far away.

Some people's lenses don't change shape so easily, so they wear glasses or contacts – an extra set of lenses in front of their eyes.

To find out more about the lenses in your eyes, turn to page 42.

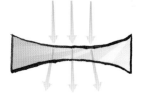

A **concave** lens refracts light outwards

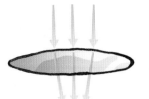

A **convex** lens refracts light inwards

Make your own magnifying glass

If you follow the instructions, you can make a very simple sort of magnifying glass using an empty plastic bottle, some water, and a pair of scissors.

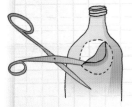

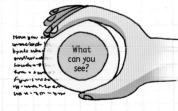

1. Cut a disc out of the bottle, from just below the neck – where the bottle is curved.

2. Pour a little water into the disc.

3. Hold it above a newspaper and move it around.

What happens?

You should find that the writing looks larger when you look at it through the water-filled disc. The water and the plastic are refracting the light and acting as a lens.

Hearing things

The reason you hear things is because of sound energy. Sounds are produced when things – such as the strings on a violin – vibrate.

The molecules in the strings vibrate and bump into any air molecules next to them, making them vibrate, too. The vibrations are passed through the air in a continuous wave. Eventually the vibrations reach your eardrums, making *them* vibrate – and you hear the noise.

Why are some sounds high-pitched and others low-pitched?

When something vibrates fast, the waves it sends out move fast, too. The waves produced when something vibrates very fast are known as **high frequency** sound waves. When something vibrates more slowly it produces **low frequency** sound waves.

High frequency waves make high-pitched, squeaky noises – like a shrill scream, or a car alarm. Low frequency waves make low-pitched, rumbly noises – like a big dog growling or a truck's engine chugging.

Wave frequency is measured in **hertz (Hz)**, so the pitch of a sound is measured in hertz, too. Humans can't hear all frequencies – our ears only pick up sounds between 20,000Hz-20Hz. Some animals, such as dogs and bats, can hear much higher frequency sounds than we can.

Sound waves with frequencies higher than 20,000Hz are known as **ultrasound**, and those below 20Hz are known as **infrasound**.

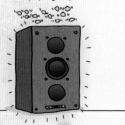

"What a quiet, well-behaved class you are!"

Studying sound

Sound waves are invisible, but physicists can use a machine called an **oscilloscope** to 'see' them. A microphone picks up vibrations and the oscilloscope changes them into wave patterns on a screen. These patterns show the sound's frequency and **amplitude** (how loud it is).

If you ever become a famous singer, you'll see your producer fiddling around with a screen like this in the recording studio, trying to get your voice to sound even better than it already is. They can adjust the amplitude, to make your voice louder or quieter, and alter the frequency, which changes the pitch — so you always sound in tune.

Ageing ears

As you get older, the range of noise frequencies you can hear gradually reduces. Most children can hear higher frequencies than their parents and teachers, for example.

Some mobile phone ring tones are deliberately high-pitched, so that children can hear them when they ring, but adults can't.

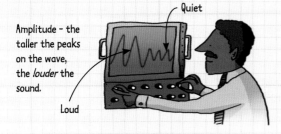

Quiet

Amplitude – the taller the peaks on the wave, the *louder* the sound.

Loud

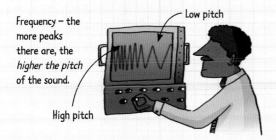

Frequency – the more peaks there are, the *higher the pitch* of the sound.

Low pitch

High pitch

Higher and lower

Here are some of the frequencies of different sounds:

100,000 – 14,000Hz – bat squeaks

5,000 – 4,000Hz – cricket song

4,500 – 100Hz – piano notes

2,048Hz – highest note a singer can reach

1,000 – 450Hz – human speaking voice

30 – 17Hz – blue whale calls

5–1Hz – tornado

Keep it down!

Sound amplitude is measured in **decibels (dB)**. A quiet whisper is about 30dB. Talking normally is about 60dB. Sounds above about 100dB can damage your hearing and even make you deaf.

How do echoes happen?

Echoes are reflected sound waves. If you shout in a big, empty room, the sound you make travels to the wall and then bounces – or echoes – back to you. The further the sound travels, the quieter it gets.

Where's the best place to hear echoes?

Sound vibrations reflect best from hard, flat, solid surfaces. But the surface has to be quite far away for you to hear a distinct echo. If it's too close, you just hear a continuous noise.

You can hear top quality echoes in big places, such as an empty church or an underground cave.

Are echoes useful?

They're very useful, especially to bats. Bats hunt at night, when their prey can't see them. But they can't see their prey, either. Instead, they send out high-pitched squeaks and wait for the sound waves to bounce back to them. By listening to the way the waves return, they can build up a picture of what's around them, and work out if food is nearby.

The bat sends out high-pitched sounds.

The sound waves hit a moth (tasty food for a bat) and bounce back.

Seeing a baby before it's born

Doctors use ultrasound – high frequency sounds that humans can't hear – to look at babies while they're still inside their mothers. Soundwaves are beamed inside the mother, and they bounce off the baby.

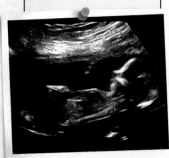

An ultrasound picture of a baby in the womb

Engineers have built machines that copy this bat method of seeing in the dark. They call the method **SONAR** – Sound Navigation and Ranging.

Battleship crews use SONAR to look for enemy submarines hidden underwater. The ship sends out a pinging sound, and waits for microphones to pick up the echoes. Most echoes bounce back off the sea bed, but shorter echoes might reveal a hidden submarine.

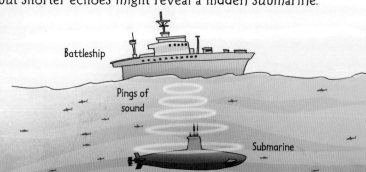

Battleship

Pings of sound

Submarine

Sound vs. light: the showdown

Light travels faster than sound. But sound can be powerful enough to make your teeth rattle, or even make you deaf.

Sound and light waves have different strengths. So if they had a 'Top Wave' contest, it's hard to say who'd win. But it might go a bit like this...

Challenge 1: Travelling around corners

He can't see us here.

But he'll HEAR us if you keep talking!

Light looks as if it has the upper hand as it speeds along towards the corner much faster than sound. But unless there's a mirror in the right place, it'll shoot right past.

Sound spreads out and even passes through things, so it has no trouble coping with the corner.

Result: Sound wins. So remember that if you're hiding from someone, you need to keep as quiet as possible even when you've found a really good hiding place.

Challenge 2: Travelling through space

Light speeds off, as usual, and keeps going strongly until the finishing line.

Sound doesn't even get off the starting block. Sound waves need a medium to travel through, and empty space isn't a medium.

Result: Light wins. Sound travels when vibrations are passed on from particle to particle. There aren't many particles in space (there isn't much of anything in space – hence its name) which is why in space, no one can hear you scream...

Challenge 3: Travelling through a window

Light slows down once it enters the glass. And it gets refracted, too, so the image it shows you might be a bit wonky, depending on the quality of the glass.

Sound actually speeds up in glass. Sound waves travel more quickly in solids (and even in liquids) than in gases like air. That's because the particles in solids and liquids are closer together, so they pass on vibrations more quickly. But the sound is muffled by the glass, so it's quieter on the other side.

Result: it's a tie! Both sound and light get through the window, but they're both altered by it.

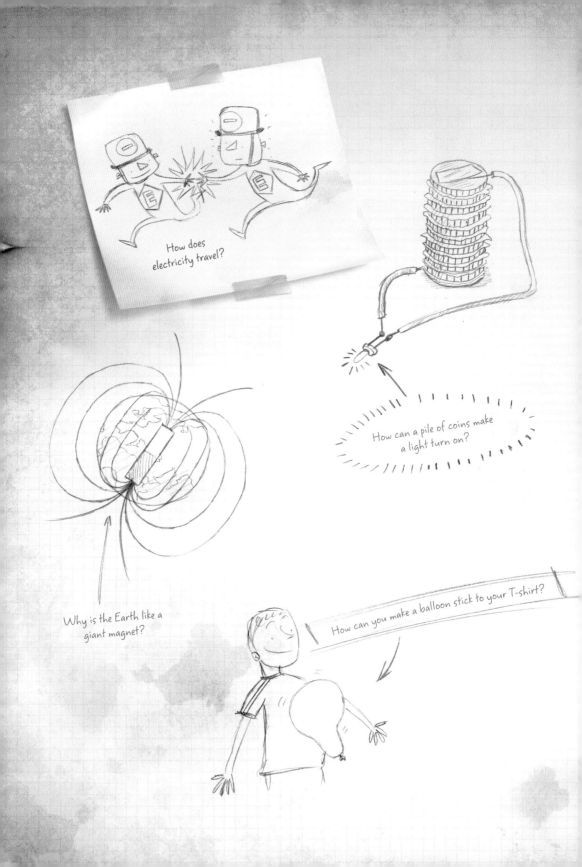

Part 4:
It's electrifying

Electricity is a kind of energy that comes in two different forms. *Static electricity* is the kind that makes your hair cling to your clothes when you pull them over your head. It's also what makes lightning flash through the sky. *Current electricity* is what flows through wires. This is the kind that's used to power televisions, computers, lights and heaters, as well as many, many other things people rely on every day.

Both kinds of electricity are related, but where do they come from? Read on to find out.

Fantastic physicist:

J. J. Thomson
1856–1940

In the late 19th century, Joseph John Thomson conducted a series of experiments using 'cathode rays' to demonstrate that electric charge flows because of tiny particles – which soon gained the name 'electrons'.

Lightning rods

Lightning striking
the Eiffel Tower in Paris

Lightning often strikes tall buildings, which can set them on fire. Tall buildings, including the Eiffel Tower, are protected by lightning rods – strips of metal that let the lightning flow through them safely to the ground. This means the electricity can spread out into the Earth without causing any damage.

Where does electricity come from?

Electricity is all to do with electrons – the negatively charged particles found in atoms. Overall, an atom has no charge, because its electrons are balanced out by positively charged protons. But *if any electrons are added or taken away*, the atom ends up with either a positive or negative **electric charge**.

How can that happen?

Believe it or not, it can happen to some objects very easily. If you rub a plastic balloon against a cotton T-shirt, some of the electrons will come off the T-shirt and stick to the balloon. This gives the balloon a slight negative charge, and the T-shirt a slight positive charge. Opposite charges attract, so you should find that the balloon sticks to the T-shirt.

Plastic and wool are both types of **insulators** – substances that build up an electric charge, rather than passing it on (similar to insulators which store up heat). This build-up of charge creates the kind of electrical energy known as **static electricity**.

Static electricity can be extremely powerful. For example, during stormy weather, water droplets in clouds rub together. This can build up a huge negative charge at the bottom of the cloud. The cloud will get rid of, or **discharge**, this build-up of charge by sending a bolt of lightning through the sky to a point of opposite charge, such as the top of another cloud, or the ground below.

Repelling and attracting

Two objects with opposite charges will attract each
other. But if they've got the same charge, they'll push
each other away, or **repel** each other.

    You can test this using two empty plastic bottles.
Rub one against your T-shirt, so it gets a negative
charge, then rest it on a table, on its side. Now charge
up the other bottle, and bring it close to the
first bottle. They should repel each
other, making the first
bottle roll away.

Here's another experiment to show how static
electricity attracts things.

    Give a balloon a negative charge by rubbing it on
your T-shirt, then hold it against a wall, and move your
hand away. The balloon should stick to the wall, even
though walls don't usually have a charge.

The balloon's negative charge
repels the electrons on the
very edge of the wall,
leaving the wall with a
slight positive charge.
So the balloon and wall
attract each other.

What about the electricity people use at home?

The electricity that flows through the wires in your
home isn't static. It's called **current electricity** and,
instead of building up in a substance, it flows through
it. But how does this happen? Turn the page to find out.

To conduct, or not to conduct?

Some substances, such as silicon,
can be insulators when they're
cold, and conductors when they're
hot. These substances are called
semi-conductors.

    Computer chips
are made from
semiconductors.
They're essential
components to
make all sorts of
machines work,
from mobile
phones to
microwaves to
MP3 players.

Two kinds of electricity

Static electricity is a build-up
of charged particles in a
substance. It's the kind of
electricity that gives you a
shock if you shuffle over the
carpet in your trainers and
then touch a metal door handle
– you're feeling the electricity
discharge.

Current electricity is the
movement of electrical charge
through a substance, and
between substances. It's what
you get from an electric socket.

How can electricity flow?

Electricity can flow through a substance called a **conductor**. Metals such as copper are good conductors, which is why electricians use them to make wires. In a metal, there are loosely held electrons which flow around the molecules in a sort of cloud (as in the picture on page 132). These electrons can pass on electrical charge very easily. The flow of electric charge through a conductor is called an **electric current**.

What creates an electric current?

Current doesn't just flow through a wire of its own accord – it needs a power source such as a **battery**.

Batteries build up a large amount of electrons – and so, a large amount of negative charge – at one end, called the **negative terminal**. The other end (the **positive terminal**) has far fewer electrons.

If you connect a wire to one end of the battery – nothing happens. But if you then connect the other end of the wire to the *other* end of the battery, the electrons at the negative terminal will pass their charge all the way along the wire to the positive terminal. In other words, a current will flow through it.

Racing electrons

Electricity flows through wires, but individual electrons don't race all the way around themselves.

Instead each one bumps into the one next to it, and so on, passing on energy a bit like a relay race, or a tumbling row of dominoes.

Fantastic physicists: Galvani and Volta 16th-17th century

Luigi Galvani noticed that a dead frog's leg twitched when it was touched by a conductor with an electric charge in it, but he couldn't work out why.

Rival scientist Alessandro Volta suggested that *charge* was flowing through it. He went on to create the first useable battery. The amount of charge a battery holds is known as 'voltage' in his honour.

The first ever battery, the zinc-carbon 'voltaic pile', was invented by Volta in 1800.

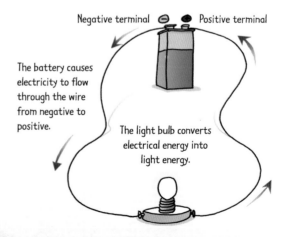

Negative terminal · Positive terminal

The battery causes electricity to flow through the wire from negative to positive.

The light bulb converts electrical energy into light energy.

How do batteries work?

A battery is a store of chemical energy that can be converted into electrical energy. The batteries most people use at home contain a paste called an **electrolyte**, and two metal terminals.

Chemical reactions in the electrolyte force electrons to build up at the negative terminal, while a positive charge builds up at the postive terminal. The difference in charge between the terminals is called **voltage**.

The voltage of a battery determines how *powerful* it is – to be specific, how much current it will drive through a conductor. Voltage is measured in **volts (V)**, often written on the side of the battery, and it can be measured using a device called a **voltmeter**.

AC/DC

There are two kinds of electric current – **direct current (DC)** and **alternating current (AC)**.

Direct current is the kind you get from batteries. It flows continuously in one direction.

Alternating current is what supplies the electricity in your house. It's provided by fast-spinning generators in power stations.

AC is more efficient because a current will always flow as long as the generator keeps spinning. But a battery will eventually run out, and need recharging.

Make your own battery

You'll need:

half a cup of salt; a cup of vinegar; 11 copper coins;
10 circles of coffee filter paper, and 10 circles of aluminium foil, each the same size as the coins

Mix the salt and vinegar together – this will be your electrolyte.

Leave the filter paper to soak in the electrolyte for a few minutes.

You build the battery in layers. Each layer has a coin at the bottom, then a circle of foil, then a circle of filter paper. Keep piling up layers **in the same order** until you end up with just a coin on top. Don't let the foil touch more than one coin, or another piece of foil.

Leave the finished battery to 'charge' for a few minutes.

To test your battery, you'll need:

Two copper wires and a light-emitting diode (LED) (you can buy these things from a DIY shop)

Connect one end of each wire to the LED by twisting it around the LED's terminals. Now tape one end of one wire underneath the battery. Tape the end of the other wire on top of the battery. When both ends are touching a coin, the LED should light up.

The current wars

In 1882, Thomas Edison was the first person to supply people with electricity. He used DC.

But then his great rival, Nikola Tesla, told the US government that AC was more efficient. Edison worried he'd lose money, and tried to persuade people AC was dangerous by using it to electrocute animals.

But in the end, AC became more popular, because Tesla was right. AC *is* more efficient than DC – and it's cheaper to supply, too.

Electricity at home

The current electricity supplied to our homes is called **mains electricity**, and it's supplied at very high voltages. So, for safety, all electric plugs contain fuses, which melt and break the circuit if too much current flows through them.

Most electric appliances also contain something called an **earth wire**. If too much voltage builds up, the earth wire carries the current into the ground, so it doesn't give anyone an electric shock.

Current triangle

Here's a magic triangle to show how to work out current, charge and time:

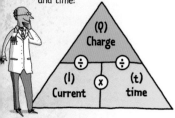

Resistance in wires

The *longer* a wire is, the more resistance it has, because the current has to flow through more of it.

The *thicker* a wire is, the less resistance it has, because there's more room in it for the current to flow.

Going around in circuits

An electric current flowing through a wire is a very basic example of a **circuit**. Most circuits include other parts, called **components**, which make use of the current that flows through them. For example, a component called a **motor** inside an electric toothbrush converts electric current into kinetic energy.

To work, a component needs a certain amount of current. If the current isn't strong enough, there isn't enough power for the component to turn on.

Calculating current

Current (I) is a measure of how much **charge (Q)** is flowing through a circuit at a particular moment. Charge is measured in **coulombs**, so current is measured in coulombs per second – more commonly known as **amperes**, or **amps** for short. You can measure current with a component called an **ammeter**, or you can work it out with this formula:

$$\text{current (amps)} = \frac{\text{charge (coulombs)}}{\text{time (seconds)}} \quad \text{or:} \quad I = \frac{Q}{t}$$

Resisting current

Just as friction slows down moving objects, **resistance** reduces the flow of current. Resistance (R) is measured in **ohms**. Insulators, such as plastics, have a high resistance, while conductors, such as metals, have a low resistance.

You can calculate resistance using this formula:

$$\text{resistance (ohms)} = \frac{\text{voltage (volts)}}{\text{current (amps)}} \quad \text{or:} \quad R = \frac{V}{I}$$

Two types of circuit

You can arrange components in two different kinds of circuit: **in series** or **in parallel**. For example, a string of fairy lights can be wired up either way. Each has different effects on the lights.

In series

Fairy lights connected in a series circuit use just one long wire, with each bulb lined up in a row, one after the other. Current passes through each one in turn, and each bulb converts the electricity to light.

    Series circuits are cheap to make, but they cause two problems. Firstly, if one bulb blows, it breaks the circuit, so *none* of the bulbs light up.

    Secondly, a series circuit with lots of bulbs has a high resistance. This reduces the voltage, so each bulb only has a dim glow.

In parallel

In a parallel circuit, each bulb is placed on its own separate section of wire. This needs more wire, but it reduces problems. The current has more than one path to travel down, so the same amount of current flows to each bulb.

This means they all glow with the same brightness. And if one bulb blows, it won't break the whole circuit.

Wire safety

Electrical wires are made of metal and covered with plastic insulators, to stop the electrical charge getting out — and giving you a shock.

Home safety

⚡ Keep electrical appliances away from water. Water is a good conductor of electricity, so if any water leaks into the device it'll conduct the current. This will stop the device working, and could give you a fatal shock if you're touching the water as well.

⚡ Make sure all wires are properly insulated. If you can see bits of metal through the plastic coating, beware — an exposed wire that's connected to the mains could give you a deadly shock or start a fire.

⚡ Devices that convert electricity into heat, such as kettles and toasters, need a lot of current. If you plug two or more of these devices into the same socket, and switch them on at the same time, it may make the socket overheat and catch fire.

More about circuits

It can be easier to think about how a circuit works if you draw a diagram of it. The diagram needs to show which parts of the circuit are connected to each other. Physicists use symbols to represent components in the circuit, and draw straight lines to show the wires.

When you're drawing a circuit diagram, use a ruler to draw the lines, and make sure there are no gaps, or it'll look as if the circuit is broken.

When a battery isn't a battery

Physicists don't actually call the batteries you use at home 'batteries'. In physics, they're called **cells**. A *battery* is when two or more cells are joined together.

The circuit symbol for a cell looks like this:

The symbol for a battery looks like this:

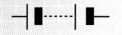

Back to front

Current is a flow of electrons from negative to positive. But in circuit diagrams, current is drawn flowing from the *positive* to the *negative* terminal. Why?

The first person to realize that current flows from one terminal of a cell to the other was French physicist André Ampère. He was working in the 18th century, before electrons were discovered. He thought that current flowed from positive to negative.

By the time his mistake was discovered, so many circuit diagrams had been drawn that physicists decided to keep drawing them in the same way.

The direction current is drawn in circuit diagrams is known as **conventional current**, but the direction current actually flows is called **real current**.

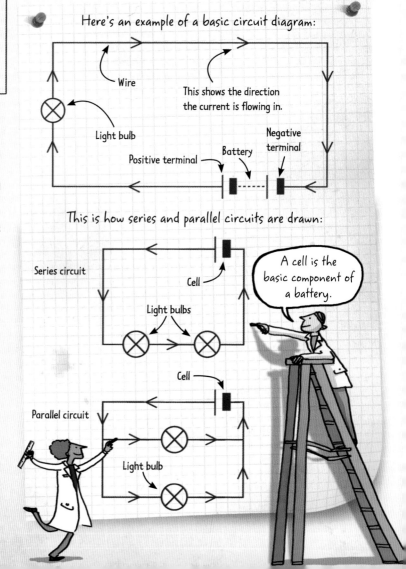

Here's an example of a basic circuit diagram:

Wire

This shows the direction the current is flowing in.

Light bulb

Positive terminal — Battery — Negative terminal

This is how series and parallel circuits are drawn:

Series circuit

Cell

Light bulbs

A cell is the basic component of a battery.

Parallel circuit

Cell

Light bulb

Here are some of the symbols for different
components you might find in a circuit.

Switch — open

When a switch is open (off), the
circuit is broken, so current
can't flow.

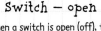

Switch — closed

When a switch is closed (on), it completes
the circuit, so current flows.

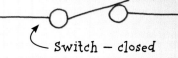

Voltmeter

A voltmeter measures the amount of
voltage in a circuit. It won't give an
accurate reasding unless it's connected
in a parallel circuit.

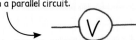

Ammeter

An ammeter measures the amount
of current in a circuit. It won't give a
proper reading unless it's connected
in a series circuit.

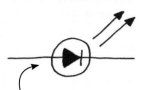

Diode

A diode is made from a
semiconductor and only conducts
electricity in one direction.

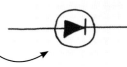

Light emitting diode (LED)

A diode that gives out light when
electricity flows through it the
right way. Uses very little energy, so
it's used in energy efficient lights.

Fuse

A fuse makes sure only a safe
amount of current flows through
a circuit.

Variable resistor

Changes the amount of resistance
in a circuit, to control the amount
of current flowing through it.

Thermistor

A type of resistor with resistance
which *decreases* as temperature
increases. Used to measure and control
temperature in heating and cooling
systems and microwave ovens.

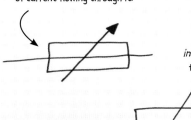

Chip chip hooray!

Modern computer chips
are tiny — no bigger than
your fingertip — but they
contain millions of circuits.
Before chips were invented,
the circuits used to make
computers work were huge.
So it was impossible to have
really small electrical devices.

Physicists are finding ways
to make circuits smaller all
the time.

Why do magnets stick to your fridge?

A **magnet** is something which can exert **magnetic force**. This means it has the ability to attract certain magnetic metals, including iron, steel, cobalt and nickel. Fridges are usually made of steel, so if you put a magnet on your fridge door, it'll probably stay there.

Magnets can attract or repel other magnets, too. That's because they have two opposite ends, called **poles** – one 'north' and one 'south' (the underside of a fridge magnet is one pole, the topside is the other).

Like electrical charges, opposite poles attract, and like poles repel. If you put one fridge magnet on top of the other, they'll stick together. But if you try to push the undersides together, they'll push each other away.

What makes a magnet magnetic?

Some substances are naturally magnetic. Magnetism was discovered thousands of years ago, when people noticed that a rock called lodestone could attract iron.

But magnets can be created, too. It's easy to magnetize iron and steel, for example (turn the page to find out how to do it yourself). The molecules in these metals act as miniature 'molecular' magnets, with their own north and south poles.

Magnetic words

Ferromagnetic – a substance that is strongly magnetic, or can be magnetized easily, such as iron.

Magnetically hard – a substance which doesn't easily lose its magnetism once it's been magnetized, e.g. steel. Used to make permanent magnets.

Magnetically soft – a substance which doesn't stay magnetized for long, e.g. iron. Used to make temporary magnets.

Imagining magnets

Inside magnetic substances, there are 'molecular magnets', each with their own north and south poles. You can use matches to see how they're arranged in magnetized and unmagnetized substances.

Imagine tipping a pile of matches onto a table. The matches are all jumbled up, just like the molecular magnets in an unmagnetized substance.

Imagine lining up all the matches so their heads face the same way. That's how the molecular magnets in a magnet are arranged.

Usually, when a bar of iron is unmagnetized, its molecular magnets point all over the place.

But when the bar is magnetized, its molecular magnets all point in the same direction.

Magnetic patterns

There's a forcefield around every magnet, called the **magnetic field**, where the magnetic force is strongest. The force created by a magnetic field makes invisible patterns called **magnetic field lines**. These lines change when two magnets meet.

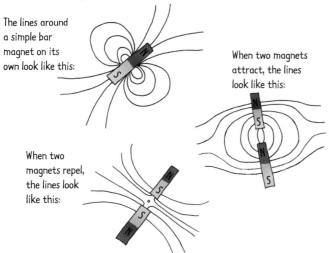

The lines around a simple bar magnet on its own look like this:

When two magnets attract, the lines look like this:

When two magnets repel, the lines look like this:

Magnetic migration

All sorts of creatures, from turtles to birds to butterflies, travel thousands of miles every year, to find cool places in summer and warmer places in winter. Often they've never made the trip before, but they almost always end up in the right place.

That's because the Earth itself is a giant magnet, and these animals can sense the Earth's magnetic field, which tells them if they're going in the right direction.

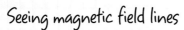

Seeing magnetic field lines

Although it's impossible to see the magnetic field itself, you can use iron filings to see the pattern of field lines it creates.

You will need:

- A bar magnet   - Iron filings   - A piece of paper

Lay the piece of paper on top of the bar magnet. Sprinkle some iron filings on top. Gently tap the piece of paper, so the iron filings jump up and then fall down on the paper again.

What happens?

The iron filings will make a pattern around the magnet, which shows the strength and direction of the magnetic force.

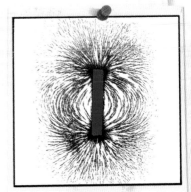

When you sprinkle iron filings over a magnet, they make a pattern like this.

How to make a magnet

You can make all the molecules in iron or steel point the same way by stroking the metal repeatedly with another magnet. Try it yourself:

You will need:

A bar magnet

Two steel needles

Destroying magnets

Magnets can be destroyed by jumbling up the molecular magnets. One way to do this is to hit a magnet with a hammer. Another is to heat it until it's red hot. But don't try either of these at home.

1. Stroke one of the needles with the bar magnet in the same direction, about 10 times.

2. Now take the needle you've stroked and touch the other needle with it.

What happens?

You should find the stroked needle attracts the other needle strongly enough to pick it up. You've made the first needle into a magnet.

See for yourself: Earth's magnetism

Use the method described above to magnetise a needle. Fill a cup with water, and place the magnetised needle on the water, in the middle of the cup.

The needle should move around and gradually come to rest. It's being attracted by the Earth's magnetic field. The needle will rest in line with the Earth's North Magnetic Pole – just like the needle on a compass.

What's the biggest magnet on Earth?

The Earth itself – it's actually a giant magnet. It has a solid core surrounded by liquid iron, which acts like a bar magnet running through the middle of the planet.

The top end of the magnetic field, or the 'magnetic North Pole', is very near to, but not quite in the same place as, the 'geographic' North Pole (the North Pole you see on a map). The other end of the magnetic field is very close to the geographic South Pole.

The needle of a compass points towards the magnetic North Pole, because it's attracted to the Earth's magnetic field – unless there's a powerful magnet nearby to distract it.

This diagram shows the pattern of the Earth's magnetic field.

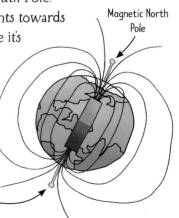

Magnetic North Pole

Magnetic South Pole

Why am I reading about magnets in a chapter about electricity?

Electricity and magnetism are very closely linked. Electric current always creates a magnetic field around it. So, when a current flows through a wire, the wire temporarily becomes a magnet, even if it isn't magnetic the rest of the time. The greater the current, the stronger the magnetic field it creates. This is called **electromagnetism**.

Electromagnetism can create really strong, temporary magnets called **electromagnets**. These are made by wrapping a long coil of wire around an iron core and passing a current through it.

Magnets can cause a current to flow, too. If you spin a magnet around inside a coil of wire, voltage builds up in the wire. If the wire is connected to a circuit, current will flow around it. The stronger the field and the faster the movement, the more voltage is produced.

Inside a power station, water is boiled into steam. This steam turns a machine called a turbine, which in turn spins a magnet around inside a coil of wire, generating an electric current that can be sent to people's homes.

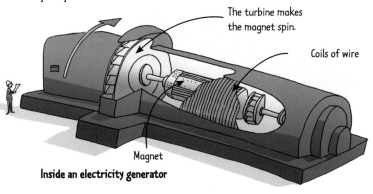

The turbine makes the magnet spin.

Coils of wire

Magnet

Inside an electricity generator

See for yourself – electromagnets

You can make your own electromagnet using some insulated copper wire, a battery, an iron nail and some paperclips.

Wind the wire around the nail, keeping the coils very close together. Wind the ends of the wire around the battery terminals. Hold the nail near the paperclips and see what happens.

You should find the nail picks up the paperclips. That's because it's turned into an electromagnet. But if you disconnect the wire from the battery, it won't work. It's only a magnet when current flows through it.

Hovering trains

Some countries, including Japan and the USA, have really fast trains called Maglev trains.

These trains have electromagnets underneath them, and they run on tracks made of electromagnets. The magnets repel each other, so the train never touches the tracks. There's no friction between the train and track, which makes Maglev trains really speedy and efficient.

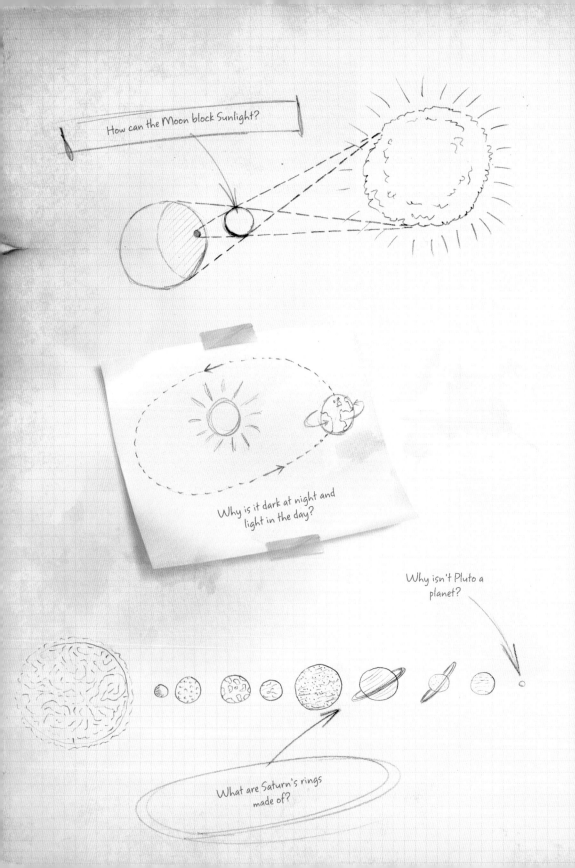

Part 5:
Lost in space

Space is vast. Really vast.
There are more stars, planets and moons out there
than even the most dedicated astronomer can count.
The study of space is a really exciting branch of
physics, known as **astrophysics**. Astrophysicists have
to invent ways to study things that are so far away
they'll probably never be able to travel to them.

Starry, starry night

A whole lot of nothing

Space, as its name suggests, is mostly just empty space. And empty really does mean empty – there isn't even any air in it, so you wouldn't be able to breathe. And away from any planets or stars, there isn't any gravity. Astronauts who take a space 'walk' actually just float.

Holes in space

When a huge star burns out and dies, it can collapse inwards, becoming a super-dense whirlpool known as a 'black hole'.

Black holes have such strong gravity that they suck everything in from a dying star – including the light. So they're only visible as 'gaps' in space.

No one knows what happens inside a black hole. Some scientists think they're portholes to parallel universes. But even if that were true, anyone entering one would be squashed into oblivion by the intense gravity before they could find out.

When you look up into the night sky, you're looking out into space. All the stars you can see are part of a group – or galaxy – named the Milky Way. If you could see it from far enough away, it would look like a swirling mass of milky-pale light. There are millions of other galaxies besides ours, and billions of other stars.

When you stargaze, you're also looking back in time. Every star (apart from the Sun) is so far away that even light – the speediest thing in the Universe – takes years to travel from them to us. In fact, astrophysicists actually measure distances across space in 'light years'. One light year is the distance light travels while a whole year passes on Earth – 9,460,730,472,600,000m.

The most distant stars in our galaxy are 100,000 light years away from Earth, and the Andromeda galaxy, which is quite near ours, is 2.5 million light years away. That means you're seeing it as it looked 2.5 million years ago.

Mind the gap!

This is a photograph of a galaxy called NGC 1300. It's similar in shape to our own galaxy, the Milky Way.

What's the Sun?

The Sun is just another star. It's not even a particularly big one – it only seems bigger and brighter than other stars because it's much closer to us. But it's still about a million times bigger than the Earth.

Like every other star, the Sun is an unbelievably hot ball of burning gases, which are squashed together, causing explosions which produce light and heat.

Why is night dark?

The Earth is constantly moving around the Sun, in a path known as an **orbit**. At the same time, the Earth constantly turns, like a spinning top, on its **axis** – an imaginary line through the middle of the planet.

A day is the time a planet takes to turn around once. On Earth, that takes 24 hours. So it's daytime on the side that's facing the Sun, and night on the other side where it's dark.

What causes the seasons?

The Earth's axis is at an angle to its orbit. When your part of the planet is tilted towards the Sun, it's summer. The Sun seems to shine more strongly, the days are longer, and nights are shorter. When you're tilted away from the Sun, it's winter. Nights are longer, days are shorter, and it's colder.

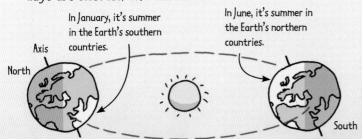

Axis
North

In January, it's summer in the Earth's southern countries.

In June, it's summer in the Earth's northern countries.

South

Don't look!

You should never look directly at the Sun – not even with sunglasses on, or through a camera or telescope. It could seriously damage your eyes.

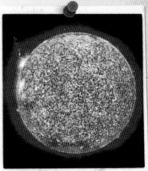

A photograph of the Sun taken through a telescope

See for yourself – the seasons

Shine a flashlight straight down at the ground. The ground will be lit up really brightly. This is how the Sun shines in summer.

Now shine the flashlight at an angle. The light will spread out more, and look paler. This is how the Sun shines in winter. When rays of sunlight are spread out, they're less warm.

What's the Moon?

The Moon is the second brightest object in the sky, after the Sun. But it's actually just a big lump of rock, and it doesn't give off any light at all. What we call moonlight is in fact sunlight, reflected off the Moon.

That's not to say the Moon isn't important. The Moon's gravity pulls on the Earth so much that it makes the sides of the planet bulge outwards a little bit. You can't really see the effect on solid land, but you can if you look at the sea: it pulls the oceans back and forth, causing the tides.

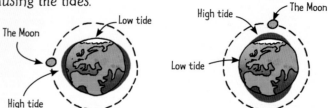

Men on the Moon

In 1961, the American President John F. Kennedy launched a space program named Apollo. He promised men would walk on the Moon before 1970.

The first Apollo spacecraft, Apollo 1, exploded on the launchpad in 1967, killing three men. But with only months until the end of the decade, in 1969, the program succeeded. Apollo 11 landed on the Moon.

The Apollo II crew – Neil Armstrong, Michael Collins and Buzz Aldrin

Neil Armstrong became the first man to walk on the Moon. He and fellow astronaut Buzz Aldrin spent two hours exploring the Moon's dusty surface.

Between 1969-1975, twelve Apollo astronauts visited the Moon. They're the only humans who've ever actually visited another place in space – so far...

Why does the Moon change shape?

If you look up into the night sky, you'll see the Moon doesn't always look the same. Sometimes it's a round full Moon, and sometimes it's a barely-there crescent. The different shapes are called the **phases** of the Moon.

But the Moon isn't really changing shape at all. As the Moon orbits around the Earth, the Sun's rays hit it at different angles. People on Earth see more or less of the Moon depending on where it is in relation to the Sun.

Astronaut Alan Bean on the Moon in 1969

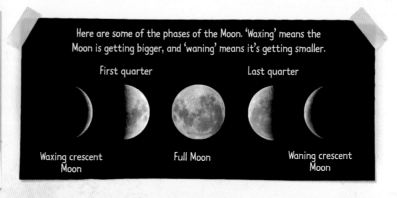

Here are some of the phases of the Moon. 'Waxing' means the Moon is getting bigger, and 'waning' means it's getting smaller.

First quarter

Last quarter

Waxing crescent Moon

Full Moon

Waning crescent Moon

Why is a year twelve months long?

The word 'month' comes from the word 'Moon'. One month is about the amount of time the Moon takes to go around the Earth.

The Moon orbits the Earth about twelve times a year, so there are twelve months in a year. But it doesn't make it around twelve times exactly. Every four years we have to adjust the length of a year so the Moon can catch up. An extra day is added to February, making a 'leap' year of 366 days.

Once in a blue moon...

In most years, there are 12 full moons, one for each calendar month. But every two or three years, there's a 13th full moon – often called a 'blue' moon – but it's actually the same colour as normal.

It was a dark and stormy day...

Sometimes, the Moon passes between the Earth and the Sun, and blocks out the Sun's light completely. This is called a **solar eclipse**. The Moon is a lot smaller than the Sun, but it's also a lot closer – so it seems to cover the Sun, and throw a shadow over part of the Earth.

During a total solar eclipse, it becomes cold and dark very quickly. Birds head to their nests, as they think night has come. In the past, people thought eclipses meant the end of the world was coming.

A life-saving eclipse

In 1503, explorer Christopher Columbus was shipwrecked on an island, and in need of food.

He knew that a lunar eclipse was about to occur, so he told the islanders that his God would get angry with them and make the Moon disappear if they didn't feed him.

Sure enough, as the Earth moved between the Sun and the Moon, the sky began to glow an angry red, and the Moon soon disappeared. Columbus got his food.

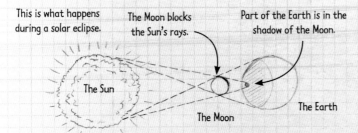

This is what happens during a solar eclipse.

The Moon blocks the Sun's rays.

Part of the Earth is in the shadow of the Moon.

The Sun

The Moon

The Earth

Lunar eclipses are less spectacular, but much more common. They happen when the Earth moves between the Sun and the Moon, blocking the Sun's light from the Moon – so the Moon seems to disappear.

Our Solar System

Planets are huge balls of matter that orbit a star. Some are made of solid rock; others are mostly made of gas. The Earth is just one of eight planets which orbit the Sun. Together, the Sun and the planets make up our **Solar System**. Our Sun isn't the only star with planets orbiting it – many other stars have them, too.

Each planet's orbit is a different size, which means it takes some of them longer to go around the Sun than others. One year is the amount of time it takes a planet to orbit the Sun once. So how long a year is depends on which planet you're on.

The centre of the Universe?

Until the 16th century, people thought the Earth was the centre of the Universe, and the Sun and the planets moved around it.

Then an astronomer named Copernicus suggested that the Earth moved around the Sun.

A scientist named Galileo agreed, and in 1632 he wrote a book about it.

Galileo's book got him in trouble with the Church, which taught that the Earth was at the centre of the Universe. Galileo was put under house arrest for the rest of his life.

Venus

The hottest planet, covered with gases so thick they would crush you to death – if they didn't poison you first.

Length of year: 225 Earth days
Length of day: 243 Earth days
Average temp.: 465°C
Moons: none

The Sun

The Sun is 99.8% of the mass of the Solar System – so everything else only makes up a measly 0.2% of it.

The asteroid belt

Thousands of bits of rock and metal which orbit the Sun between Mars and Jupiter. They can be as tiny as a pea, or as big as a city.

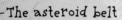

Mercury

Small rocky planet with no air to breathe.

Length of year: 88 Earth days
Length of day: 59 Earth days
Temperature: -170° to 427°C
Moons: none

Saturn

Completely made of gas, surrounded by rings made of lumps of rock and ice.

Length of year: 29 Earth years
Length of day: 10.5 Earth hours
Average temp: -178°C
Moons: 60 (that we know of)

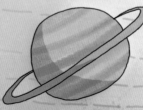

Pluto

Until 2006, scientists classed far-off Pluto as a planet, but they now they call it a 'dwarf planet', because it's much smaller than the eight main planets.

Many moons

A moon is a lump of rock that orbits a planet, just as planets orbit the Sun. The Earth only has one moon, but some planets have lots. Jupiter has at least 63, and there may be more astronomers haven't spotted yet.

Big and far away

The planets on this page, and the distances between them, aren't shown to scale.

Neptune

Stormy planet with winds as fast as a jet plane.

Length of year: 164 Earth years
Length of day: 16 Earth hours
Average temp: -236°C
Moons: 13

Jupiter

The biggest planet in the Solar System. The large red spot on its surface is a storm that's been raging for hundreds – maybe thousands – of years.

Length of year: 11.9 Earth years
Length of day: 9.9 Earth hours
Average temp: -153°C
Moons: at least 63

Comets

Lumps of ice and rock, about 1-5 kilometres across. Comets have a solid core surrounded by a cloud of dust and gas. When they pass near the Sun, they reflect sunlight and glow, so we can see them.

Comets leave a trail of dust and rock, which rains down on Earth in a meteor shower when they pass through Earth's orbit.

Earth

Delightful planet, mostly covered in water, home to lots of interesting creatures, including humans.

Length of year: 365.25 days
Length of day: 24 hours
Temperature: from about -88°C to 58°C
Moons: one

Uranus

This planet has an axis that's much more tilted that the Earth's axis. It's practically on its side.

Length of year: 84 Earth years
Length of day: 17.24 Earth hours
Average temp: -213°C
Moons: 27 moons (that we know of)

Mars

If humans ever had to leave Earth, Mars would probably be the best place to move – even though it's horribly cold, and doesn't have any air. In fact, the American space agency NASA is currently planning a mission to visit Mars. If it goes ahead, the astronauts would be the first ever to have visited another planet.

Length of year: 685 Earth days
Length of day: about 40 minutes longer than a day on Earth
Average temp: -23°C
Moons: two little ones

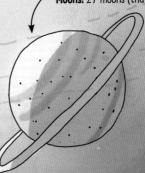

Physics through the ages

People have been studying how the Universe works for thousands of years. The word 'physics' comes from a Greek word, *physis*, meaning nature. All kinds of things were considered to be physics until the 16th century, including philosophy and chemistry. Here's the story of physics so far:

about 800,000 years ago

Early people learn how to create fire using friction: they rub dry sticks together until they get hot enough to catch fire.

about 2,500 years ago

Democritus argues that everything is made from tiny, indivisible units, which he calls *atoms*.

about 2,200 years ago

Archimedes discovers displacement by getting into a full bath and splashing water over the sides.

about 2,000 years ago

Arab scientist Ibn al-Haytham, also known as Alhazen, writes the *Book of Optics*. He's the first person to realize that light travels in a straight line.

1609

Galileo builds the first really powerful telescope. He works out that the planets move around the Sun – but most people don't believe him.

1660s

Isaac Newton develops a theory of gravity, studies the spectrum of light and begins his work on the Laws of Motion.

1800s

Alessandro Volta discovers that electric current is a flow of charge, and invents the 'Voltaic pile' – the first battery.

1820

Danish physicist Hans Christian Ørsted discovers that magnetic fields produce an electric current. This leads to the development of

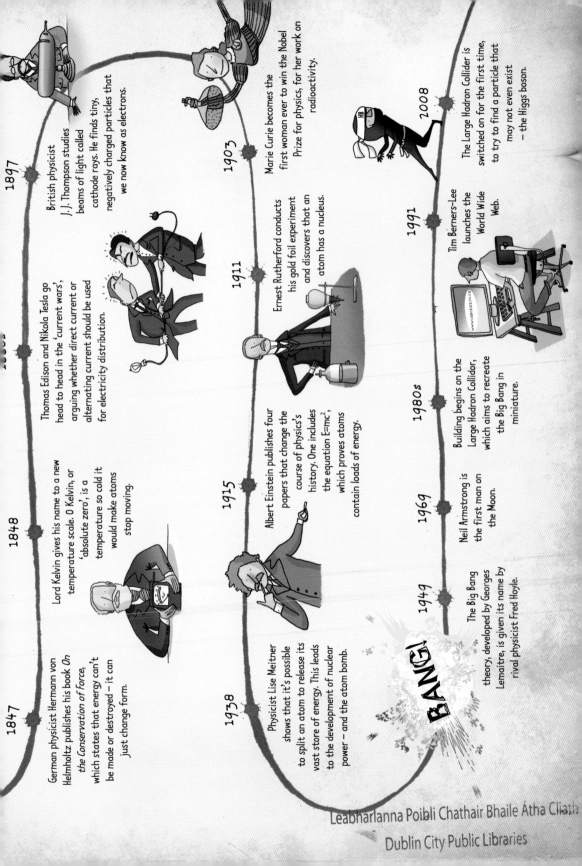

1847

German physicist Hermann von Helmholtz publishes his book *On the Conservation of Force*, which states that energy can't be made or destroyed – it can just change form.

1848

Lord Kelvin gives his name to a new temperature scale. 0 Kelvin, or 'absolute zero', is a temperature so cold it would make atoms stop moving.

Thomas Edison and Nikola Tesla go head to head in the 'current wars', arguing whether direct current or alternating current should be used for electricity distribution.

1897

British physicist J. J. Thompson studies beams of light called cathode rays. He finds tiny, negatively charged particles that we now know as electrons.

1903

Marie Curie becomes the first woman ever to win the Nobel Prize for physics, for her work on radioactivity.

1911

Ernest Rutherford conducts his gold foil experiment and discovers that an atom has a nucleus.

1915

Albert Einstein publishes four papers that change the course of physics's history. One includes the equation $E=mc^2$, which proves atoms contain loads of energy.

1938

Physicist Lise Meitner shows that it's possible to split an atom to release its vast store of energy. This leads to the development of nuclear power – and the atom bomb.

1949

The Big Bang theory, developed by Georges Lemaître, is given its name by rival physicist Fred Hoyle.

BANG!

1969

Neil Armstrong is the first man on the Moon.

1980s

Building begins on the Large Hadron Collidor, which aims to recreate the Big Bang in miniature.

1991

Tim Berners-Lee launches the World Wide Web.

2008

The Large Hadron Collider is switched on for the first time, to try to find a particle that may not even exist – the Higgs boson.

More about science

Now that you know what biology, chemistry and physics are all about, turn the page to find out more about how scientists work. There are also some useful reminders about scientific formulas and equations, and a glossary listing what some of the harder words in this book mean.

what is science?

Science comes from the Latin word, *scientia*, meaning 'knowledge'. It is the study of how things work, and is often divided into three areas:

Biology is the study of life.

Chemistry is about the substances that make up the world.

Physics is the study of the laws that rule our Universe.

How does science work?

Scientists come up with ideas that explain something about the world. They base those ideas on things they've seen themselves, or that other scientists have written about.

Then they have to see if their ideas are right. To be a real scientist, it isn't enough to say that what you *think* is true, or that you believe it, or that it's common sense. You have to *prove* it's right (or at least, not wrong), by doing experiments that back it up. When an idea can be tested through experiments, it's called a **hypothesis** (unlike the many ideas people have which can't be tested scientifically).

Top scientists write about their experiments in journals, so other scientists around the world can try them too. If other experts agree there is enough evidence, the hypothesis becomes a **theory** – meaning it's the accepted, tested and most likely explanation of why something is the way it is.

How do experiments work?

An experiment must be a fair test of an idea.

1. Hypothesis
This is where you explain what your idea is. It also usually includes predictions of what you expect the results of the experiment to be.

2. Method
This describes how you're going to do the experiment. It includes a **control**, which is the 'normal' situation; and the experiment, which is like the control but with one key difference. That way, if the results vary, you know it must be because of that one thing.

3. Results
These record the outcome of the experiment (including the control).

4. Conclusion
This is where you interpret the results. Did they support the hypothesis? Have you changed or rejected your hypothesis after seeing the results?

Here's an example of a simple scientific experiment...

1. Hypothesis
'Adding salt to ice makes it melt faster.'

2. Method
Place two ice cubes in separate glasses. Sprinkle a teaspoon of salt on ice cube B, but none on ice cube A. Time how long the ice cubes take to melt. Do they melt at the same speed, or does one melt faster than the other?

3. Results
Ice cube B melts faster than ice cube A (the control).

4. Conclusion
The only difference between the ice cubes was that one was exposed to salt and one wasn't. So ice cube B must have melted faster because of the added salt. This result supports the hypothesis.

However, there might be reasons why this experiment wouldn't work. For example, ice cube B might be slightly warmer or smaller than the control, ice cube A. If it's already warmer or smaller, this ice cube might take less time to melt. It's really important to make sure that the salt is the *only* difference between the ice cubes.

Are scientists ever wrong?

Yes, scientists get things wrong all the time. They may misinterpret experiments, get bad results, or not be able to test ideas until the right technology is invented.

But what every good scientist wants most of all is to discover how things really work – even if that means admitting to mistakes along the way. So, if their ideas are proved wrong, they're always prepared to change what they think, and move on.

'The one who seeks truth ... submits to argument and demonstration'

This was the philosophy of one of the first people to use fair, rigorous experiments.

Ibn al-Haytham, an 11th-century scholar, based his theories about light and vision on his own observations, rather than what people usually assumed was true.

He argued that scholars shouldn't trust anyone's ideas without carefully considering the evidence for themselves.

Science factfile

Here are some quick reminders of the symbols and equations used in this book.
If you want to remind yourself what any of the words mean, check the glossary.

Symbol	Meaning	Symbol	Meaning
°C	degrees Celsius	ρ	density
°F	degrees Fahrenheit	J	joules, a unit of work
K	Kelvin	W	watts, a unit of power
+ (as in Na⁺)	a positively charged ion	N	newtons, a unit of force
- (as in Cl⁻)	a negatively charged ion	Pa	pascals, a unit of pressure
⤳	light energy	λ	wavelength
Δ	heat energy	Hz	hertz, a unit of frequency
e⁻	an electron	c	wave speed OR speed of light
m/s	metres per second		
m³	metres cubed, a unit of volume	t.i.r.	total internal reflection
		dB	decibels, a unit of sound level
m/s²	metres per second squared, a unit of acceleration	Q	electrical charge
		I	electric current
kg	kilograms	DC	direct current
kg/m³	kilograms per metre cubed, a unit of density	AC	alternating current
		LED	light-emitting diode

A formula shows how to calculate one quantity if you know others. It looks a bit like a calculation, but with symbols instead of numbers. If you replace enough of the symbols with actual measurements, you'll be able to find out what's missing. For example, you can work out a car's speed (s) if you know the distance (d) it travels in a given time (t), using the following formula.

$$s = \frac{d}{t}$$ So, if the car travels 6m in 2 seconds... $$s = \frac{6}{2} = 3 \text{ m/s}$$ ...its speed is 3 m/s.

Magic triangles

Sometimes a formula is made up of three quantities, which can be written as a 'magic triangle'. To find the quantity at the top, multiply the two below. And to find either of the quantities below, divide the top by the remaining quantity.

Here's how a magic triangle would work, if it had real numbers in it instead of symbols:

$$6 = 2 \times 3$$

$$2 = \frac{6}{3} \quad \text{and} \quad 3 = \frac{6}{2}$$

Here are some real magic triangles that scientists use:

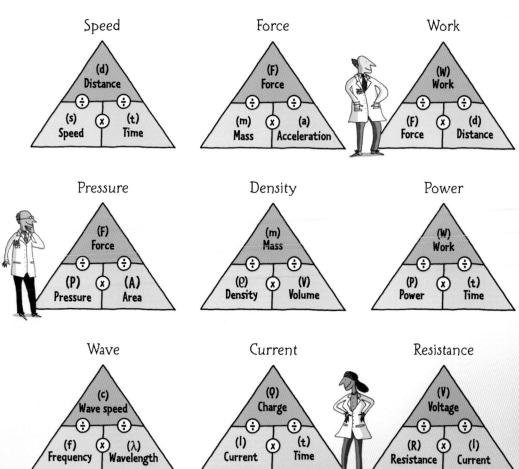

Chemical equations

Scientists, especially chemists, work with all kinds of different substances – each one with its own name and symbol. Different substances react in different ways, and scientists write the reactions as **equations**, laid out in a line. An arrow shows the direction of the reaction.

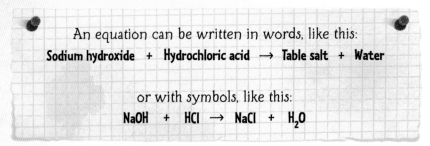

An equation can be written in words, like this:

Sodium hydroxide + Hydrochloric acid $\longrightarrow$ Table salt + Water

or with symbols, like this:

NaOH + HCl $\longrightarrow$ NaCl + H_2O

Balanced equations have numbers by each symbol, to show how many of those atoms or molecules there are compared to all the others. (Although if there's only one of them, then no number is shown.)

In balanced equations, each side must show the same number of each kind of atom. In the equation above, both sides show one atom of Na (sodium), O (oxygen) and Cl (chlorine), and two of H (hydrogen – shown on the right as H_2).

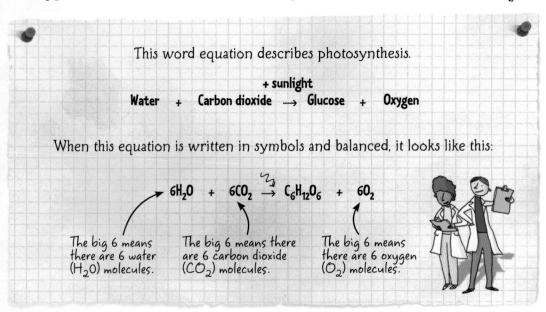

This word equation describes photosynthesis.

+ sunlight

Water + Carbon dioxide $\longrightarrow$ Glucose + Oxygen

When this equation is written in symbols and balanced, it looks like this:

$$6H_2O \ + \ 6CO_2 \ \rightarrow \ C_6H_{12}O_6 \ + \ 6O_2$$

The big 6 means there are 6 water (H_2O) molecules.

The big 6 means there are 6 carbon dioxide (CO_2) molecules.

The big 6 means there are 6 oxygen (O_2) molecules.

Inside atoms

How substances react is all down to atoms, and the particles inside them.

Neutrons sit in the **nucleus** and have no charge.

Protons sit in the nucleus and have a positive charge.

Electrons form shells around the nucleus and have a negative charge.

There's always the same number of protons and electrons in an atom, so overall, atoms have no charge.

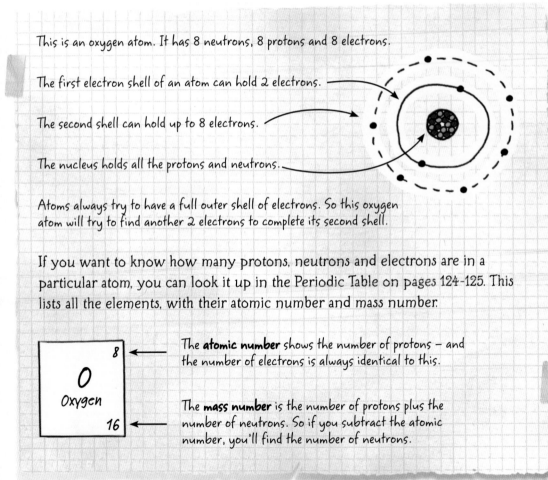

This is an oxygen atom. It has 8 neutrons, 8 protons and 8 electrons.

The first electron shell of an atom can hold 2 electrons.

The second shell can hold up to 8 electrons.

The nucleus holds all the protons and neutrons.

Atoms always try to have a full outer shell of electrons. So this oxygen atom will try to find another 2 electrons to complete its second shell.

If you want to know how many protons, neutrons and electrons are in a particular atom, you can look it up in the Periodic Table on pages 124-125. This lists all the elements, with their atomic number and mass number.

8
O
Oxygen
16

The **atomic number** shows the number of protons – and the number of electrons is always identical to this.

The **mass number** is the number of protons plus the number of neutrons. So if you subtract the atomic number, you'll find the number of neutrons.

Glossary

Words in *italics* have their own separate entries.

acceleration The rate at which an object's *velocity* changes.

acid A *substance* that forms positive *ions* of hydrogen (H^+) when *dissolved* in water.

activation energy The minimum amount of *energy* *substances* need to *react* together.

adaptation When a *species* alters over time to become better-suited to the place where it lives.

algae *Protists* which make their food through *photosynthesis*. Some kinds join to form seaweeds.

alkali A *base dissolved* in water.

alloy A *mixture* formed from two or more *metals*, or from a *metal* and a *non metal*.

alpha particle A form of *radiation* made up of two *protons* and two *neutrons*.

alternating current (AC) *Current electricity* which constantly changes direction. The most widely used type of current.

amplitude The height of a *wave*.

angiosperm A plant which flowers and produces seeds inside a *fruit*.

antibodies Chemicals made by some white blood *cells*, which attack and disable invading germs.

artery A blood *vessel* which carries blood away from the heart.

atom The smallest building block of an *element*.

atomic number The number of *protons* in the *nucleus* of an *atom* of a certain *element*.

axis An imaginary line around which something (for example, a planet) spins.

bacteria Single-celled *organisms* with a simple *cell* structure and no *nucleus*.

base A *substance* that forms negative *ions* of hydroxide (OH^-) when *dissolved* in water.

boiling point The *temperature* at which a *substance* changes *state* from a liquid to a gas.

bond A link between *atoms* or *ions* in a *molecule*.

by-product Another reaction *product* that is not the main or useful product.

catalyst A chemical that speeds up the *rate of reaction*, but is not a *reactant*.

cell The basic unit of life, made of structures floating in cytoplasm and bound by a membrane.

centre of gravity The point through which the Earth's *gravity* appears to act on an object.

chemical equation A way of writing down the *reactants*, *products* and conditions of a reaction.

chemical reaction The breaking and forming of *bonds* that changes *reactants* into *products*.

chemical symbol One or two letters that stand for an *element's* name, for example He for helium.

chlorophyll The green substance in *chloroplasts* which absorbs energy from light for *photosynthesis*.

chloroplast The structures inside plant *cells* which contain *chlorophyll*.

chromosome A long strand of genetic information found in the *nucleus* of a *cell*. Human cells contain 46 chromosomes. Each chromosome is made up of sections called *genes*.

circuit A closed loop of wire around which *current electricity* can flow.

classification A way of sorting *organisms* into groups based on shared characteristics.

cloning When an *organism's genes* are copied to make an identical organism. Many organisms use cloning to reproduce.

combustion The burning of a *substance* in air.

compound A *substance* made up of two or more different *elements* that have *bonded* together.

concave lens A *lens* with at least one surface bending inwards.

condensing When a gas changes into a liquid.

conducting When hotter *molecules* transfer heat to cooler *molecules* by bumping into them.

conductor A *substance* which allows heat or electricity to move through it.

convection When heat is transferred by moving *molecules*.

convex lens A *lens* with at least one surface bending outwards.

covalent bond A *bond* that involves the sharing of *electrons* between *atoms*.

crystal A regular, repeating arrangement of *atoms*, *molecules* or *ions* inside a solid.

current electricity A flow of charged particles.

decomposition reaction A reaction in which a *compound* breaks down into smaller parts.

density How much *mass* an object has in relation to its *volume*.

direct current (DC) *Current electricity* which only flows in one direction. Supplied by batteries.

displacement The *volume* of water (or another substance) pushed out of the way by an object.

displacement reaction A reaction in which one *element* replaces another in a *compound*.

dissolve To mix a *substance* into a liquid, forming a *solution*.

distillation A purification process that isolates different *substances* using their different *boiling points*.

DNA (deoxyribonucleic acid) A very long molecule that contains coded instructions for all that happens in a *cell*, and much of the *structure* and operation of the whole *organism*.

ecosystem A combination of a place and its conditions, and all the *organisms* that live there.

electrolysis A process where a liquid *compound* is split apart by passing *current electricity* through it.

electromagnet A *magnet* which only attracts metals when *current electricity* flows through it.

electromagnetic spectrum A family of *energy waves*, including heat and light, which all travel at the *speed of light*.

electron A tiny, negatively charged particle that orbits an *atom's nucleus*.

element The simplest type of *substance*, made up of only one sort of *atom*.

embryo An early stage in the formation of a new *organism*, when it has basic body structures, but before its *systems* have started to work together properly.

endothermic reaction A *reaction* that takes in a lot of heat and gives out only a little.

energy The ability to do *work*.

enzymes Chemicals made by *cells* to speed up reactions.

epithelium A *tissue* that lines a cavity inside the body.

evaporating When a liquid changes into a gas.

evolution When *species* change into new species over time. It mostly happens through *natural selection*, although other processes can play a role.

exothermic reaction A reaction that takes in only a little heat and gives out a lot.

extinct A term describing a *species* that has died out.

fertilization When a male and female *gamete* fuse together to make a *zygote*.

force A push or a pull which changes the motion or shape of an object.

fossil The remains or traces of a long-dead *organism*, turned to stone after millions of years spent buried underground.

freezing point The *temperature* at which a *substance* changes *state* from a liquid to a solid.

frequency The number of *waves* that pass a particular point every second. In sound, frequency determines how high- or low-pitched a noise is.

friction A *force* which opposes the motion of two objects rubbing against each other.

fruit Part of a plant that grows after *fertilization* of the *ovules*, to surround one or more seeds.

gamete A sex *cell*, holding half the *genes* of a normal *cell*. A new individual forms when a male and female *gamete* fuse.

gene Part of a *chromosome* which holds instructions for one or more characteristics. Humans have over 200,000 genes.

glucose A type of sugar used to provide energy. Animals get it from food, and plants make their own.

gravity A *force* which pulls all objects together. On Earth, it pulls everything downwards.

greenhouse effect An increase in the average temperature on Earth, caused by a build up of gases in the atmosphere that don't allow heat to escape.

groups The columns of the *Periodic Table* numbered I-VIII. *Elements* in the same group often have very similar *properties*.

gymnosperm A plant which produces seeds, but not flowers or *fruits*.

indicator A *substance* that turns a specific colour when mixed with an *acid* or a *base*.

inertia An object's resistance to changing *velocity*.

inhibitor A *substance* that decreases the *rate of reaction*.

inorganic A term used to describe a *compound* that doesn't contain any carbon.

insulator A substance which resists heat or electricity moving through it.

invertebrate An animal without a backbone.

ion An *atom* that has either lost or gained some *electrons*, giving it a positive or negative electrical charge.

ionic bond A *bond* formed by the giving or taking of *electrons* between *atoms*.

kinetic energy Movement *energy*.

kingdom The first, and largest, subdivision that biologists divide living things into; for example, the plant and animal kingdoms.

lattice A regular, interlocking network of *atoms*, *molecules* or *ions* inside a solid.

lens A transparent substance with at least one curved surface which *refracts* light, usually to help people see better.

machine An object which makes it easier to do *work*.

magnet An object that attracts some metals and attracts or repels other magnets.

magnetic field The area around a *magnet* in which objects are affected by *magnetic force*.

magnetic force The *force* which makes a *magnet* attract some metals and attract or repel other *magnets*.

magnetic poles The opposite ends of a *magnet*, where the *magnetic force* is concentrated.

mammal A group of *vertebrates* who have hair, make milk to feed their babies, and most of whom give birth.

mass The amount of *matter* in an object.

mass number The total number of *protons* and *neutrons* in the *nucleus* of an *atom* of a certain *element*.

matter The physical stuff that the Universe is made up of.

medium A *substance* which *energy* travels through.

meiosis A kind of cell division which results in *gametes* with half a set of *genes*.

melting point The *temperature* at which a *substance* changes *state* from a solid to a liquid.

metal An *element* that conducts electricity and heat.

metalloid An *element* that shares *properties* with both *metals* and *non metals*.

microbe A tiny living thing that can only be seen with a microscope. Most are single-celled *organisms*.

mitosis A kind of cell division which results in two *cells*, each with a full set of *genes*.

mixture A collection of *elements* and/or *compounds* that have not bonded together.

molecule Two or more *atoms* bonded together. These *atoms* can be of one or more *elements*.

momentum The *mass* of an object multiplied by its velocity.

natural selection The way in which the most successful individuals' *genes* spread through a *species*, gradually causing a new *species* to evolve.

nervous system The *system* made up of the brain and nerves, which relays and reacts to messages.

neuron A nerve *cell*, used to carry messages around the body.

neutral A *substance* that is neither an *acid* nor a *base*, OR particles that have neither a positive nor a negative electrical charge.

neutralization reaction A reaction between an *acid* and a *base* that forms a *neutral* salt.

neutron A small, *neutral* particle found in the *nucleus* of an *atom*.

niche A *species'* slot in an *ecosystem*, including how it uses the available resources. Each species has its own niche.

non metal An *element* that has no metal-like *properties*.

nucleus Either the structure of a *cell* which holds its *chromosomes*, or the centre of an *atom*, made up of *protons* and *neutrons*. The plural of nucleus is nuclei.

nutrients Vital substances that *organisms* can't make for themselves, so must obtain from soil or food.

organ A collection of *tissues*, joined together into a structure that does a particular job (such as a heart).

organic A term used to describe a *compound* that contains carbon.

organism Any self-contained living thing.

oscillation When something vibrates up and down, or forwards and backwards.

ovule A female *gamete* of a flowering plant, found within the flower.

oxidation When a *reactant* loses *electrons*.

Periodic Table A list of all known *elements* in order of increasing *atomic number*.

periods The rows of the *Periodic Table*. Going across the periods from left to right, *atoms* have more protons, neutrons and electrons.

pH A measure of how strong an *acid* or *base* is. A strong *acid* has a pH of 1 and a strong *base* has a pH of 14. A *neutral substance* has a pH of 7.

photosynthesis The process by which plants make their own food from water and carbon dioxide, in a reaction powered by *energy* from sunlight.

pollen Tiny powdery grains, which are a flowering plant's male *gametes*.

pollination The transfer of *pollen* to a stigma (often on another plant), to fertilize an *ovule*.

potential energy Stored *energy* that something has when *work* has been done on it.

power The rate at which *work* is done, or *energy* is converted.

pressure The strength of *atoms* or *molecules* squashing against something, when a *substance* pushes, or exerts a *force*, on another substance.

producer Any *organism* which makes its own food rather than eating other organisms.

product A *substance* formed by a *chemical reaction*.

prokaryote Single-celled *organisms* with simple *cell* structures and no *nucleus*. *Bacteria* are prokaryotes.

properties The ways in which a *substance* behaves (physical properties) or *reacts* (chemical properties).

protist A single-celled *organism* with a complex *cell* structure and *nucleus*. *Protozoa* and *algae* are protists.

proton A small, positively charged particle found in the *nucleus* of an *atom*.

protozoa *Protists* which get their food from digesting other *organisms*.

radiation Particles, light or heat rays given off by a *substance*. Not all radiation is harmful.

radioactive A term used to describe an unstable *substance* that emits harmful *radiation* as it breaks down.

rate of reaction The speed at which *reactants* turn into *products*.

reactant A *substance* that takes part in a *chemical reaction*.

receptor A nerve ending or *cell* which detects information about the outside world.

redox reaction A *reaction* involving the *oxidation* of one *reactant* and the *reduction* of another.

reduction When a *reactant* gains *electrons*.

reflection When *waves* bounce off a solid surface.

refraction When light changes direction after passing from one *medium* into another.

resistance A *subtance's* ability to resist the flow of electricity.

respiration The process that releases *energy* from food; it usually needs oxygen and makes carbon dioxide.

reversible reaction A *reaction* that can be reversed so the *products* change back into the *reactants*, usually by altering the *temperature* or *pressure*.

semiconductor A substance which only *conducts* electricity under certain circumstances.

sexual reproduction A way of reproducing in which a male and female *gamete* fuse, creating a new individual with a unique set of *genes*.

shell The path an *electron* takes as it moves around the *nucleus* of an *atom*.

Solar System Our Sun and the planets and moons that orbit around it.

solute A *substance* which is dissolved in a *solvent*.

solution A *mixture* of *substances* in a liquid.

solvent A liquid which *dissolves* another *substance* OR the liquid part of a *solution*.

species A group of *organisms* that can breed together, producing children that can also breed.

speed How fast something moves, worked out by dividing the distance travelled by the time taken.

speed of light In a *vacuum*, light travels at 300,000 km/s, making it the fastest thing in the Universe.

sperm A male *gamete* of an animal.

spore A basic reproductive *cell*, made without *fertilization* by the simplest plants.

state The form a *substance* takes – solid, liquid or gas.

static electricity Electric charge which is held on the surface of a *substance*, and doesn't flow.

substances The different types of stuff the Universe is made of. Any solid, liquid or gas is a substance.

system A collection of *organs* which together do a particular job in the body, such as digestion.

temperature A measure of how hot something is, usually given in $^{\circ}C$ (degrees Celsius) or K (Kelvin).

tissue Many *cells* of the same type, grouped together to form part of an *organism*.

transpiration Loss of water from a plant through its leaves, making it draw up more water from its roots.

ultrasound High *frequency* sounds that humans can't hear.

vaccinaton Infecting someone with a harmless form of a germ, to make them produce *antibodies* that will safeguard against the germ in the future.

vacuum A space that doesn't contain any *matter*.

vein A blood *vessel* which carries blood to the heart.

velocity The *speed* and direction an object is moving.

vertebrate An animal with a backbone.

vessel A tube which carries liquid around an *organism*, such as blood or sap.

virus A very simple particle with some characteristics of a living *organism*.

voltage Forces *electrons* around a *circuit*.

volume How much space a *substance* takes up.

wave A wave transports *energy* from a place of high energy to a place of low energy by making a *medium* oscillate.

weight The pull of *gravity* on an object.

work Work is done when a *force* moves an object.

zygote The first *cell* of a new *organism*, made when a male and female *gamete* join.

Index

Acknowledgements

Every effort has been made to trace and acknowledge ownership of copyright. If any rights have been omitted, the publishers offer to rectify this in any future editions following notification. The publishers are grateful to the following individuals and organizations for their permission to reproduce material on the following pages (t=top, b=bottom, l=left, r=right, m=middle)

p10 © Visuals Unlimited/Corbis; **p11** Art Wolfe/Science Photo Library (SPL); **p17** GK Hart/Vikki Hart; **p22** © Kevin Schafer/Corbis; **p23** Hans Eggensberger; **p25** John Durham/SPL; **p26** Steve Gschmeissner/SPL; **p27** © Jupiterimages/Brand X/Corbis; **p29** David Barlow Photography/Artem Model; **p30** James Cavallini/SPL; **p32** Lee D. Simon/SPL; **p46** James Stevenson/SPL; **p48** SPL; **p50** D. Phillips/SPL; **p60** Winfried Wisniewski/FLPA; **p61** © Phil Degginger/Alamy; **p62** © Frans Lanting/Corbis; **p64** © Nick Garbutt/naturepl.com; **p65** (t) Steve Gschmeissner/SPL; (b) © Hiromitsu Watanabe/amanaimages/Corbis; **p68** © Phillippe Clement/naturepl.com; **p72** John Reader/SPL; **p73** (t) © Layne Kennedy/Corbis; (b) © Lester V. Bergman/Corbis; **p84** © Sally A. Morgan; Ecoscene/Corbis; **p87** © Norbert Wu/Minden Pictures/FLPA; **p90** © Steven David Miller/naturepl.com; **p91** (t) © Tom Mangelsen/naturepl.com; (b) © Suzi Eszterhas/Minden Pictures/FLPA; **p110** Charles D. Winters/SPL; **p117** Charles D. Winters/SPL; **p159** © Robert Malone/Alamy; **p166** © Thom Lang/Corbis; **p167** (bl) SPL; (br) Stefan Diller/SPL; **p174** Millard H. Sharp/SPL; **p176** © Weatherstock/Corbis; **p177** © Stephen Frink/Corbis; **p178** © Nick Greaves/Alamy; **p187** (tr) Keith Kent/SPL; (m) Allan Morton/Dennis Milon/SPL; **p197** Maximilien Brice, CERN; **p215** Hiroyuki Matsumoto/Getty; **p219** © Sylvia Cordaiy Photo Library Ltd/Alamy; **p224** © Bernd Mellmann/Alamy; **p225** (t) © Marco Cristofori/Corbis; (b) Philip and Karen Smith/Getty; **p232** © John Lund/Corbis; **p235** Ted Kinsman/SPL; **p237** Pasieka/SPL; **p240** Erich Schrempp/SPL; **p244** courtesy of Alex and Emily Frith; **p248** Jean-loup Charmet/SPL; **p257** Cordelia Molloy/SPL; **p262** NASA/ESA/STSCI/Hubble Heritage Team/SPL; **p263** European Space Agency/SPL; **p264** (tl) NASA/SPL; (bl) NASA/SPL; (bm) Thierry Legault/Eurelios/SPL

Series designer: Stephen Moncrieff   Art director: Mary Cartwright
Image manipulation: John Russell   Picture research: Ruth King
With thanks to John Gillespie, MSc
and Lucy Bowman, Conrad Mason and Fiona Patchett